FRIDAY
IS THE NEW
SATURDAY

T0347043

FRIDAY

IS THE NEW

SATURDAY

HOW A FOUR-DAY WEEK
CAN SAVE CAPITALISM

PEDRO GOMES

Cover illustration: iStockphoto/francescoch

First published 2021
This paperback edition first published 2024

FLINT is an imprint of The History Press
97 St George's Place, Cheltenham,
Gloucestershire, GL50 3QB
www.flintbooks.co.uk

British Library Cataloguing in Publication Data.
A catalogue record for this book is available from the British Library.

ISBN 978 1 80399 661 5

Typesetting and origination by The History Press
Printed and bound in Great Britain by TJ Books Limited, Padstow, Cornwall.

Trees for L🌱fe

To my father, for teaching me how to think.
To my mother, for showing me how to do.
To my sister, for inspiring me to write.

Contents

Acknowledgements

As a schoolboy, I was always better at dealing with numbers than with words. I never had any desire to write a book. The need to explain my view on the four-day working week, and clear the misconceptions around it, forced my hand. When I persuaded myself to do it, I thought it would be a painful and a solitary endeavour, much like running a marathon. I was wrong. Research was exciting and putting all my thoughts together, inventing analogies and building such a big narrative was invigorating rather than painful. Plus, it was like cycling a grand tour, rather than running a marathon. The glory appears to be individual, but behind the winner there is the teammates' support. I had to sit down, research, read, think and write, but in going over the final draft, I found many fragments of my family, friends and colleagues with whom I discussed my ideas, plus the red pen of the editors who helped me much along the way.

For a start, the book has only come about thanks to my agent, Jonathan Conway, and Laura Perehinec at Flint. Thank you for believing in this project. Jonathan's amazing work raised the book to a much higher standard. Nick Humphrey and Dan Coxon copy-edited the proposal and the final draft, and Jezz Palmer made the book real.

My colleague Ron Smith, a fountain of wisdom, joy and dedication, and Alejandro Librero-Cano, my friend and former student, carefully read the embarrassing first version of each chapter, much harder to read than the final manuscript. Their many comments on the economic arguments and the pitch of the writing helped me immensely in striking the right balance.

Many of my friends – men and women, young and old, left- or right-leaning, from different countries – have read and commented on the book or indulged me in long discussions, helping me see the four-day working week from their unique viewpoint. Cristina Pinheiro and Tito Casquinha read early versions and encouraged me to keep going. The comments – with a helpful dose of scepticism – of Matthias Burgert, François Pouget and Jorge de Castro helped me polish the arguments. Tommaso Garibaldi, Stephen Wright, Sandeep Kapur, Carolyn St Aubyn, Marcelo Ferman, Sue Lawrence, Dave Clayton, David Ford, Agustin Casas, Yarine Fawaz, Matilde Pinto Machado and Maya Mendiratta read later versions of the draft or individual chapters. Two accomplished writers, João Medeiros and Richard Davies, guided me through the publishing process and advised me on the art of writing. João, a lifelong friend, is a tough but rousing coach. Tito Fernandes, Shambhu Manandhar and my Graduate Diploma in Economics students shared with me their inspiring stories.

My friend Pietro Garibaldi encouraged me to write my ideas in a book in the first place. Rachel Ngai and Francesco Caselli, both great teachers and great scholars I admire, saw a presentation of my arguments while I was still writing this book. Christopher Pissarides took time from his busy schedule to read the book before it went to the printing press. I am indebted to all four for having endorsed the book in its early stages. Many of my initial thoughts materialised while supervising Suhair Hindiyeh, a master's student at Birkbeck. Discussions with other fellow economists at Birkbeck and elsewhere helped me polish the arguments: Colin Rowat, Andy Ross, David Schroeder, Roald Versteeg, Yunus Aksoy, Ken Hori, Jean-Baptiste Michau, Ivy Sabuga, Issam Samiri and Paul Wohlfarth. My students from the MSc of Politics, Philosophy and Economics 2020 class endured more than eight hours of online detailed exposition of my arguments, often past 9 p.m., and made many comments and suggestions that I incorporated in the book. Marie Licht drew, on request, two of the comic strips. My friends Sarolta Laczó, Dylan Morrissey (and Figgy), Theodore Kyriakou, Marie-Laure Morelli, Mário Pereira, Rui Panêlo, Delphine Morin, Kenny Labrosse, Mafalda Pinto, Carlos Morais and Patricia Melo helped me in various ways.

Finally, I owe much to my wife, Amélie, and my daughter Nina. Besides having to put up with an absent-minded husband, Amélie, who finds economics extremely boring, patiently read preliminary drafts in what can only be described as proof of love. Nina lost several hours of play with daddy. When she starts working, she will realise it was a small price to pay for having a three-day weekend. I hope she'll want to spend some of those Fridays with her parents. Amélie and Nina have forgiven me for dedicating this book instead to my sister Rita, and to my parents Joaquim and Manuela. I only got to this point in my life, where I have the knowledge, capacity, comfort and inspiration to write this book, because of the unconditional love and support they have given me throughout my forty years of existence.

Praise for *Friday is the New Saturday*

'As societies become richer there is demand for more time off work and better-quality hospitality and entertainment services. Pedro Gomes makes a compelling case that our societies are now ready to institutionalise this ongoing trend: formalise a week made up of four working days and three weekend days. He shows that extending the laws, regulations and customs that now govern Saturday to Friday will not cause havoc but will make us a happier lot. If this sounds boring, you can be sure that it is far from it. Written in an easy style, with humour, the book tells stories from economics, history and even the author's own experience with childcare, that directly or indirectly support the four-day week. Social institutions change slowly, unless a big shock, like a war or a pandemic, comes and shakes them up. Fingers crossed that this book will shake up the five-day working week without the need for another war or a new covid virus.'

Sir Christopher Pissarides,
2010 Nobel Laureate in Economics

'Pedro Gomes presents a compelling approach to the topic, rooting his arguments in a range of economic theories, history and data – focused on the improvement of society.'

> *Financial Times Business Books of the Month:*
> *August Edition (2021)*

'I also recently read Pedro Gomes's *Friday is the New Saturday*, a breezily written polemic for shifting to a four-day workweek. It left me convinced that the idea, at least, deserves more consideration as our society has become richer and should enable us to consume more of everything – including time with our children.'

> *Jason Furman, Professor of Economics, Harvard University,*
> *in* Wall Street Journal, *Books of the Year*

'The idea of a shorter working week has recently received eloquent endorsement from a new book called *Friday is the New Saturday* by the economist Pedro Gomes. One of the striking things about this book is that Gomes argues that working as hard as people currently do has such a deleterious effect on their productivity that when working hours are reduced, total output may not fall. In some sectors it could actually rise. If he is right about this, then there is no trade-off between working hours and incomes. We are faced with the prospect of having more leisure without losing any income. I think Gomes is on to something ...'

> *Roger Bootle,* The Telegraph

'One of this summer's bestsellers is *Friday is the New Saturday: How a Four-Day Working Week Will Save the Economy* by Pedro Gomes. He argues that giving workers more freedom to decide their hours will increase productivity, propel innovation, support families and lead to better life choices.'

> *Alice Thomson,* The Times

'Gomes notices that, just like a hundred years ago when the working week went from six to five days, in the next few years we may see the definitive change to the four-day working week. Over the course of almost three hundred pages, Gomes presents argument after argument as to why we shouldn't fear this change, but rather embrace it with its many advantages. You don't have to agree with every one of them to learn from them all and be inspired by the author's enthusiasm.'

Ricardo Reis, A.W. Phillips Professor of Economics,
London School of Economics

'The long-run decline in hours worked during the week is a basic fact. There is no reason to think that the current setting, with approximately five days of work with approximately eight hours per day, cannot be reduced or changed. The four-day week might simply be the social innovation that contemporary capitalism urgently needs. Pedro Gomes makes the most persuasive economic case for the four-day week I have seen. The book should be on the bookshelves of every socially curious reader.'

Pietro Garibaldi, Professor of Economics,
University of Turin

'In the 20th century, the five-day working week replaced the six-day week. The fall in working hours was accompanied by a massive improvement in living standards because of new technologies, which enabled people to work less and enjoy more leisure. Pedro Gomes' book provides considerable food for thought about moving to the next stage, in light of new technological developments that make it possible to establish a new standard of a four-day working week.'

Rachel Ngai, Professor of Economics,
Imperial College London

Introduction

An Idea to Shape the Course of History

'Ideas shape the course of history.'

John Maynard Keynes

You might find it surprising to learn that economics has much in common with religion and love, but it is true. You cannot find better motivators of human behaviour – they can each bring happiness and build the foundations for well-being, but they can also blind, create discord and provide justification for harmful actions. Just as many things done in the name of religion are not done for God, and many things done in the name of love are not done for romance, many things done in the name of economics are not done for the economy.

This book is about one proposal that has been dismissed in the name of economics, but that would bring about a powerful economic renewal if enacted: the four-day working week. Since 2018, there has been a surge of interest in the idea. It first came about as a radical new management practice implemented by a few quirky firms. Articles soon followed in respectable publications like *The Guardian*, *The Economist*, the *Financial Times* and the *New York Times*. At the same time, the idea was picked up by some progressive think tanks like the New Economics Foundation and Autonomy. It then found its way into the manifesto of the UK Labour Party for the 2019 general election, and during the 2020 coronavirus pandemic it has been spoken about by Jacinda Ardern, prime minister of New Zealand, as a possible way to jump start her nation's economy. Since then, more companies are jumping on board with trials being conducted all over the world. Still, the idea raises much scepticism and is either viewed as a radical left-wing fantasy or branded as unworkable. After all, if we have always worked for five days each week, why change?

The purpose of this book is to break this narrative and explain the many compelling economic arguments in support of the four-day working week. These ideas come from both the left and right of the ideological spectrum – in fact, no economic theory stands against it. Moreover, it could be implemented much more smoothly than we might imagine. We should do it for – not in spite of – the economy.

This book is divided into three parts. The first part explains that although the four-day working week seems like a recent idea, it is not. There was a serious proposal in the US in 1970 called '4/40' (i.e. four days and forty hours of work per week), which was adopted by a number of firms. History also repeats itself in its criticisms. Most of today's arguments against the four-day working week were discussed in the US between 1908, when firms first started moving from a six-day to a five-day working week, and 1940, when the five-day working week was adopted nationwide.

My concept of a four-day working week is about much more than the enlightened 4/40-style management practice that has dominated headlines recently. I propose the four-day working week as something bigger: government legislation implemented across the entire economy. Such legislation would reduce the regular working week to a coordinated four days, from Monday to Thursday. All economic activities conducted during the working week would be organised over those four days, and all economic activities conducted over the weekend would operate from Friday to Sunday – hence my rallying cry: 'Friday is the new Saturday'.

There are many merits of flexible working arrangements (driven by workers), and the management practices supporting them (implemented by firms), and a number of my arguments can also be made to promote them. However, as we shall see, such arrangements are inferior to a four-day working week implemented by government legislation. Only in this way can the full economic benefits for society of reducing the working week be achieved.

The book's second part lays out the eight economic arguments for the four-day working week. Why should we support it?

- Because it is possible.
- Because it will fuel the economy through demand for leisure industries.
- Because it will increase productivity.
- Because it will unleash innovation.
- Because it will reduce technological unemployment.
- Because it will raise wages and reduce inequalities.
- Because it will give people more freedom to choose what to do with their time.
- Because it will reconcile a polarised society.

To explain the economics behind each of these arguments, I have enlisted the help of four of the most influential economists in history: John Maynard Keynes, Joseph Schumpeter, Karl Marx and Friedrich Hayek. I will view the economy through their eyes. These four political economists lived in different times and held diverging views on how to solve the problems facing societies. However, although they are thought of as torchbearers of competing ideologies, they have much in common. I believe that each of them, if they were alive today, would wholeheartedly support the idea of the four-day working week as an invaluable step towards improving society. As Winston Churchill famously said, 'If you put two economists in a room, you will get two different opinions; unless one of them is Lord Keynes, in which case you would invariably get three quite different opinions.' I do not expect everyone to be persuaded by all of my arguments, but I hope that some of them will hit home.

My eight arguments will be more or less persuasive depending on your own ideological preferences, but they are all underpinned by sound economic reasoning and supported by the data. Ultimately, the core of each argument relates to what people would do with their extra day off work. They might rest more, which would increase their efficiency during their four working days. They might enjoy leisure activities that involve spending, which would stimulate consumption. They could decide to work, so they would be exercising their individual freedom. They could use the day for retraining and acquiring new skills to help them move to a more rewarding or promising occupation. Or they could devote their time to their passion and create the innovations of the future. I don't presume to know what people would do, but whatever choice people made, they would be contributing to the economy. In the words of the Nobel-Prize-winning economist James Tobin, 'every leisure act has an economic pay-off to someone'.

There are those who believe that five is the ideal number of days to work per week, but don't wonder why that number hasn't changed in eighty years when almost everything else has – the speed we communicate, the types of jobs we do, the technology available to us, the number of years we study, the structure of our families, the role of women in society, the duration of our lives, the nature of our social interactions. They do so for the same reason that their great-grandparents believed six working days per week was the ideal number: because it was the status quo. This is the only credible argument against the four-day week: the fact that changing habits and institutions is never easy. Change is disruptive and the adaptation to a new way of organising society is costly. But the Covid-19 pandemic has weakened this argument; we are looking for a new normal, and we want it to be better. This offers us an unprecedented opportunity because the world – workers, firms and politicians – is open to new forms of organising the economy.

The final part of this book examines the practical details of implementing the four-day working week, in both the private and public sectors, and discusses its implications for the environment and GDP, and the equality between men and women. A transition to a four-day week could be made much more smoothly than one might imagine. If you are wondering whether everyone would take a 20 per cent pay cut by working a day less, the answer is no. The large majority of workers would not have any wage cuts. Surely this is too good to be true, or some form of economic dark magic? I can assure you it is neither. There are several possible adjustment mechanisms that will protect wages, ranging from increases in productivity, adjustments of hours worked in the remaining four days, reductions in oversized profits, price increases, subsidies and, most importantly, time. A transition period of approximately five years between the announcement of the four-day working week and its implementation would give workers, firms and the government enough time to prepare, restraining wage growth during this period to avoid cuts when the implementation takes place.

The four-day working week is an idea that can be embraced across the political spectrum and its implementation can be shaped by different ideologies. It is inevitable that the adjustments imposed will be different in the US than in France, because American and French citizens have different views on workers' rights and the importance of entrepreneurship. Also, within a country, different industries, occupations and firms could apply distinct combinations of these options. These negotiations would involve different stakeholders, such as unions, industry and consumer associations, and also the government.

In its early stages, implementing a four-day working week will be disruptive, but we should not take our eyes off the prize. Its implementation is a civilisational leap, desirable both for the economy and for the benefit of humanity. It will unshackle humankind, propelling our productivity and innovation, and giving us the freedom to flourish.

Let me finish this introduction with a disclaimer of three personal flaws. First, I am an economist, and a mainstream one. I love teaching and researching economics, and find nothing more captivating than studying economic science's theoretical models to investigate the complexity of people and their interactions in society, or applying statistical methods to an original dataset to discover new facts. How does people's behaviour change with different incentives? How do we improve societies with the right policies and damage them with the wrong ones? Economics is an incredibly useful science, despite its failings. In its call for a four-day working week, this book is also a story of some of the best ideas I have learned from the greatest economists, and how they can be combined to show that, far from being a radical proposal, the four-day working week would be a great achievement of economic science.

My second personal flaw relates to my own ideology. Being left- or right-wing is no more than a choice of how to view the world, yet much of today's ideological debate feels worse than the rivalries between fans of opposing sports teams; you pick a side and stick to it, hating your opponent above all else. I prefer to form my own opinions by looking for the best solution to a problem, no matter where it comes from. Like any economist, I believe in the power of free markets to coordinate the actions of people to achieve the best possible use of scarce resources. This is Economics 101, taught to all first-year university economics students. But like any good economist, I know that markets fail to achieve the best use of resources when firms don't face competition, when not all economic agents have the same information, or when firms pollute too much and do not pay for the consequences. Free markets also fail in the production of *public goods* like parks or roads, and they are powerless to enforce the law. At least in these cases, there is a role for the government. We teach this to students in their second and third years of an economics degree, but as the models become more complex, fewer students absorb their gist. In a world that is ever more polarised, this book is about bringing together different ideologies in an attempt to save an economic system that has brought prosperity during the last eighty years but is faltering. That, as you will see, is one of the beauties of the four-day week.

My third personal flaw is that I will not apologise for the other two flaws. In this book, I will use economics to think about the world, drawing on insights from economic theory, history and data. Do not expect an ideological book; I won't provide a blind glorification of free markets or a relentless criticism of capitalism. (You won't have trouble finding plenty of other books doing that.)

Twenty years ago, while studying for my undergraduate economics degree in my native Portugal, the idea of the four-day working week was planted in my brain when I read *Essays in Persuasion*, a collection of some of John Maynard Keynes's work. In one of the essays, 'Economic Possibilities for our Grandchildren', published in 1930, Keynes predicted that within 100 years people would be working fifteen hours per week. Keynes made some pretty successful predictions throughout his career, but surely a fifteen-hour working week will not be one of them.

Keynes's logic relied on the idea that technology would continue to improve as quickly as it had since the start of the Industrial Revolution in the eighteenth century, and that people would share the gains in productivity by consuming more and working less. He believed that we would be able to afford to work less *and* that we would want to work less. The first part of his argument was right: between 1929 and 2000, living standards in the West, measured by real GDP per capita, increased by between four and six times. However, the second part of his argument was wrong: in the same period, hours worked per week fell from forty-seven to an average of forty-two for men and thirty-nine for women. Societies have chosen to keep working, but we are always able to change our minds. This book is my attempt to change yours.

PART ONE

Understanding the Four-Day Working Week

1

History Repeating

'Progress comes from technical invention, and we shall be ever grateful to the discoverer of fire, the inventor of the electric dynamo, and the perfector of hollandaise sauce. But there are also momentous social inventions. Indeed, as society becomes more affluent, these may become increasingly vital. Without language we should still live in the cave, and all honour to that unknown genius who discovered that disputes of precedence could be settled by the toss of a coin. The four-day week is precisely such a social invention.'

Paul Samuelson, in his Foreword to 4 Days,
40 Hours, *published in 1970*

In 1970, Paul Samuelson received the Nobel Prize in Economics. The Nobel Committee stated that 'More than any other contemporary economist, Samuelson has helped to raise the general analytical and methodological level in economic science. He has simply rewritten considerable parts of economic theory.'

An American of Polish origin, Samuelson received his PhD from Harvard, and spent his lengthy and distinguished career at the Massachusetts Institute of Technology (MIT), living long enough to write obituaries of all the other important economists of the twentieth century. Rightfully considered the father of modern economics, he developed so many different economic fields that it was impossible even for the Nobel Committee to select his single most important contribution. He influenced how economists understand the decision-making of consumers, the well-being of an economy, the workings of financial markets, the role of governments in providing public goods, the winners and losers of international trade, and how we perceive the economy as a dynamic process.

Samuelson was pivotal in increasing the use of mathematics in economics. He saw mathematics as the only language that could be used to tell logically coherent stories and express reasoning, and he came to personify the attempt of economics to distinguish itself from other social sciences, approximating it to the rigour of physics and the other 'hard' sciences. The adoption of mathematics became the defining feature of modern economics. Articles that had many words and few equations now have many equations and few words. For better and for worse, it is thanks to Samuelson that economists, proud of their intellect, are known for having over-inflated egos; they are disdained by other social scientists for over-simplifying a complex reality; they are mocked by natural scientists because of the unrealistic assumptions they make; and they are ignored by everyone else because their science seems impenetrable.

Today, Samuelson is widely admired for his ability to unify opposing views. He was, in his own words, a 'dull centrist'. His textbook *Economics: An Introductory Analysis* has sold over 4 million copies worldwide and trained generations of economists. The book incorporates the two main branches of economics: *microeconomics*, which studies the behaviour of individual actors, such as consumers, firms or specific markets; and *macroeconomics*,

which studies the whole economy within a country or region – how all firms, all households and the government interact. One branch studies a single tree, while the other studies the forest. Both are intertwined, but while microeconomics has a bottom-up approach, the approach of macroeconomics is top-down. Because of the inherited complexity of the interaction of so many actors, macroeconomics tends to be more controversial and is often more dogmatic. In his textbook, Samuelson combined two opposing views of macroeconomics. There was classical economics, the dominant paradigm up until the Great Depression in the 1930s, which focused on the capacity of firms to produce goods and ignored the role of spending by consumers. Conversely, Keynesians believed that recessions are caused by insufficient spending, and their approach was adopted to deal with the persistently high levels of unemployment that resulted from the Great Depression. The combination of these opposing views, now known as the *neoclassical synthesis*, reflects Samuelson's ability to unify.

In 1970, Samuelson wrote the foreword to *4 Days, 40 Hours*. A collection of articles by social scientists and management experts edited by Riva Poor, then a student at MIT's Sloan School of Management, the book analysed a novel and promising management practice implemented at the time by more than thirty companies: a four-day working week comprised of forty hours, without reducing pay to workers. The book approached the four-day working week from a microeconomic angle. It reported how firms that implemented '4/40' saw a rise in productivity and a reduction in costs, an increase in worker happiness, morale and job-satisfaction, and a reduction in staff turnover and absenteeism. It described how employees reacted to the change and what they did with their extra day of weekend, including resting, spending time with family, travelling, engaging in hobbies or sports, reading more, pursuing further education, or taking a part-time job.

Samuelson, in the year he was recognised as the father of modern economics, not only endorsed the four-day week but went so far as to call it a 'momentous social invention'. Samuelson argued that it offered a new choice in an area where people had few options – what to do with their time – and that it could even change the structure of the family through levelling up the division of labour between husband and wife. However, although the most brilliant economist of his time categorically supported the idea, the four-day working week did not take off.

A decade later, in 1981, another book on the four-day working week was published: *A Shorter Workweek in the 1980s*. The author, William McGaughey, describes himself as 'a philosopher, story-teller, landlord, labour economist, world historian, political candidate, arrestee and family man'. His book approached the four-day working week from a macroeconomic angle, as a policy prescription. It advocated the shorter working week as a solution for unemployment, by promoting work sharing. It also sought to counter the most serious objections to a shorter working week, namely that it would aggravate inflation, the economic bogeyman of the time, by raising firms' costs, or that people might choose to increase their incomes by working longer rather than pursuing leisure.

McGaughey wrote a second book on the subject in 1989, *Nonfinancial Economics: The Case for Shorter Hours of Work*. This time he enlisted a heavyweight as co-author: Democratic Senator Eugene McCarthy. McCarthy was an economics professor before embarking on a career as a politician. He served in the US House of Representatives for ten years before becoming a senator in 1959. He was a maverick. Against the odds, he challenged the incumbent Lyndon Johnson for the Democratic nomination in the 1968 presidential election, galvanising the anti-Vietnam War movement. After a tight first primary, Johnson announced that he would not seek re-election and Robert Kennedy entered the race. McCarthy and Kennedy each won several primaries before Kennedy was killed. That year's Democratic National Convention, marked by violence, picked Vice President Hubert Humphrey as its nominee. McCarthy sought the presidency a further four times, but never garnered the same momentum. In 2005, *The Economist* wrote in his obituary: 'Irishness, daring, puckish humour, wilful solitariness, a sense of the pervading importance of higher things, were all delivered with professorial elegance by a man once described as "Thomas Aquinas in a suit".'

In his first term as senator, McCarthy was the chair of a Special Committee on Unemployment, convened to consider the implications of automation. Among the various options to deal with worker displacement due to labour-saving technologies, the report stated that it might become necessary to reconsider the work-time option, should unemployment remain high. Many of these ideas were repeated in his co-authored book published some thirty years later, which also recycled several chapters of McGaughey's original. The book argued that the four-day working week was the right policy to address increasing automation and the spread of labour-saving technologies. Its deeper philosophical point was that many jobs in the economy reflect pure waste. This waste has taken many forms, from excessive government regulation to the production of goods that could only be sold through significant advertising or by being exported cheaply to foreign countries, and from the conspicuous consumption of products we don't need through to wars, the ultimate waste. The economy was full of fat, and reducing the working week would make it leaner.

Senator McCarthy is not the only high-profile politician to have supported the four-day working week. After the chaos of the 1968 Democratic primaries, Vice President Hubert Humphrey lost against Richard Nixon. This might have been good news for the four-day week, as Nixon himself, while Vice President in 1956, had foreseen in the 'not too distant future a four-day work week' and a 'fuller family life for every American'. However, by the time Richard Nixon was president, he had changed his mind. (No wonder McCarthy later said that 'Nixon is the kind of guy who, if you were drowning twenty feet from the shore, would throw you a fifteen-foot rope.')

After a few decades in oblivion, the four-day working week made a comeback. In 2018, Robert Grosse, a Professor of Business Administration at Arizona State University and former President of the Academy of International Business, wrote *The Four-Day Workweek*. His book is a modern take on *4 Days, 40 Hours*; instead of calling for a rearrangement of the forty hours into four days, it proposes a reduction to thirty-two working hours. Grosse reaffirms the link between reducing working hours and increasing productivity. He also analyses the implementation of the four-day week and the trade-off between productivity gains and wage cuts. Academic in tone and full of statistics, his book acknowledges a possible role for the government in providing incentives for workers and firms that switch to a four-day week, but overall it takes a microeconomic view – it is directed at 'forward-thinking executives and leaders'.

In 2020, another book on the subject was published. *The 4 Day Week* is also written from the microeconomic perspective, but it is told from a personal perspective. The author, Andrew Barnes, is the CEO of Perpetual Guardian, New Zealand's largest statutory trust company with £100 billion in assets and 240 employees. In 2018 he implemented what he called 'the 100-80-100 rule' at the firm. Workers received their wages in full and worked 80 per cent of the time, provided they delivered the agreed output. And they did. Barnes now travels the world, telling audiences how the 'five-day week is a nineteenth-century construct that is not fit for purpose in the twenty-first century'. He did not implement the four-day working week for charity or for lifestyle reasons after a near-death experience; he is a businessman and he did it for profit.

These five books demonstrate the two approaches we can take to the four-day working week, and the range of actors who might lead the revolution. The books by Poor, Grosse and Barnes take the bottom-up microeconomic approach, listing the benefits to firms and workers of reducing working hours. Implicitly, they assume that workers and firms should lead the revolution, and that whatever they want will be provided by the market. The books by McGaughey and McCarthy present a top-down macroeconomic perspective. They list the benefits of a four-day working week for society, and do not expect markets to convert to it spontaneously. Instead, they argue that governments should lead the revolution through legislation.

It is a time of growing publicity for the four-day working week – more firms are implementing it with astounding results, new politicians are supporting it, unions are getting behind it too, together with several think tanks. Will the four-day working week finally take off?

There are grounds for optimism, but it is worth remembering that firms have been experimenting with the four-day working week and that for at least fifty years there have been calls for it from many serious economists and politicians. Doubters of the four-day working week can simply point to these previous failed attempts and discard the idea as an impractical fantasy. If it didn't work before, why should it work now?

To understand why the four-day working week has not taken off before, we must look beyond the hype and learn why the considerable arguments in its favour have only ever persuaded a small minority. So, what can we learn from history to find better arguments for a four-day working week in the twenty-first century?

2

Singing an Old Song

'The biggest problem is not to let people accept new ideas, but to let them forget the old ones.'

John Maynard Keynes

Working five days a week is not written in our genes, the scriptures or the stars. The working week is an economic, social and political construct. Until the beginning of the twentieth century, people in the Western world worked six days each week and rested on Sundays. In 1908, a few small businesses in the US implemented a revolutionary practice: the five-day working week. In 1922, the National Association of Manufacturers published a bulletin called *Will the 5-Day Week Become Universal? It Will Not.* They gave eight reasons against the radical proposal:

- It would greatly increase the cost of living.
- It would increase wages generally by more than 15 per cent and decrease production.

- It would be impractical for all industries.
- It would help meet a short-term sales decline but would not work permanently.
- It would create a craving for additional luxuries to occupy the additional time.
- It would mean a trend towards leisure and the Arena – Rome did that and Rome died.
- It would be against the best interest of those who want to work and advance.
- It would make us more vulnerable to the economic onslaughts of Europe, now working as hard as she can to overcome our lead.

The objections to the four-day working week today are simply repetitions of these same arguments. They can be grouped into four categories: economic, operational, ethical and comparative. The first and second reasons are economic. They are misguided because they take a static view of the economy and of the relationship between workers and firms. They assume nothing else will change in response to the four-day working week; workers will not change the energy they put into production, managers will not change their practices, and consumers will not change their demand for goods. In fact, the opposite is true – economies are dynamic and are constantly adjusting.

These economic reasons also ignore the distinction between *average* and *marginal productivity*, one of the crucial concepts in economics. The longer you work, whether in hours or days, your added contribution – your *marginal productivity* – declines. Workers are less productive in the eighth hour of work than in the seventh, and less productive on a Friday than on a Thursday.

Arguments three and four concern the practicality of shortening the work week. Recently, we could read in *The Telegraph*: 'We all know that the four-day week proposal is unaffordable, impossible, imaginary' or 'It is too operationally complex'. A 'crackpot plan' said Boris Johnson, then the UK Prime Minister. These are lazy arguments made by people averse to change and unwilling to judge a proposal by its merits. Moreover, there is no economic substance to an argument of just following the status quo.

Arguments five to seven are ethical in nature. Their modern equivalent is 'Under the four-day working week, people are just going to watch TV and get dumb.' These types of arguments are paternalistic and patronising, and behind them lies the view that leisure is somehow perverse or evil. At the beginning of the nineteenth century, the workday lasted from sunrise to sunset, and the first shorter-hours movement aimed to reduce the maximum working day to ten hours. In 1825, the master carpenters in Boston responded to the demands of the journeymen whom they employed: 'We learn with surprise and regret that a large number of those who are employed as journeymen in this city have entered into a combination for the purpose of altering the time of commencing and terminating their daily labour from that which has been customary from time immemorial.' They considered such a combination 'fraught with numerous and pernicious evils' and would expose the journeymen themselves 'to many temptations and improvident practices' from which they were 'happily secure' when working from sunrise to sunset. In other words, workers would spend their free time drinking, gambling, fighting and fornicating.

The philosopher Bertrand Russell, in his 1932 timeless essay *In Praise of Idleness*, summarised it well:

> The idea that the poor should have leisure has always been shocking to the rich. In England, in the early nineteenth century, fifteen hours was the ordinary day's work for a man; children sometimes did as much, and very commonly did twelve hours a day. When meddlesome busybodies suggested that perhaps these hours were rather long, they were told that work kept adults from drink and children from mischief. When I was a child, shortly after urban working men had acquired the vote, certain public holidays were established by law, to the great indignation of the upper classes. I remember

hearing an old Duchess say: 'What do the poor want with holidays? They ought to work.' People nowadays are less frank, but the sentiment persists, and is the source of much of our economic confusion.

At least the biblical argument widely invoked those days against the five-day working week – that God only rested on Sunday – cannot be recycled against the four-day working week. Amen!

Finally, the eighth argument is about external competition. Today it would sound something like: 'China already produces goods so cheaply that switching to a four-day week will spell a further loss of competitiveness. We cannot afford it now.' This argument relies on the narrow view of the world economy as a zero-sum game, ignoring how all countries benefit from international trade and cooperation. What's more, who thinks we will retain our leadership (whatever that means) over China by working a six-day week instead? The economic clout of China accelerated precisely after they adopted the five-day working week in 1995.

Despite these widely held negative opinions, in 1926 Henry Ford, the founder of Ford Motor Company, surprised his fellow industrialists by implementing a five-day week across his US and overseas factories, covering 99 per cent of his workforce. It was an astonishing decision, and in his statement putting forward his reasons he made a powerful business case for it, deftly rebutting all the common criticisms. He contradicted the economic arguments, finding that his workers 'come back after a two-day holiday so fresh and keen that they are able to put their minds as well as their hands into their work'. Management, he continued, responded by improving processes and increasing efficiency, because 'the harder we crowd business for time, the more efficient it becomes'. He dismissed the ethical concerns about increased leisure time, stating that 'there is a profound difference between leisure and idleness'. He then flipped the external competition argument on its head, claiming that the move would strengthen rather than weaken the position of the US relative to their European competitors, and gave the example of Germany, which had increased the 'hours of the labor day under the delusion that thus the production might be increased' when in fact 'it is quite possibly being decreased'. Finally, he gave a powerful economic argument in favour of the five-day working week, claiming that increasing leisure 'will raise demand for the goods produced by the American Industry, workers will demand more food, more and better goods, more books, more music – more of everything.' Above all, by successfully implementing the policy, Ford showed the feasibility and practicality of the five-day week. I will come back to his statement several times, because two of my eight arguments in the four-day working week's favour closely follow his reasoning.

Did other industries line up to follow Ford? Not at all, but his decision still made an impact. In 1929, the National Industrial Conference Board, a US business association, published *The Five-Day Week in Manufacturing Industries*. They estimated that by 1928, only 2.6 per cent of wage earners in the US were working five days, 80 per cent of whom were employed by the Ford Motor Company. The report discussed several of the benefits found by companies that implemented the shorter working week, such as increased productivity, reduced overhead costs and improved worker attendance and punctuality. They concluded that the 'evidence does, however, remove the five-day week from the status of a radical and impractical administrative experiment and places it among the plans which, however revolutionary they may appear to some, have demonstrated both practicability and usefulness under certain circumstances'. Still, the five-day week continued to have many detractors. In 1936, Harold Moulton, the president of the Brookings Institution, an influential American think tank, wrote that 'the shorter work week would prove to be nothing short of a calamity to the wage earners of the country'.

When *The Economist* wrote in 2018 that 'growing calls for a four-day week are likely to go unheeded', I was disappointed by this lukewarm reception. Then I remembered that one of the reasons I love *The Economist* is its editorial consistency; over eighty-five years before, on 20 June 1936, *The Economist* had written in a similar tone that the forty-hour week is a 'demand which will arouse general sympathy, but must at the same time present very serious difficulties'. That gave me cause for optimism – just two years after that article, the five-day working week moved from the micro- to the macroeconomy in the US, with the introduction of the Fair Labor Standards Act of 1938. This law prescribed a five-day, forty-hour working week as the standard, and set up an enforcement system through overtime penalties for firms for each hour of a worker's time beyond the scheduled forty. The law first applied only to firms engaging in interstate commerce and allowed two years for the adjustment to take place. Its coverage expanded over the following decades. Wall Street only stopped trading on Saturday mornings in September 1952. The legislation also introduced a minimum wage and limited child labour. Such an ambitious and multi-dimensional overhaul of labour law was a consequence of the deepening of the US recession at the time, and the Fair Labor Standards Act was a central plank of Franklin Roosevelt's New Deal. The day before he signed it, Roosevelt said that: 'Except perhaps for the Social Security Act, [it] is the most far-reaching, far-sighted program for the benefit of workers ever adopted here or in any other country. Without question it starts us toward a better standard of living and increases purchasing power.' On the eve of the Second World War, the five-day working week had finally taken off in the US.

The UK's progress towards the five-day week was slower and driven by industry rather than the government. Between 1946 and 1963, a five-day working week was agreed in the printing, building, mining, construction and electrical industries, and later in shipbuilding and engineering. It was also adopted by some of the nation's largest employers, such as Tate & Lyle. Yet by 1963 only half a million workers in the UK had achieved a forty-hour week, out of a total workforce of more than 20 million. It was not until the 2003 EU Working Time Directive that all

UK workers were covered by a maximum hours' regulation, of forty-eight hours per week.

A remarkable aspect about the criticisms of the five-day week is that they completely disappeared whenever it was implemented. Think about it. There has never been an attempt to go back to working six days. Surely this can only happen when the success of a measure is so obvious to so many people, and when there are hardly any losers. How unusual is it for such deep social or economic transformation to be so consensual? The European Union has never been able to rid itself of its critics. The National Health Service, an ingrained institution in the UK, has faced calls for privatisation from some politicians. In the US, Obamacare was implemented, but its foundations were attacked at the first opportunity. The five-day working week was much more than an achievement of the workers' movement, it was a social innovation that improved the way we organise the economy in the twentieth century.

There is one remaining argument of critics of the four-day week, and it comes from those who argue that there is an ideal number of days we should work per week – not too many, and not too few. They claim that five is the magic number and has been unchanged for eighty years, like a constant in physics or mathematics. The idea of a magic number is common in economic policy, when we are balancing costs and benefits. For instance, some economists believe the corporate tax rate should go up to increase tax revenues while countering inequality, and others think it should go down to incentivise the investment of firms. Regarding the inflation target of central banks, which is about 2 per cent, some economists say it should be 4 per cent and others that it should be zero. When we are talking about an ideal amount, you usually have people making the case in both directions. If the five-day week is still that magic number, there should at least be some work extremists calling for a six-day week. But, in an age when fanatics dominate large parts of the digital world, I haven't found even one person who thinks we can solve our economic malaise by making everyone work an extra day.

In the current criticisms of the four-day working week, history is repeating itself. If firms, workers and policy makers had believed the criticisms in the past, we would all still be working twelve-hour shifts for six days a week. Would detractors of the four-day working week seriously defend a return to the old days? If not, what makes the five-day working week more special than the four-day week, other than it being the status quo? If it was possible to change from six to five days, surely it's possible to change it to four.

To escape the status quo, we have to start afresh and analyse the benefits and the drawbacks of the four-day working week, without falling into the empty rhetoric of the antagonistic 'sporting rivalry' style of discussion. Let's start with a clean slate, and to do that I first want to make clear what a four-day working week actually means.

3

What is the Four-Day Working Week?

'If you always do what you've always done, you'll always get what you've always got.'

Henry Ford

My definition of the four-day working week is simple. Whatever economic activities take place during the week should be done over four days, from Monday to Thursday. All economic activities that take place over the weekend should be done over three days, from Friday to Sunday. All economic activities that take place throughout the seven days, for instance in hospitals, hotels and pubs, should still be done over seven days, but the standard working week should have only four days. Who should be the driver? I propose that it should be the government implementing the four-day working week through legislation, similar to the US's Fair Labor Standards Act of 1938.

I have deliberately kept my definition generic. One of the biggest mistakes of proponents of the four-day week in the past has been to make their definitions too precise. Riva Poor's 4/40 proposal added that there should be no reduction of total weekly hours worked. Robert Grosse added that the hours worked per day should not increase in the other weekdays, essentially prescribing a 4/32 system. If you add 'without loss of pay', it further complicates the message. These are important issues, but they are related to the implementation of the four-day week rather than to the concept itself. Think of it like a marriage. First, a couple decides whether they want to tie the knot. Then, they argue over how many people to invite to the wedding, whether they will dance to a band or a DJ, and what flowers they'll have. These are important decisions, but nobody calls off a wedding because of them. It's the same with the four-day week. Two countries might implement it in different ways. The British might prefer red roses, the Americans blue chrysanthemums, and the French white lilies. Within a single country different industries or different occupations might make different adjustments. I will devote the third part of this book to these issues of implementation, but first I need to convince you to marry this idea.

A common misconception is that the economy stops over the weekend, but it's not true; it merely shifts gear. Quite a few people work over the weekend. I know this first-hand, as my wife is an obstetrician and gynaecologist in the NHS. It is an impressive job that makes me feel that what I do is useless. While I spend hours struggling with Greek letters in a differential equation or finding a misplaced semicolon in a computer code, she uses a seventeenth-century metal salad server, a nineteenth-century plumbing aid or a timeless scalpel to bring babies into the world. As babies don't think about working hours when deciding when they want to be born, one weekend per month my wife works twelve-hour shifts, either during the day or at night. Please don't feel sorry for her, that's easy compared to my job of looking after our 5-year-old daughter for the whole weekend. On Saturday morning I take her to ballet and then do the weekly shopping. In the afternoon we bounce on the trampoline at Kidzone. On Sunday we go swimming, grab a bite to eat at the local farmers' market, and then it's on to the Museum of Childhood or the cinema to watch *Frozen 2* ... again! During that weekend, I encounter hundreds of people who are working. In fact, according to the Labour Force Survey, 20 per cent of all employees work on a Saturday and 15 per cent work on a Sunday. As a comparison, on any given weekday, roughly two thirds of us are working.

The four-day working week is often associated with microeconomic practices such as flexible working arrangements between firm and workers. These include flexibility in the number of hours worked (such as part-time work or job shares), in the scheduling of hours worked, and in the place of work, like working from home. My wife, like 25 per cent of all workers in the UK, works part-time. She works 80 per cent, so she is effectively on a four-day working week. In other countries, the rate of part-time work is even higher. According to Eurostat, the institution that produces official European Union statistics, Belgium, Germany, Austria and Norway all have higher part-time rates than in the UK, and the Netherlands leads the way with close to half of all workers being part-time.

A common argument is that part-time workers are only part-time because they can't find a proper full-time job, but this is categorically false. According to the UK Labour Force Survey, a large majority of part-time workers – 70 per cent – do not want a full-time job, and only 12 per cent do. The remainder are students. There is a distinct gender aspect to part-time work: 40 per cent of women are part-time workers, compared to only 12 per cent of men. This is one of the key statistics to support Paul Samuelson's claim that the four-day working week could help balance the separation of tasks in a household between men and women. Women would benefit more from the four-day week, as men would be compelled to work fewer hours and do more housework.

Other beneficiaries of the four-day week are younger and older workers. There is a particular pattern when charting the ages of part-time workers: a *U-shape*. Part-time work is very high – 90 per cent – for 16-year-olds who are employed, and it goes down progressively, until it reaches 15 per cent for workers aged 25 to 29. It stabilises at around 20 per cent, until it shoots up again at age 54. About 60 per cent of workers aged 65 to 69 are working part-time and, unsurprisingly, all employed workers between the ages of 90 and 95, estimated in the survey to be more than 5,000 people, work part-time. The four-day week would benefit younger workers, as they could take advantage of weekend part-time jobs to earn wages and gain experience, as well as older workers who could prolong their working lives.

Another interesting fact is that part-time employment is not a well-heeled London thing; the part-time rate in England's capital is 20 per cent, the lowest of all twelve UK regions. The highest part-time rates are found in the South West with 29 per cent, and in Wales, Scotland and the North East with 27 per cent. Part-time work is more common in certain sectors: between 40 and 50 per cent of workers in food and drink service, retail, domestic personnel, sport, amusement, recreation, services to buildings and landscape, and creative arts and entertainment are part-time. There is an equal balance of part-time workers between the private and public sectors.

At the moment, taking up a part-time role is a bottom-up decision, usually initiated by workers. This adds to four-day week management practice, initiated by firms, which is most often reported in the news, such as in this *Washington Post* article from November 2019:

Microsoft launched a four-day workweek experiment earlier this year in one of the most unlikely places: Japan. But in a country known for its culture of extreme overwork, the shorter week had a big boost on productivity. [It is] the latest example of a growing global movement to experiment with the concept of a four-day workweek as tight labor market conditions continue, technology offers increased flexibility, and reports proliferate that some workplaces have seen beneficial results from working four days and then being off for three.

Where these cases differ from my own definition of the four-day working week is that they are led by firms and workers rather than by the government. Yet there have been top-down legislative approaches to reduce working time of the type that I propose, in addition to the US Labor Standards Act. The best-known example is the implementation of the thirty-five-hour working week in France in 2000. The Aubry Law established as overtime all time worked after the standard legal limit of thirty-five hours per week. The purpose was not to reduce the working week to four days, but to reduce the working day from eight hours to seven. Everyone should finish working one hour earlier. One of the aims of the law was to reduce the unemployment rate through work sharing, an argument that is scorned by most economists because it views production as fixed and does not contemplate the possible adjustments of an economy's moving pieces – the behaviour of workers, managers and consumers. Researchers who have studied the impacts of the Aubry legislation have found that the law had little effect on employment, and total hours worked per week only reduced slightly because people engaged in more overtime to earn extra money or to increase their holiday allowance.

There are two key aspects that make my definition of the four-day working week superior to both the bottom-up flexible working arrangements (like Microsoft in Japan) and policies that reduce a population's daily working hours (like France's Aubry Law): coordination and commuting.

Coordination between agents is a key element of economic activity. Economic theory and data advocate the benefits of agglomeration economies – the geographic clustering of economic activities, such as tech companies in Silicon Valley in the US, the Milan fashion industry, and Aerospace Valley in southwest France. Many of the same arguments for coordination across space can also be made for coordination across time. When I am working, I am more productive if I can be in contact with my manager, my co-workers, my suppliers and my clients. If firms implement an uncoordinated four-day week or workers become part-time, losses occur because of the difficulties in collaboration and delays in communication and decision-making. We want to buy, produce and sell at the same time that others are buying, producing and selling.

Management scholars argue that, in recent decades, firms have become more collaborative. In a typical work week, the percentage of time spent on the phone, email or in meetings is between 70 and 85 per cent for white-collar workers and can reach 95 per cent for top executives, many of whom spend all day in meetings and briefings. Teamwork makes a firm more productive but requires some coordination of hours. In a recent study, researchers analysing a large number of Danish firms and workers found evidence of a positive association between the overlap of workers in the workplace and the productivity of the firm and the wages of workers.

Coordination is important among co-workers, but also across companies. The most common problems described by firms that adopted the four-day week in the early 1970s were to do with shipping and the need to educate their customers to the fact that they were closed on Friday. The four-day week as a management practice cannot avoid the trade-off between coordination within and between firms. The biggest decision of managers is therefore whether to give workers a day off across different days of the week, which worsens coordination within firms, or give all workers the same day off, which makes the coordination with suppliers and customers more difficult. The four-day week implemented through legislation avoids this problem of uncoordinated implementation, because it changes the status quo, acting like a synchronisation device for all economic agents.

Coordination also matters for leisure. What are the benefits of not working on Wednesday if my wife and friends are all working? Researchers from the universities of Stanford and Wisconsin-Madison have argued that time is a *network good* – its value depends on the number of other people in your social network who are also free. They support this hypothesis with data from the American Time Use Survey, stating:

that both workers and the unemployed experience remarkably similar increases in emotional well-being on weekends and have similar declines in well-being when the workweek begins. The unemployed look forward to weekends much the same as workers. Weekend well-being is not due to time off work *per se* but rather is a collectively produced social good stemming from widely shared free time on weekends. The unemployed gain comparatively little benefit from their time off during the week, when others go to work.

Along the same lines, Stephen Jenkins of the London School of Economics has used UK data from the 1990s to show that partners tend to synchronise their working hours and engage in leisure activities depending on the availability of companions outside of their household. He concludes that 'although working longer hours may accelerate growth in GDP per capita in the short run, both income and social life may suffer in the longer run'. Coordination of leisure is also the reason why couples tend to synchronise the timing of their retirements.

According to the late Harvard economist Alberto Alesina, coordination of work and leisure is the reason why weekends exist in the first place. To avoid overloading roads during the week, and restaurants and museums over the weekend, as well as to make more intensive use of expensive machinery, it would be more logical if everyone rotated their days off. This form of organising economic activity was never adopted, because the benefits of coordination of economic activity overcome by far the costs of congestion and lower utilization of machinery.

And it wasn't for lack of trying. In 1929, the Soviet Union installed the *nepreryvka* or 'continuous working week'. Joseph Stalin disliked the religious aspect of Sundays and thought that machines should never stop. Workers were divided into groups, represented by a colour-coded symbol, and would rotate their days off. The experiment was a failure on every count. Productivity fell, the constant rotation of tasks meant that no one would take responsibility, machines broke down faster, and family life suffered. 'What is there for us to do at home if our wives are in the factory, our children at school, and nobody can visit us ...? It is no holiday if you have to have it alone,' summed up a reader of the communist newspaper *Pravda*. In 1940, Stalin abandoned *nepreryvka* and reinstituted a six-day week with one common rest day.

Coordination has an international dimension too. Small countries with strong economic ties with the rest of the world, like the Netherlands, face larger costs of unilaterally adopting a four-day working week when compared to larger countries. Even if most of its labour force works part-time, coordinating on a third day of weekend could worsen the interaction with their trading partners. Would a German manufacturer prefer to contract the financial services of a company from the Netherlands that's only open four days a week, or one from Luxembourg that is open five days? International coordination implies that the transition towards a shorter working week is likely to start in large economies with strong domestic markets, like the US, Canada, the UK, France, Germany or the European Union as a block. But it also implies that, once the first countries adopt it, others will soon follow like a trail of domino pieces – after all, why would the financial services company in Luxembourg need to operate on Fridays, when all its German customers are off?

The second key benefit of my definition of a four-day working week is less commuting. Let us do a back-of-the-envelope calculation. According to the UK's Trades Union Congress, the average worker in Britain spent, before the pandemic, fifty-nine minutes commuting per day. Multiply that for forty-seven five-day weeks of work and you get a staggering 230 hours spent commuting per year, equivalent to twenty-eight days of work. Multiply that for the 25 million full-time workers in the UK and the time lost to commuting is an eye-watering 750 million working days (or, if you prefer, 750 million days of lost leisure). The four-day working week would rescue 150 million days of lost time.

Besides the time cost, commuting entails a direct monetary cost – on average, a UK worker spends £1,738 a year on their commute. There is also a well-established indirect cost in terms of health outcomes. People with long journeys to and from work report much lower subjective and physiological well-being. Research by the behavioural economist Nobel Prize winner Daniel Kahneman has shown what any Londoner who takes the Central Line to work in rush hour already knows: commuting is our least enjoyable daily activity. Longer commuting is associated with higher rates of depression, stress, high blood pressure, heart disease, stroke, visits to the doctor and 'pulling a sickie'. Commuters also tend to exercise and sleep less; the more time you spend in your car or on public transport, the less time you spend in the gym or in bed.

The widespread use of flexible working arrangements is evidence that society is ready for the four-day working week. According to the 2019 UK Labour Force Survey, 15 per cent of all workers are self-employed, up from 12 per cent in 2001, meaning that they already have the freedom to choose how much to work. Under the four-day working week they would keep this freedom – no one would stop them. Out of the remaining 85 per cent, one quarter of people work part-time and only a small minority would want to work more hours. On the other hand, out of the remaining full-time workers, 40 per cent of them want to work fewer hours, 16 per cent already work fewer than thirty-six hours, and about 20 per cent of them have some type of arrangement such as flexitime, annualised hours contracts, term-time working, job-sharing, a nine-day fortnight, 4.5-day weeks, summer hours or on-call working. Society will keep pushing, but it cannot give that final push by itself. Just as my wife and her obstetric toolkit are needed for difficult births, we need the help of the government to deliver the four-day working week. And, as she would tell you, whatever the pain you might go through, it will be a distant memory the moment a new life is front of your eyes.

4

How to Propose?

'In the days of Manchester liberalism, the labour contract was a matter between the individual worker and employer. Any "labour policies", either by the society or by the organisations, were non-existent. Luckily, this has been changed.'

Ragnar Frisch

In 1895, when Alfred Nobel, a Swedish inventor and businessman, left his fortune to create prizes for extraordinary scientific or cultural contributions, he did not envisage thère being a prize for economics. It was only in 1969 that the Riksbank, the central bank of Sweden, created the Prize in Economic Sciences in Memory of Alfred Nobel. So, who were the economic geniuses who beat Paul Samuelson, the father of modern economics, to the first Nobel Prize? It was Ragnar Frisch, a Norwegian economist, together with a Dutch economist, Jan Tinbergen.

Ragnar Frisch was the founder of a third branch of economics – econometrics. He defined it as follows:

Intermediate between mathematics, statistics and economics, we find a new discipline which, for lack of a better name, may be called econometrics. Econometrics has as its aim to subject abstract laws of theoretical political economy or 'pure' economics to experimental and numerical verification, and thus to turn pure economics, as far as possible, into a science in the strict sense of the word.

After Frisch's death, Samuelson wrote: 'Ragnar Frisch dominated analytical economics from the early 1930s founding of the Econometric Society to his wartime internment in a Nazi concentration camp. He combined fertility and versatility with depth.' His versatility, together with the lack of a clear association with any school of thought, makes it hard to classify him in the history of economics, but his impact was profound. Together with Joseph Schumpeter, he was one of the sixteen founders of the Econometric Society, an exclusive club of academic economists that publishes *Econometrica*, still one of the most prestigious economics journals. Frisch himself was editor-in-chief from its inception in 1932 until 1955. It was Frisch who introduced the concept of the 'economic model', the bread and butter of economists, through an unusual visual metaphor:

The observational world itself, taken as a whole in its infinite complexity and with its infinite mass of detail, is impossible to grasp. Taken in its entirety, in its immediate form of sense impressions, it resembles, so to speak, a jelly-like mass on which the mind cannot get a grip. In order to create the points where the mind can get a grip, we make an intellectual trick: in our mind we create a little model world of our own, a model world which is not too complicated to be overlooked, and which is equipped with points where the mind can get a grip, so that we can find our way through without getting confused. And then we analyse this little model world instead of the real world.

Frisch was particularly gifted in naming new concepts. He was also responsible for coining the terms 'macroeconomics' and 'microeconomics'. Between them, macroeconomics, microeconomics and econometrics make up the trio of core courses in any postgraduate economics programme.

Frisch thought that government had an important role to play in implementing macroeconomic policy. He, like many other economists, was scarred by the Great Depression. 'The mass unemployment prevailing in most countries in the 1930s led to a monstrous situation: standards of living declined in the midst of plenty', he wrote in 1949. 'Food and other consumption goods were deliberately destroyed while people hoped and prayed that something would turn up.' Frisch believed that the economy could be improved by means of macroeconomic policy, and he worked for many decades with Norwegian public institutions developing macroeconomic models to be used in policy. He did not disdain private enterprise – he was a great friend and admirer of the work of Joseph Schumpeter – but simply thought that some changes must come from the top.

Econometrics enables economics to leave the realm of theory and use data to validate or disprove theories in the real world. Economists typically think about the use of data in three ways. The first is purely descriptive. What is the percentage of the growth rate of the economy that is accounted for by start-ups, or the average commuting time of a Japanese worker? Economists usually show these numbers in graphs or tables and use them to highlight the importance of a certain phenomenon. Sometimes we use them to highlight an observation that is inconsistent with a particular theory – a *puzzle*.

A second way of using data in economics is to establish associations between two or more variables. A higher unemployment rate in an area is associated with a larger support for Brexit. Working fewer hours is associated with higher productivity across firms. Spending less time commuting is associated with more happiness. The association is often shown in scatter plots and can be useful in generating interest in particular economic mechanisms. Its limitation is simple: *association* does not mean *causality*. For instance, do lower hours raise productivity, or do increases in productivity enable lower hours? Besides this *reverse causality*, the association could be caused by a third variable, or it might simply be associated by chance – something that often happens when we are comparing two series over time. The consumption of cheese in the US is associated with the number of suicides by hanging, the sales of ice cream with forest fires, and a scatter plot could link my daughter's height to the US stock market index. Economics seminars can be violent spectacles, with one economist calling them a 'contact sport'. I have seen more economics seminars go embarrassingly downhill because of poor wording than because of poor economic reasoning. If an economist ever talks about an association as causality, even with a logical explanation, their reputation will be tarnished.

The third way of using data in economics is to establish a causal relation between variables. This is extremely difficult to achieve. In natural sciences one can run experiments, setting up a control and treatment groups and comparing their outcomes. In economics, particularly in macroeconomics, it is more complicated, but this is where econometrics has really helped. It has shown economists how to make causal statements. There are several ways of doing it.

One is to use what we call *instrumental variables*. Suppose we want to know whether having more customers throughout the day will make taxi drivers work shorter or longer hours. Looking at the

association between the number of customers and the hours driven is no good, because there is a problem of reverse causality – cab drivers who work longer hours will naturally serve more customers. To solve it, we can use information on the weather. In particular, we can use rainy days as an instrumental variable – rainy days usually attract more customers for cabs and do not depend on any economic variable. Using mathematical formulas that econometricians derived, we are able to pin down how an increasing demand for cab rides affects cab drivers' decision of how many hours they will work. According to Richard Thaler, winner of the 2017 Nobel Prize in Economics, they work fewer hours. On rainy days, once they reach their target income, taxi drivers prefer to go home earlier. (At least, the New York cab drivers of Thaler's study do.)

Another route to making causal statements is to explore *natural experiments*, for instance the implementation of laws that affect some groups of workers, firms and regions but not others. Between 2004 and 2011, the South Korean government reduced its work week from forty-four to forty hours, gradually expanding it from larger to smaller businesses. This allowed researchers to measure its impact by comparing workers in firms of different sizes who had different *exposure* to the law. Using this methodology, Daniel Hamermesh, a leading expert in labour economics, found that life satisfaction in Korea increased among those workers most likely to have been affected by the legislation, suggesting that 'legislated reductions in work hours can increase workers' happiness'. Researchers from the National University of Singapore have also shown that working one fewer hour per week increased the frequency of visits of workers to their elderly parents by 6.5 per cent. They concluded that 'reducing work hours may serve as an effective policy intervention for improving the well-being of not just workers and their nuclear families, but also their extended families'; a sensible social argument for the four-day working week.

Finally, economists can also set their own experiments. Intrigued by Richard Thaler's conclusions, two economists from the University of Zurich conducted an experiment with bicycle messengers in Switzerland, paying an extra 25 per cent commission for successful deliveries over four weeks. They found that, unlike the New York cab drivers, messengers performed more shifts and, despite being less productive in each shift, increased the total number of deliveries.

The most rigorous experiments are called *randomised controlled trials*. These were pioneered by Abhijit Banerjee, Esther Duflo and Michael Kremer, winners of the Nobel Prize in 2019, who used them to test which policies are effective in alleviating poverty. Randomised control trials involve setting a treatment group where a particular policy is implemented and a control group where it is not, and assigning subjects randomly to each of the groups. This method is considered to be the most credible method of uncovering causal evidence and is now widely used in development and health economics. However, it is much harder to use in labour economics or macroeconomics, and much more expensive to run in the US than in India.

Economists working with data face an uphill battle to publish their research. They have to be clever in designing their study, and they are scrutinised for all possible theoretical mechanisms that could invalidate or weaken what economists call *identification* – establishing a causal link – however implausible. Even Richard Thaler's study faced critiques. Cab drivers might work fewer hours on rainy days because of the dangers associated with driving under difficult conditions. The problem is that most of the time, to achieve such clean results, the setting of the study must be very specific (i.e. in South Korea, in 2000, lowering weekly hours from forty-four to forty in some firms), which raises another problem – what is its *external validity*? Maybe some companies in a region in Sweden implemented the four-day week and their productivity improved, but would you expect similar effects in British or French companies? Another problem is *selection*. The firms that have implemented the four-day week are different from other companies. Would you expect the same improvements in productivity in all other firms if the Swedish government mandated a four-day week to the whole economy? Such difficulties limit our ability to use data to make general statements.

Economists are all too aware of these problems, and are unforgiving. If a researcher does not put a strong case for causality, all their other evidence will be ignored or branded as speculative. The paper will never be published, and the author won't be promoted. If the researcher's claim of causality is strong, the setting will most likely be very particular, and one can question whether the conclusions are general enough. I have rarely attended an applied economics seminar in which all the audience came out fully convinced by both the specific and the wider arguments.

This causality fundamentalism has much improved the science of economics, but at a cost. It has removed research from areas where clear empirical work is not possible. No economist can ever provide empirical evidence showing the effects of a country-wide implementation of the four-day week – it is impossible. Pointing out that within four years of the introduction of the Fair Labor Standards Act in 1938, the unemployment rate fell from 20 per cent to zero, and that it coincided with the beginning of the golden age of the US – the birth of many multinational companies, a baby boom and the obliteration of populist movements – does not persuade economists because that period overlapped with the Second World War. All the *suggestive* evidence is dismissed because it is not causal. The many accounts of positive outcomes of firms that have implemented the four-day week are also not accepted in economics, because one can claim that these were special firms to begin with. This is why the four-day working week has generated academic research in sociology, political science, business administration, law, ecology and gender studies, but no explicit research in mainstream economics.

The four-day week is one of the 'sins of omission' that, according to George Akerlof, a Nobel Laureate, 'lead economic research to ignore important topics that are difficult to approach the "hard" way'. One such lapse was the failure to predict the 2007 global financial crisis that led to the Great Recession. Most of the ingredients had been precisely studied in various literatures, ranging from macroeconomics to finance or real estate. The problem was that, even if someone had put the pieces together, a narrative with so many moving pieces would be seen as jelly-like in the eyes of economists, and too 'soft' to be published. Another 'sin of omission' in economics is global warming; the lack of interest by the majority of economists gives ammunition to those who see it as a hoax, justifying continuous inaction to one of humanity's biggest threats.

In Part Two of this book, I attempt to put all the pieces together, building an economic narrative for the four-day working week. To achieve this, I will go back to the techniques of the economists before Samuelson and Frisch and rely on an old-fashioned blend of economic theory, historical examples, opinions of brilliant minds, stories of successful firms, anecdotal evidence and logic. Still, as an economist, I am a descendant of Frisch, and I have inherited his need to quantify any statement as far as possible. I cannot simply say, 'There are many people working part-time in the UK' without being compelled to provide numbers to show the exact dimension of the phenomenon. I will therefore document as much evidence as possible for these different mechanisms, and will make clear whether the evidence is merely descriptive, associative or causal. Some of you might not share my enthusiasm for data and numbers, but it is part of my DNA as an economist.

PART TWO

The Eight Reasons Why

5

The First Reason: Because it is Possible (Keynes)

'The Principle of Unripe Time is that people should not do at the present moment what they think right at that moment, because the moment at which they think it right has not yet arrived.'

F.M. Cornford

John Maynard Keynes was born in 1883, the son of Florence Ada Keynes, a remarkable woman and one-time Mayor of Cambridge, and John Neville Keynes, an eminent economist at the University of Cambridge. Keynes attended Eton College and then King's College at Cambridge University, breeding grounds for England's elite, accumulating prizes for his academic achievements. At Cambridge, he was elected President of the Cambridge Union and was a star-member of the Apostles, a secret society of intellectuals. After completing his undergraduate studies in mathematics, he spent two years as a civil servant, after which he returned to King's with a fellowship. His academic reputation grew rapidly, and in 1911 he was appointed editor of the *Economic Journal*, a role he would hold for thirty-four years.

One of my favourite passages from John Maynard Keynes's writing is his description of a master-economist's talents:

> He must be mathematician, historian, statesman, philosopher – in some degree. He must understand symbols and speak in words. He must contemplate the particular in terms of the general and touch abstract and concrete in the same flight of thought. He must study the present in the light of the past for the purposes of the future. No part of man's nature or his institutions must lie entirely outside his regard. He must be purposeful and disinterested in a simultaneous mood; as aloof and incorruptible as an artist, yet sometimes as near to earth as a politician.

Keynes wrote these words in 1924, in the obituary of his Cambridge University mentor Alfred Marshall. He went on to add, 'much, but not all, of this ideal many-sidedness Marshall possessed'. Keynes was not known for his modesty, so it is quite plausible that he was describing himself. If Marshall fell short of fulfilling all of these attributes, Keynes possessed them all. As *The Economist* wrote after his death, Lord Keynes 'was civil servant, pamphleteer, don and college bursar, editor, company chairman, patron of the arts, government spokesman and adviser, member of the Upper House – he touched no career that he did not brilliantly adorn'.

During the First World War, Keynes consulted for the British government on financial issues, and when the hostilities were over he was appointed one of the UK's representatives at the Versailles Peace Conference. Joseph Schumpeter could not hide his admiration for Keynes, who would have:

> conquered a place in history even if he had never done a stroke of scientific work, as he would still have been the man who wrote *The Economic Consequences of the Peace* (1919), bursting

into international fame when men of equal insight but less courage and men of equal courage but less insight kept silent.

In the book, Keynes expressed his strong disagreement with the terms of the Treaty of Versailles on the grounds that it was too punitive on Germany, predicting that it would bring economic chaos to Europe and lay the groundwork for authoritarian regimes.

Even Friedrich Hayek recognised Keynes as 'one of the most intelligent and most original thinkers ever; an intuitive, real genius, with a wide knowledge in many subjects ... except Economics!' They were ideological rivals, after all.

Keynes published 'Economic Possibilities for our Grandchildren' at the start of the Great Depression. While pundits were speculating about economic Armageddon, Keynes prophesied that within a century the economic problem would be solved and people would be working fifteen hours per week. This bold conclusion was reached on the basis of two assumptions – we would be able to work less, and we would want to work less. Keynes laid out his argument:

> In quite a few years – in our own lifetimes, I mean – we may be able to perform all the operations of agriculture, mining, and manufacture with a quarter of the human effort to which we have been accustomed [...] I would predict that the standard

of life in progressive countries one hundred years hence will be between four and eight times as high as it is today. [...] For many ages to come the old Adam will be so strong in us that everybody will need to do some work if he is to be contented. We shall do more things for ourselves than is usual with the rich to-day, only too glad to have small duties and tasks and routines. But beyond this, we shall endeavour to spread the bread thin on the butter – to make what work there is still to be done to be as widely shared as possible. Three-hour shifts or a fifteen-hour week may put off the problem for a great while. For three hours a day is quite enough to satisfy the old Adam in most of us!

Keynes's prediction that the standard of living would be four to eight times higher was spot on. In the ninety years that separate us from his article, the US has multiplied its GDP per capita by six and most European countries have multiplied it by five, despite the effects of a devastating world war and other crises. Not everything would be plain sailing, warned Keynes – technological progress comes with technological unemployment, but he viewed this side effect as temporary.

Keynes was neither a fortune teller nor a science-fiction writer. He understood that the technological frontier would keep expanding, but not even in his wildest dreams could he have foreseen the new technologies that were coming our way. The development of the internal combustion engine powered cars, tractors, aeroplanes, submarines and monster trucks. Electricity powered everything else, boosted by nuclear energy. There was a burst of new materials: sheet glass, concrete, stainless steel and aluminium were used to construct buildings and skyscrapers, nylon improved clothing, rubber allowed for washing machines and condoms, and plastic has been used everywhere. Fertilisers, pesticides and herbicides improved crop yields, which together with antibiotics, blood transfusions and X-rays prolonged our lives. Radio, telephone, TV and the internet revolutionised communication. Electronics, satellites, rockets and interplanetary probes allowed us to go to the moon and have made us dream of space travel and colonisation.

The increase in living standards was accomplished by these astounding technological innovations, but it was accelerated by improved management practices, the legal structure of limited liability, efficient financial systems, international trade, intellectual property rights legislation and sound economic policies. This all took place within a mixed capitalist system that varied from freer markets to more state intervention, depending on which dead economist was in fashion.

Keynes's mistake was in the second part of his argument. In a static economy, leisure can only increase at the expense of lower consumption, but in a growing economy this is not the case. With rising productivity, societies face a choice of whether to increase leisure or consume more. Suppose a new technology doubles productivity and all workers can produce twice as much in their five-day working week. Societies can choose either to keep working the same number of hours and double consumption, or to maintain its consumption and work half as much, or any combination of the two. Keynes believed people would welcome the technological improvements by both increasing consumption *and* working less.

In pre-historical times, it is thought that a hunter-gatherer worked for about four hours per day – about 1,650 hours per year. That was enough to get all the food for his meals and wood to keep him warm at night. With farming came work that was more irregular: winter months were quieter than the harvest season. A pre-industrial farmer worked for about 2,000 hours per year. With industrialisation, it seemed wasteful not to keep machines running, so men, women and children began to work much longer hours. In 1840, a typical factory worker toiled for 3,300 hours per year.

Throughout Keynes's life, reducing working hours was as much of a priority for workers' unions as increased pay. In the UK, a series of Factory Acts introduced by Parliament during the nineteenth century determined the reduction of working hours per day, first for women and children, and later extended to men. Keynes lived throughout the period where workers – men, women and children – reduced their working week from sunrise to sunset on six days a week, to the five-day, forty-hour week first seen in Henry Ford's factories. The Bank of England estimates that the weekly working hours of a full-time worker fell from sixty-five hours in 1860 to forty-eight hours in 1930. Keynes extrapolated from this that people and societies would want to continue reducing their working hours, as well as increasing consumption. However, in the UK the average weekly hours of full-time workers fell by only six hours over the next nine decades, to forty-two in 2017.

The total annual hours worked reflects not only the average working week, but also the number of holidays and the share of part-time employment. Given the rise of part-time working, the total annual hours spent working has been falling. Since 1950, in the US and the UK, the average hours per worker fell from 2,000 hours per year to about 1,700 today. An even more striking example is Germany, where average hours fell from 2,400 to 1,400. So Keynes wasn't completely wrong – the predicted tendency to work less is there, but it has been uncoordinated and expressed asymmetrically across the workforce, being driven by women in part-time work.

One of the most twisted arguments against a four-day working week is a great example of the Cambridge academic F.M. Cornford's satirical *Principle of Unripe Time* – that although the idea might be great, 'the time is not yet ripe'. In 1956, the then US Vice President Richard Nixon pledged that the four-day working week would come soon. In 1963, President John F. Kennedy predicted it for the end of the century, and since the 1970s procrastinators regularly assured us that it will happen once we become a bit richer. Just recently, Andy Haldane, the former Bank of England chief economist, predicted a four-day working week will become the norm in 2050, and Jamie Dimon, the CEO of JPMorgan, said that the next generation would work not four, but three days and a half. Yet we have experienced astonishing economic growth over the past ninety years, and if we had kept a proportional pace of the decline in working hours we could have very well fulfilled Keynes's prediction of a fifteen-hour working week. Instead, we have kept stalling and postponing. After all the technological progress and increases in GDP per capita of the last decades, we can surely afford it now. The time has come.

In 1964 there was an attempt in the US Congress to amend the Fair Labor Standards Act to further reduce the standard working week to thirty-five or thirty-two hours. During the hearings before the Select Subcommittee on Labor, Mr Ira Nunn, representing the National Restaurant Association, stated: 'It is inconceivable that productivity can be increased by 14.3 per cent in the near future,' promptly adding, 'Over the past years, business has noted a tremendous increase in productivity; and this increase has been passed along to workers in the form of higher wages. This is clearly what the workers prefer.' In short, productivity has increased much in the past, but will not increase in the immediate future. Can you guess how many years it took labour productivity in the US to increase 14.3 per cent, the amount needed according to Mr Nunn to allow firms to survive the thirty-two-hour week? According to the US Bureau of Labour Statistics, it took only four years. By 1968, productivity had increased by more than 14.3 per cent. In fact, since 1943, it took only about six years to achieve such productivity rises. The four-day working week is within our reach. All we need is four to six years.

When I was a graduate student in London, I watched Champions League football matches in a pub called The Famous Three Kings. It was a large pub with several rooms, with a different match showing in each. One Wednesday evening, a few minutes before the matches started, the pub landlord told customers over the loudspeakers: 'Today, we'll show Manchester United in the front room, Chelsea in the back room, and we have Bayern Munich vs AC Milan upstairs in German and downstairs in Italian. Why? Because we can!' This seemed like a pretty good reason to me.

So why should we implement the four-day working week? Because we can. We have reduced the working week before. We can surely do it again. Over the past five decades, we as a society have chosen not to reduce our working hours significantly. But this is a choice, not a law of economics. We can change our minds. As Keynes said, 'When the facts change, I change my mind. What do you do, sir?'

6

The Second Reason: Because It Will Fuel the Economy through Demand for Leisure Industries (Keynes)

'Many economists today seem to have forgotten this fact. Leisure is not, as they suppose, a drain on the economy, but a lubricant. Leisure is like the rain that nourishes abundant consumer crops. It is obvious that if people literally do not have the time to use a product, they will have no need to buy it; and that, in turn, makes them less likely actually to buy it.'

Eugene McCarthy and William McGaughey
Nonfinancial Economics: The Case for Shorter Hours of Work

Although Keynes rapidly rose to fame with the publication of *The Economic Consequences of the Peace*, his longer-lasting impact has been in rewriting macroeconomic theory with his *General Theory of Employment, Interest and Money*, published in 1936. To understand Keynes's contribution, we first need to grasp some fundamentals of microeconomic theory.

The beating heart of any economy is trade, which involves buyers and sellers. Sellers supply goods or services – they are producers. Buyers demand goods or services – they are consumers. Lots of people buying and selling make up a market, and micro-economics studies a particular market. How do consumers decide how much to buy? How do sellers decide how much to produce? How do they interact in the market? Microeconomics teaches us the law of supply and demand, one law which cannot be repealed or amended. The price of a good adjusts to equate supply and demand. For example, if the demand for hand sanitiser is larger than supply, its price will increase. The increase in price will simultaneously deter some buyers and encourage sellers to produce more. If sellers, for any reason, cannot increase production – what economists call *inelastic supply* – the higher demand for a good will translate into a higher price, without a change in the quantities traded. One good example of inelastic supply is housing – when demand for housing increases, the supply of housing cannot adjust quickly, so it is mainly reflected in increased house prices.

The economic activity combined over many markets makes up the whole economy. That is the subject of macroeconomics – not individual production and expenditure decisions, but the aggregate supply and demand of an entire economy. *Aggregate supply* is the total production of goods and services. All production has to be bought by someone, and this is what economists call *aggregate demand*. Breaking it down into different components – consumption by households and the government, and investment by firms – is the starting point of macroeconomic analysis, and the foundation of the standardised system of national accounts that measures economic activity – a country's gross domestic product (GDP). Aggregate supply equals aggregate demand. Even if the economy produces more than what is demanded, the remainder is added to firms' inventories, so it is labelled in the accounts as investment.

What macroeconomists often disagree about is how the economy adjusts. Does supply adjust to demand, or demand adjust to supply? Think of an antique weighing scale. On the left side – the supply side – you place iron weights. On the right side – the demand side – you place different vegetables: carrots ('c' for consumption), garlic ('g' for government consumption, and because its intense smell and flavour is loved by some and loathed by others), and asparagus (for investment – I couldn't find a vegetable beginning with the letter 'i', so I've chosen one that looks similar). How do we get the two sides to balance? Do we first place a weight and then add the vegetables? Or do you put the vegetables on first and then adjust the weights?

Before Keynes, macroeconomists placed all the emphasis on the production side of the equation – the aggregate supply. They focused on the *factors of production* – what firms use to produce goods and services – and what policymakers can do to increase them. The main factors of production are the hands and the brains of workers (which economists call *labour*), and the tools, machines and structures used to produce goods and services (which economists call *capital*). Robert Solow, a Nobel Prize winner, joked, 'If God had meant there to be more than two factors of production, he would have made it easier for us to draw three-dimensional diagrams.' An important clarification is that capital for an economist does not mean money or wealth – it refers to real goods that can be bought within an economy, like tools, machines or factories. We boost capital when we invest, such as when a farmer buys a tractor, an accountant buys a computer or a chef builds a new restaurant. For an economist, buying shares in Apple or Tesla in the stock market is not investment. That is merely a change of ownership of a particular firm; it does not alter an economy's underlying productive capacity.

Supply-side macroeconomists, like classical economists, believe that output can only be increased by improving the factors of production or *technology* – how good we are at putting capital and labour together. For them, aggregate demand does not matter. In the words of Jean-Baptiste Say, a nineteenth-century French classical economist:

> The encouragement of mere consumption is no benefit to commerce; for the difficulty lies in supplying the means, not in stimulating the desire of consumption and we have seen that production alone, furnishes those means. Thus, it is the aim of

good government to stimulate production, of bad government to encourage consumption.

A classical economist would first place a 1kg weight onto our antique weighing scales – the production in the economy as allowed by the factors of production – and would then add the vegetables. If they are not balanced, an 'invisible hand' would add or take some carrots and asparagus away until they were equal.

Macroeconomic theory tends to change after calamitous economic events. When economies fell to the Great Depression, classical theory could not explain why 25 per cent of workers could not find jobs and why it took so long for the unemployment rate to fall. Keynes proposed a theory that stressed the role of aggregate demand. Firms are not going to produce if they don't have customers to buy their goods, and unemployed workers are not good customers. In his view, we first put the vegetables onto the scale and then adjust the weights. If we only have 700g instead of 1kg, we will not be using all the available resources – machines will remain idle and workers will be unemployed. He granted that the tendency of the economy would be for prices to fall to restore full employment in the long run, to which he added, with his usual rhetorical mastery, 'in the long run we are all dead'. Keynes viewed recessions as driven by low aggregate demand, in particular of consumption and investment. These types of demand depend to a great extent on expectations about the future – what he called 'animal spirits'. He argued that while the aggregate economy could stay unbalanced for a long time, macroeconomic policy could restore full employment by stimulating the economy through aggregate demand. And that could be done by governments, which control directly one of the components of aggregate demand: government spending.

Keynes's powerful insight was that GDP would respond to an increase in government spending by a ratio of more than one to one. If the government hires more workers, they will buy more goods and services – they will go to a restaurant, buy books from a bookshop or get that painful tooth filled by the dentist. These expenditures would be income to the chef and her staff, to the bookseller and the authors and publishers of the books sold, and to the dentist and his assistant. With a higher income, each of these beneficiaries would increase their own consumption and keep the economy moving. Government spending therefore has a multiplier effect through private consumption; if we are 300g short of 1kg, we do not need 300g of garlic to restore full employment – if the multiplier is two we need 150g, a 'buy one, get one free' offer, and if the multiplier is four we only need 75g, 'four for the price of one'. It was this economic reasoning that drove the initial policy response to the financial crisis of 2007–08, with the quick approval of the Stimulus Bill in the US and similar measures elsewhere.

How do supply-side macroeconomists view the effects of increasing government spending on output? Their theory predicts a zero effect, because it won't change the amount of labour, capital or technology in the economy. The only consequence of such a profligate government would be to raise prices and put pressure on interest rates to curb inflation, and therefore to discourage investment – what economists call *crowding out*. This was the economic logic behind the supporters of 'austerity' during the European debt crisis. If we fix government finances (by cutting government spending), investment will be *crowded in*, and with more machines assembled and more factories built we will raise production in the long term.

These two economic theories perfectly illustrate the difference between economics and accounting or mathematics. If an

accountant or mathematician, knowing that aggregate supply is equal to aggregate demand, is asked what happens if government spending increases by £1 million, their logic would claim that production would also increase by £1 million. But economics is a science that studies human behaviour, and human behaviour is not static or fixed. From the two opposing theories, classical economists predict a zero effect on output, while Keynesians predict an effect much larger than £1 million – all would agree that the effect would never be around £1 million.

Who is right? Dogmas apart, neither of them. Most economic theories are right under certain circumstances and wrong under others. Samuelson, that self-styled dull centrist, brought the two views together, arguing that the Keynesian theory was plausible in the short run and the classical theory was more plausible in the long run. The difference between the short and the long run is in the eye of the beholder. The short run could be anything from a few months to ten years, while the long run could be anything from five years until the end of time.

The Keynesian view dominated macroeconomic thought from the 1940s until the 1960s, and came into discredit during the 1970s following a succession of recessions where high unemployment coexisted with high inflation, an impossible combination according to the Keynesian theory. Still, it was quickly resuscitated in 2007 at the start of the Great Recession, and most economists recognise that the swift, short-term Keynesian policy response avoided a much deeper recession of the scale and length of the Great Depression. Aggregate demand matters.

Returning to the four-day working week, how could it stimulate the economy through aggregate demand? To make my case, I won't rely on the rhetorical mastery of Keynes or any other economist. Instead, I'll return to Henry Ford who, according to *Forbes* magazine, is 'the most influential businessman of all time'. When explaining his company's implementation of the five-day working week in 1926, he said:

The industry of this country could not long exist if factories generally went back to the ten-hour day, because the people would not have the time to consume the goods produced. For instance, a workman would have little use for an automobile if he had to be in the shops from dawn until dusk. And that would react in countless directions, for the automobile, by enabling people to get about quickly and easily, gives them a chance to find out what is going on in the world – which leads them to a larger life that requires more food, more and better goods, more books, more music – more of everything. [...] Just as the eight-hour day opened our way to prosperity, so the five-day week will open our way to a still greater prosperity. [...] There is another angle, however, which we must largely reckon with – the positive industrial value of leisure, because it increases consumption. Where people work longest and with least leisure, they buy the fewest goods. No towns were so poor as those of England where the people, from children up, worked 15 and 16 hours a day. They were poor because these overworked people soon wore out – they became less and less valuable as workers. Therefore, they earned less and less and could buy less and less.

Business is the exchange of goods. Goods are bought only as they meet needs. Needs are filled only as they are felt. They make themselves felt largely in leisure hours. [...] The five-day week simply carries this thought farther. The people with a five-day week will consume more goods than the people with a six-day week. People who have more leisure must have more clothes. They must have a greater variety of food. They must have more transportation facilities. They naturally must have more service of various kinds.

This increased consumption will require greater production than we now have. Instead of business being slowed up because the people are 'off work', it will be speeded up, because the people consume more in their leisure than in their working time. This will lead to more work. And this to more profits.

And this to more wages. The result of more leisure will be the exact opposite of what most people might suppose it to be.

These are not the words of an academic sitting in his ivory tower speculating about how the economy works, nor are they the words of a left-wing radical in the Occupy movement. These are the words of an entrepreneur who built a business empire, not by exploiting a monopoly like many of his peers, but by building cars better, faster and cheaper than anyone else. The reverence that these words merit should be proportional to the vast number of cars that Ford sold throughout the twentieth century.

Henry Ford was ahead of his time – his statement is pure Keynesian economics, ten years before Keynes's *General Theory*. We need money to consume, *but we also need time*. We feel our needs and consume more in our free time than while working. A 2009 survey carried out by Gallup found that Americans spend 20 per cent more money on Saturdays and Sundays than on an average weekday. If we are always working, we might make a lot of money, but we won't spend it. We might save more, but saving does not move the economy, it slows the economy down – *the paradox of thrift*, as Keynes called it. Too much saving inflates house prices that are already at historically high levels, lowers interest rates that are also at historically low levels, and fuels all sorts of financial bubbles. Ben Bernanke, former Chair of the US Federal Reserve and 2022 Nobel Laureate, blamed the global savings glut from 1996 to 2006 for the dot-com bubble at the end of the last century, and then the housing bubble and other imbalances that led to the financial crisis of 2007. Japan's lost decade in the 1990s has been attributed to excess savings accumulated because of stagnant spending, for instance on clothing and footwear, transport, health, communication, and restaurants and hotels.

With more leisure time we would spend more on certain goods, which was exactly what happened after the implementation of the US's Fair Labor Standards Act. Cinema attendance rocketed and, by the mid-1940s, 60 per cent of the US population were going to the cinema weekly. The demand consolidated the Hollywood movie industry and kept it a world leader until today. Between 1957 and 1960, while GDP grew by 14 per cent in the US, consumer spending on foreign travel, books and maps, theatre and opera, and amusements such as bowling increased at about twice that rate.

The new consumer needs predicted by Henry Ford gave rise to many companies still operating today. Richard and Maurice McDonald opened the first McDonald's in California in 1940. Carl's Jr, another fast-food brand, started as a hot dog cart the following year. Coach New York, now a famous luxury bags and accessories brand, also began in 1941. Best Western, a chain with more than 4,000 hotels worldwide, was created from an informal network of independent hotels in California in 1946. In that same year, Estée Lauder started making cosmetics, Paul Iams began producing dried dog food, and Earl Tupper founded the Tupperware Company. Dick's Sporting Goods, the US's largest sporting goods retailer, opened in 1948 as a fishing supply store. American Broadcasting Company, owner of eight TV stations, was founded in 1943 as a radio network. Fender, one of the world's most popular guitar makers, was founded in 1946. One year later, Atlantic Records began its run as one of America's most successful record labels. All these brands were born to satisfy the newly acquired needs of consumers with much time on their hands, eager for 'more food, more and better goods, more books, more music – more of everything'.

The introduction of the five-day working week in China in 1995 has been singled out as an important cause of the subsequent boom in their domestic tourism market, now the largest in the world. Between 1990 and 2006, the number of domestic travellers quintupled and the average spending per capita in domestic tourism increased sevenfold. Theme parks, like the Splendid China Folk Village or the Chimelong Ocean Kingdom, were built together with sports facilities and cultural venues. Entertainment and art performances proliferated. The tourism and related industries now account for more than 10 per cent of Chinese GDP.

What about now? If we had a three-day weekend, where would we spend our money? I don't presume to know the answer, but let me indulge in some speculation. Intellectuals would read more newspapers and books, and visit galleries, concert halls and theatres. Outgoing types would drink in the pub with friends more often, go to concerts or festivals, or out for dinners at restaurants and on to nightclubs, followed by after-hours kebabs and Ubers home. Those who take it easier might head to the cinema. Fitness enthusiasts would have time to exercise more, so would need to replace their running shoes more often, and they might join a gym, go to the swimming pool or buy a racing bike to participate in a triathlon. Some might explore new activities, like fencing, rock climbing or chess-boxing (yes, it's a thing). Why not buy a sailing boat? Sports enthusiasts would go to stadiums, subscribe to TV packages and might bet a bit more. The landlord of The Three Kings would consider adding another screen to his pub. Travellers would take more city breaks now that they would last for three days; some might organise the trip by themselves, while others would hire a travel agency or a tour operator. They'd stay in hotels or rent an Airbnb, go to local restaurants and shop in local markets. As for the less adventurous, they could stay at home, playing *Call of Duty* or watching a superhero blockbuster on Netflix.

The power of these fifteen industries was recognised by Joseph Schumpeter, the star of the following two chapters: 'A little reflection will show that workmen's demand for the "services" of their own labor power is actually a very important factor in the shaping of the process of production.' According to the Labour Force Survey, taken together, these service industries account for at least 20 per cent of the UK's employment, so one should expect a significant boost. Anyone with a stake in these industries should be leaping into the four-day week faster than Spider-Man jumping off a building.

Clearly, workers would spend less on some other things – they wouldn't buy so many suits, or coffees at the cafe near the office.

Some chain restaurants would close in business districts but they would reopen elsewhere. There are those who might not have enough spare income to spend, if they are already struggling to make a living. These people are unlikely to be able to raise their consumption, but they would also be the ones who would get more employment opportunities as leisure industries boom. Which workers would benefit? These service industries have double the rate of part-time workers – 40 per cent – than the remaining seventy industries. Young workers would benefit the most, as almost 25 per cent of workers in these industries are under 25, compared to 8 per cent in the remaining industries. This would allow young people to gain experience in the labour market. It would also help older part-time workers stay in the labour force longer; the service industries represent 20 per cent of the employment of workers aged 65–80, and 40 per cent of workers aged 80–85. Finally, it would benefit women and workers with lower qualifications: 67 per cent of workers in this sector do not have higher education (54 per cent in the remaining industries) and 51 per cent are women (46 per cent in the remaining industries).

Since the financial crisis, we are facing a *secular stagnation* – a period with a persistent stagnant economy and little economic growth. The term was coined during the Great Depression by Alvin Hansen, a Harvard professor dubbed 'the American Keynes'. Some economists, like Nobel Laureate Paul Krugman and Larry Summers, a former US Treasury Secretary, argue that the root of the present secular stagnation is again lack of aggregate demand. Firms have few profitable investment opportunities, and even when the interest rate was close to zero and they had billions of dollars in cash reserves, they didn't want to invest. Like gravity in space, many conventional laws of economics are inverted under secular stagnation. Gauti Eggertsson, a macroeconomist from Brown University, and Jean-Baptiste Michau, a French economist, have shown that, beside the paradox of thrift, an economy trapped in secular stagnation faces the *paradox of toil*. If workers decide to work more, for instance by moonlighting in a second job, they have a negative effect on wages and lower aggregate demand so, paradoxically, aggregate employment in society falls.

The solution, Keynesians declare, is for the government to spend its way out of the secular stagnation, just as it did to escape the Great Depression, courtesy of the New Deal and the Second World War – a view that influenced the unprecedented fiscal expansion of President Biden. But Keynesians are not Keynes. Keynes never said government spending was the only way to restore the balance between demand and supply. In fact, in a letter to his friend T.S. Eliot, Keynes wrote that 'full employment policy by means of investment' was 'only one particular application of an intellectual theorem. You can produce the result just as well by consuming more or working less.' In light of this, I can offer an alternative interpretation of how we got out of the secular stagnation in the 1930s. Could the Fair Labor Standards Act have contributed to jump-start the US economic engine? As I explained, we cannot make a causal statement because of the confounding effect of the Second World War, but the timing is suggestive. Although the US Federal Government doubled spending between 1933 and 1936, when President Roosevelt signed the Fair Labor Standards Act in June 1938 the unemployment rate was still at 20 per cent. By the end of 1941 (thirty months later), the unemployment rate had dropped to 3.6 per cent, while government spending had only increased from $8 billion in 1938 to $15 billion. Government spending to finance the war only exploded between 1943 and 1945, when it reached $74 billion, but the unemployment rate had already reached zero way before, in June 1942. The dramatic fall of unemployment began precisely when the Fair Labor Standards Act was signed and preceded the boom in spending.

Shortening of the working week can rescue us again. At least, it deserves a chance to be considered as a serious policy alongside increasing government spending. As Henry Ford argued, one day less of work will lead to more demand, which will lead to more economic activity, so that 'the result of more leisure will be the exact opposite of what most people might suppose it to be'.

The Third Reason: Because It Will Raise Productivity (Schumpeter)

'The capitalist achievement does not typically consist in providing more silk stockings for queens but in bringing them
within the reach of factory girls in return for steadily decreasing
amounts of effort.'

Joseph Schumpeter

Joseph Schumpeter had three goals in life: to be 'the best horse-
man in Vienna, the best lover in Austria and the best economist
in the world'. He told his students at Harvard University that
he had achieved two of his goals. One of his students was Paul
Samuelson, who wrote after his death in 1950:

There were many Schumpeters: the brilliant enfant terrible of
the Austrian School who before the age of thirty had written
two great books; the young Cairo lawyer with a stable of horses;
the Austrian Finance Minister; the social philosopher and
prophet of capitalist development; the historian of economic

doctrine; the economic theorist espousing use of more exact methods and tools of reasoning; the teacher of economics.

When Schumpeter joined Harvard University, in 1932, he had lived in eleven different cities in five countries. He was a showman, and he would spend hours dressing up in the morning to carefully match the patterns and colours of shirt, tie, jacket and handkerchief. He was also a ladies' man, entertaining friends with provocative stories of orgies and advanced sexual techniques. One of Schumpeter's former lovers would write letters asking him for detailed advice on how to improve the sexual performance of her inexperienced husband. It is impossible to know which of his three goals he didn't achieve, although he would occasionally say that things didn't look well for the horses.

Being overshadowed by Keynes does not take away the honour of being one of the greatest economists of all time. Schumpeter also possessed all the characteristics of the master economist. He was the most cited economist of his time, and the most knowledgeable. His last book, *History of Economic Analysis*, edited posthumously by his third wife Elizabeth Boody Schumpeter, also an economist, is a 1,000-page masterpiece that summarises the history of economics and economic thought from Ancient Greece until 1950. Schumpeter and Keynes were opposite types of economists. Keynes was an economist–engineer, setting his mind to solve immediate problems. How to determine war compensations? How to jump out of the Great Depression? How to pay for the war? How to set up the post-war international financial system? In contrast, Schumpeter was an economist–scientist, wanting to discover how the world works and understand the essence of capitalism and the reasons for its long-run success. 'I am not running a drug store,' Schumpeter once said, 'I have no pills to hand out; no clear-cut solutions for any practical problems that may arise.' Contrast it to Keynes's motto: 'If economists could manage to get themselves thought of as humble, competent people on a level with dentists, that would be splendid.' Economics needs both mindsets.

What I find the most remarkable about Schumpeter is his acceptance of different methodologies in economics. While not being mathematical himself and struggling with anything beyond standard maths, he was, for the most part of his career, one of the most fervent defenders of the use of mathematics in economics. This contrasted with Keynes, who having been gifted in mathematics – he was a wrangler* – was sceptical towards its use in economics. Schumpeter, instead, with his weight on the profession, enabled and promoted the massive change brought by Samuelson and Frisch. Schumpeter placed his passion for economics and its development above his own ego. He supervised Samuelson's PhD thesis and, together with Frisch, founded the Econometric Society and *Econometrica*. The correspondence between Schumpeter and Frisch reveals a sincere friendship that, given their age, location, background, political ideology and personalities, would seem quite unlikely. They exchanged long letters, where Frisch described his attempts to express Schumpeter's ideas mathematically, and the replies where Schumpeter gave economic intuition to the equations. They complemented each other, yet no paper ever came out of their friendship. But Schumpeter's methodological diversity was broader. He believed that to understand the economy in all its complexity, one needed

---

* Just an elitist Cambridge word to mean he had a First in maths.

multiple approaches and methods. He emphasised the importance of economic history in the formulation of theories and in his work incorporated insights from philosophy, law, sociology, psychology, business and political science. He thought economics would become a better science if economists would accept and incorporate, rather than attack and ostracise, other methods. Economics embraced mathematics, but the rest of Schumpeter's methodological diversity got lost along the way.

Schumpeter, like Keynes, viewed economic growth as a way for more consumption together with fewer hours of work. Like all economists before Keynes, Schumpeter placed the limelight on the supply side – the production of goods and services. His greatest economic insight is that innovation, technology and efficiency are the centre stage of economic progress and that *entrepreneurs* are their main actors. The word *entrepreneur* was coined in 1800 by Jean-Baptiste Say, but for most economists before Schumpeter the focus was on the dichotomy between the factors of production, capital and labour, and their owners – capitalists and workers – central in the writings of Marx. For Schumpeter, capital owners and workers are only supporting actors. It is leadership that matters, not ownership. The entrepreneur, not the capitalist, reforms and revolutionises the processes of production, by introducing new goods, new qualities of goods or a new method of production, either by experimentation or scientific discovery; opening of a new market; conquering of a new source of supply of raw materials; inventing new intermediate goods; or reorganising an industry. Whatever the innovation coming from entrepreneurs, it sustains long-term economic growth, even if it destroys the value of established companies, in what he called *creative destruction*, his most famous concept. Streaming killed Blockbuster, digital photography killed Kodak, and the smartphone killed Nokia.

Such a positive view of the entrepreneur was not unheard of, but it was unusual. Even Adam Smith had a negative view of businessmen. He wrote in *An Inquiry into the Nature and Causes of the Wealth of Nations* that:

The proposal of any new law or regulation of commerce which comes from [capitalists] ought always to be listened to with great precaution, and ought never to be adopted till after having been long and carefully examined, not only with the most scrupulous, but with the most suspicious attention. It comes from an order of men whose interest is never exactly the same with that of the public, who have generally an interest to deceive and even to oppress the public and who accordingly have, upon many occasions, both deceived and oppressed it.

Marx was more laconic – he just called them vampires.

Which view is right? We don't have difficulties finding examples of both. The one entrepreneur who personifies Schumpeter's ideal is Henry Ford. Schumpeter, in a letter to Frisch explaining how he viewed the economy not as a recurring process, a *Groundhog Day*, but as an evolutionary process similar to biological mutations, wrote that entrepreneurial activity makes 'economic things change instead of making them recur. And its effects are not recurring – Ford can never be repeated – but "historic" and definitely located in historical time. They are also irreversible.' Henry Ford was unique. Compare him to other businessmen of his time who made unimaginable fortunes: Washington Duke, Leland Stanford, Cornelius Vanderbilt, Andrew Carnegie or Andrew Melon. These millionaires are not known for how they built their fortune, but, if anything, for spending a small fraction of their wealth on setting up a university. And there is, of course, John Rockefeller, the richest man in the US by 1913, with a fortune of $900 million. These *robber barons* got rich by controlling entire industries. Being the only seller – *monopoly* – means you can charge high prices, and being the only buyer – *monopsony* – means that you pay little to your suppliers and workers. Many benefited from large shady government contracts. They are closer to Adam Smith's businessmen and Marx's vampires, perfectly described by Calvin.

Contrast them with Henry Ford. Alone, he built an automobile in his workshop. He sold it and kept building more automobiles,

better and faster. He then installed the first moving assembly line for mass production, reducing the time it took to build a car from more than twelve hours to two hours and thirty minutes. He achieved it by breaking the assembly of the car into small steps and training each of his workers to do just one. He even hired motion experts to design those tasks more efficiently and built machines to do some automatically. He created a new product, produced at a manic efficiency, and sold it at the lowest price with only a small margin. He made his fortune not by providing more cars to rich men, but by bringing them within reach of factory workers in return for steadily decreasing amounts of effort. Didn't he take the words out of Schumpeter's mouth?

Why did Henry Ford, obsessed with producing at the cheapest cost, reduce the working week to five days for his workers? According to the National Association of Manufacturers, this would have raised the costs of production and reduced the number of cars coming out of his assembly lines. But Henry Ford did it *for* – not in spite of – productivity. Although workers would spend fewer hours in his factories, their productivity per hour would increase enough to compensate for the reduction in hours, meaning they would produce the same number of cars. Ford pointed to two main reasons for the rise in productivity: better workers and better management. Regarding the workers, he explained:

It is not necessary to bring in sentiment at all in this whole question of leisure for workers. Sentiment has no place in industry. In the olden days those who thought that leisure was harmful usually had an interest in the products of industry. The mill owner seldom saw the benefit of leisure time for his employees, unless he could work up his emotions. Now we can look at leisure as a cold business fact.

It is not easy so to look at leisure, for age-old custom viewed leisure as 'lost time' – time taken out of production. [...]

That the devil finds work for idle hands to do is probably true. But there is a profound difference between leisure and idleness. We must not confound leisure with shiftlessness. Our people are perfectly capable of using to good advantage the time that they have off – after work. That has already been demonstrated to us by our experiments during the last several years. We find that the men come back after a 2-day holiday so fresh and keen that they are able to put their minds as well as their hands into their work.

Perhaps they do not use their spare time to the best advantage. That is not for us to say, provided their work is better than it was when they did not have spare time. We are not of those who claim to be able to tell people how to use their time out of the shops. [...] We think that, given the chance, people will become more and more expert in the effective use of leisure. And we are giving the chance.

Ford made clear that implementing the five-day working week was a well-thought-through business decision grounded on extensive experimentation, not on sentimental or humanist reasons. He dismissed all those moralist considerations about the ethics of work and found in trials that more rested workers could produce more in five days than tired workers in six.

Workers are least productive on the last day of the week, a fact that relates to an essential concept in economics, the concept of *marginal productivity* – how much more a worker produces if he works one extra hour per day, or one extra day per week. Economists think that most jobs face diminishing marginal productivity. The last hours of the day are typically less productive because a worker is already tired. Also, fatigue kicks in on the last day of the week, so workers tend to be less productive, working more slowly and making more mistakes. This is still true today, as illustrated by the blunt statement of the director of Soc-Med, a social media agency, to *Forbes*: 'If we are being honest with ourselves, Friday afternoons can be very unproductive and we end up just being there, unless there is a major project going on.'

But Ford's argument went further. He realised that workers on Saturday were too tired, but also that if they rested instead, they would begin the following week more engaged, motivated and productive. In those days, workers needed physical rest. Factory workers suffered from repetitive motion disorders, immortalised by Charlie Chaplin screwing nuts at an ever-faster pace in the movie *Modern Times*. Another example documented in academic literature was the acceleration of the production of ammunition in the UK during the First World War. Initially personnel worked seven days, eighty hours per week, but after several studies on the productivity of workers in different schedules, the official recommendation limited the hours to sixty-seven, because longer hours would not yield higher output. Working too many hours without enough rest might boost production initially, but if prolonged in time, workers will just be permanently tired, slower, more prone to making mistakes. Several recent studies on the performance of medical interns, nurses and police officers find a positive association between long hours and low efficacy, accidents and injuries.

Mistakes on assembly lines can be extremely costly, either because they require production to be stopped or because defective products might have to be excluded. On an assembly line with fifty workers, if each worker makes just two mistakes per 1,000 pieces, close to 100 pieces will be defective. Mistakes are also costly outside assembly lines. The recall of more than 40 million cars to replace defective airbag inflators bankrupted Takata Corporation, an 80-year-old Japanese company with $6 billion revenue, in 2018. And how costly was the 2019 grounding of the Boeing 737 Max because of control problems? Both were the outcomes of a cascade of human errors in different stages of design and production that culminated in a 'single point of failure', an illustration of the so-called 'Swiss cheese model of accidents', often used to analyse disasters in aviation or medical incidents.

Let's look at a hypothetical example. Imagine a team of three obstetricians in charge of an emergency birth. To guarantee the best possible care, ten critical tasks must be completed, such as checking the position of the baby or monitoring their heart rate. Each task is reviewed by the three doctors to make sure there are no slip-ups; doctors are humans and, even when they are at their best, they overlook one task. The chances that a crucial task is missed by all three doctors are one in 1,000. However, if the doctors are tired (as is often the case at the end of a long shift) and each one overlooks two tasks, a 'poor obstetric outcome' is eight times more likely. Instead of happening once every three years, it happens almost three times *every* year. The individual probability of making a mistake only doubled, but the probability of failure of the mission increased eightfold. When workers are tired, 'single points of failure' happen much more frequently.

Nowadays, the problems are not as much physical as they are psychological. Health institutions paint a dark picture. In the UK, one in four people experience mental health issues each year. More than 40 per cent of people have experienced depression, and more than one quarter have had panic attacks in their lifetime. Mental illnesses are more common, long-lasting and impactful than other health conditions, and they are the second-largest source of burden of disease in England. While there are several reasons behind the rise of mental illnesses, working conditions are one of the major causes.

Extreme prolonged stress can lead to burnout. In 2019, the World Health Organization defined occupational burnout as a syndrome resulting from chronic workplace stress, with symptoms of 'energy depletion or exhaustion; increased mental distance from one's job, or feelings of negativism or cynicism related to one's job; and reduced professional efficacy'. If you think this doesn't concern firms, read what *Forbes*, in one of its many articles on stress and burnout, had to say about it: 'Executives, owners and founders have to take on this productivity-punishing fact: stress is robbing your business, and your employees, right now.' Schumpeterian entrepreneurs understand the danger.

At any time, one in six workers will experience depression, anxiety or stress. In 2018, these three illnesses were responsible for 44 per cent of all cases of work-related ill health and half of all working days lost due to health issues in the UK. This is often hidden. One in five people take a day off due to stress, yet 90 per cent of them cited a different reason for their absence. It is responsible for up to 91 million working days lost. Human resources experts blame burnout for half of employee turnover. About 300,000 people with a long-term mental health condition lose their jobs every year. Estimates of the economic costs of mental health problems vary, depending on the methodology, but are always large. Studies place the costs for the UK somewhere between £34.9 billion and £100 billion each year, up to 4.5 per cent of its GDP. For the US, Harvard Business School estimates that stress-related burnout imposes a healthcare cost of $125 billion to $190 billion a year.

Do you think this is bad? It is worse in other countries, particularly in Asia. Death by overwork is so common in Japan and South Korea that they have their own words for it: *karoshi* (過労死) and *gwarosa* (과로사). It is usually the result of a heart attack or a stroke, due to long working hours and stress, in a sad parallel with the death by exhaustion common in Victorian times. The first case of *karoshi* in Japan was reported in 1969, but it only became a public health issue much later. It is hard to know its true extent but, every year, there are more than 500 legal claims to recognise a death as *karoshi* and attribute compensation to the family. The number of cases where compensation was awarded has more than tripled in the last twenty years. Suicides are another extreme manifestation of overwork. Between 2009 and 2019 in Japan, 24,000 people committed suicide due to problems related to their working situation.

No one is immune to extreme work pressures, not even economists. According to their biographers, Keynes and Schumpeter died from a heart attack and cerebral haemorrhage respectively, after a period of intensive work (Keynes negotiating Bretton Woods and Schumpeter working on his magnum opus). News of suicides occasionally rock the profession. A recent survey of PhD students in top US economics departments found that 25 per cent of them suffer from depression or anxiety and 11 per cent have frequently contemplated suicide or self-harm.

Sleep deprivation is another consequence of overwork that reinforces the trends in mental illness and impacts productivity. A report by the Rand Corporation, a prestigious independent think tank, quantifies the economic costs of sleep deprivation. Ten years ago, 35 per cent of Brits, 45 per cent of Americans and 55 per cent of Japanese slept less than seven hours per night. More recent studies find that 70 per cent of Japanese sleep fewer than seven hours and 30 per cent admit to having to drink alcohol to sleep. The report quantifies the causes of lack of sleep. Mental health problems reduce sleep by seventeen minutes, unrealistic time pressures at work by eight minutes, irregular hours by three minutes, and longer commuting about ten minutes. For comparison, contrary to what you might expect, having dependent children only takes five minutes of your sleep time.

Sleep deprivation is associated with leading causes of death like cardiovascular diseases, diabetes and hypertension, and impairs cognitive ability, causing traffic accidents, mistakes and loss of productivity at work. Lack of sleep increases mortality risk by up to 13 per cent. Several of the big human-caused catastrophes, like the Chernobyl nuclear explosion, the *Exxon Valdez* spill and the Space Shuttle *Challenger* explosion, were linked to sleep-related disorders and deprivation. Because of absenteeism due to sickness, higher probability of death and lower productivity, sleeping disorders remove $411 billion from the US economy, more than 2 per cent of GDP; $138 billion from the Japanese economy, 3 per cent of GDP; and $50 billion from the UK economy, close to 2 per cent of GDP. Some businesses are waking up to the economic cost of sleep deprivation. The US sleep-health industry is worth $40 billion. In Japan, firms are paying workers for sleeping more than six hours a night, installing sensors in their mattresses.

Why are burnout and sleeping disorders becoming the repetitive motion syndrome of the twenty-first century? This is a fundamental question towards understanding why implementing the four-day working week is more urgent now than it was fifty years ago. Mental health conditions are becoming more damaging because jobs are changing, and societies are changing.

Economists studying the impacts of present-day technological changes have found that the rapid improvements in computer technology and automation have brought ever cheaper machines that can replace humans in occupations involving mainly routine tasks, such as bookkeeping, clerical work and repetitive production tasks. In contrast, occupations involving non-routine tasks are on the rise. These can be of two types. There are non-routine abstract jobs, performed by highly skilled workers who are helped – not replaced – by machines: doctors, engineers, managers, economists and programmers. Machines also don't substitute non-routine manual jobs like waiters or salesmen, mainly low-skilled. As the economy-wide demand for middle-skill routine occupations has declined, non-routine jobs are thriving. In the US, in forty years the share of workers in routine occupations fell from 60 to 40 per cent. Conversely, employment in abstract non-routine occupations increased from 25 to 45 per cent.

A routine factory job is physically intense, but a non-routine job can be mentally draining. Pay attention to the following list of jobs that stand out for their impact on mental health, compiled by the news website *Business Insider*: veterinarians, emergency medical technicians, construction workers, childcare workers, doctors, nurses, restaurant workers, humanitarian workers and lawyers. *Forbes* has a similar list that includes: broadcasters, taxi drivers, public relations executives, senior corporate executives, newspaper reporters, event coordinators, police officers, airline pilots, firefighters and military personnel. All of them have in common a low content of routine tasks. They are highly non-routine, either abstract or manual. These types of jobs will be on the rise in the foreseeable future, so don't expect the burden of burnout to decrease any time soon, unless we do something about it.

Even if jobs were not changing, societies have transformed themselves. In the past fifty years, women left the kitchen and entered the labour market. In the UK, the employment rate among women aged 25–54 is up from 57 per cent in 1975 to a record 78 per cent in 2017. Naturally, the proportion of couples with children where only one adult works has almost halved, from 47 per cent to 27 per cent in 2015. This, together with the rise of divorce and single parenthood, has created a growing percentage of workers who face heightened time pressures and increased conflict between work and their private life. 'Stressed, Tired, Rushed: A Portrait of the Modern Family', wrote the *New York Times* in 2015. Anyone in this situation knows exactly what the article is talking about.

Few of you will know a rather obscure Portuguese musician, Latin Grammy award winner José Cid, who in 1978 created a masterpiece, *10,000 Anos Depois Entre Vénus E Marte*, considered a pioneer album of progressive rock. As progressive rock did not sell much in Portugal in those days, Cid made a living creating pop music of more dubious quality. Around the same time, he composed a tacky song, 'A pouco e pouco', that describes a day in the life of a couple in the 1970s. The husband has an office job with long hours, but when he comes back home his wife has cleaned the house and done the shopping, his favourite food is on the table and the kids are in bed. Next morning, when he wakes up, breakfast is ready, his shirt is cleaned and ironed, and his shoes polished. Compare this to a day in the couple's life half a century later. Naturally, both partners are working. They rush through breakfast, drop the kids at school, work intensive jobs, coordinate on picking up the kids, and come back home only to go shopping, collect shirts from the dry cleaner, cook, have dinner, put the kids to bed, clean and organise the house, reply to some work emails and fall asleep halfway through a Netflix series. Instead of reducing the stress, time at home just mounts the pressure. Surveys cited by the *New York Times* find that 40 per cent of mothers and 50 per cent of fathers feel they are spending too little time with their children. Three out of five full-time working mothers say they don't have enough leisure time, and more than half of the fathers say the same. Parents with a college degree suffer more: 65 per cent find it difficult to balance job and family. Can you imagine the lives of single mums who represent 20 per cent of households with dependent children in the UK?

In some countries, grandparents traditionally take an active role in caring for their grandchildren, relieving the pressure on parents. But, with women having children later and later, and often moving to another city, together with the increase in the retirement age, this support will be less and less effective.

We all understand the importance of rest in football or in elite sports. Without rest, players have more injuries, make more mistakes, and the team cannot reach its full potential. But resting is fundamental in every occupation. The changing nature of jobs and the instantaneous communication, brought by the internet, have intensified work in the last thirty years, so we need more rest. However, the changing role of women in society and the evolution of demographics means we are resting less than before. Together, these structural changes are putting pressure on mental health and making workers less productive. The economic motor is running too fast, but we are not getting any more speed. We need to change gear. The four-day week would reduce this pressure and raise workers' productivity. This idea is counter-intuitive, because we would be working less to produce more, but don't be fooled. Anyone with a creative job knows that inspiration doesn't come when someone is exhausted. It is better to switch off and come back with a fresh mind.

Coming back with a fresh mind was not the only reason why productivity in Ford's factories increased with the five-day working week. Management also improved:

> We have decided upon and at once put into effect through all the branches of our industries the 5-day week. Hereafter there will be no more work with us on Saturdays and Sundays. These will be free days, but the men, according to merit, will receive the same pay equivalent as for a full 6-day week. A day will continue to be 8 hours, with no overtime. [...]
>
> This decision to put into effect the short work week is not sudden. We have been going toward it for three or four years. We have been feeling our way. We have during much of this time operated on a 5-day basis. But we have paid only for 5 days and not for 6. And whenever a department was especially rushed it went back to 9 days – to 48 hours. Now we know from our experience in changing from 6 to 5 days and back again that we can get at least as great production in 5 days as we can in 6, and we shall probably get a greater, for the pressure will bring better methods. A full week's wage for a short week's work will pay. [...]
>
> The harder we crowd business for time the more efficient it becomes. [...]
>
> Management must keep pace with this new demand – and it will. It is the introduction of power and machinery in the hands of management which has made the shorter day and the shorter week possible. That is a fact which it is well not to forget.

Naturally, services can not go on the 5-day basis. Some must be continuous and others are not yet so organized that they can arrange for 5 days a week. But if the task is set of getting more done in 5 days than we now do in 6, then management will find the way.

Just as you apply stress to your body to build muscle, the pressure of time pushes managers to improve efficiency. Shortening the working week will distinguish good managers from bad managers better than any MBA – who is a Henry Ford, and who is one of Adam Smith's businessmen? Schumpeterian managers will see the new reality as an opportunity to get ahead. They will streamline processes, change the patterns of meetings, buy new software or new machines, or alter their products. They will maintain production by increasing productivity, keeping prices unchanged. To keep their profits, bad managers will reflect the shorter working week with higher prices. Firms with good managers will attract more customers, gaining market share, while firms with bad managers will lose out, fostering the creative destruction and renewal of the economy. It is as simple as that – competition will work and better firms will get ahead. As was the case a century ago, nowadays we have good and bad managers. Expect the bad managers to oppose the four-day week, and good managers to embrace it.

The relation between automation and labour market conditions is one of reverse causality. Higher automation affects unemployment and wages, but also higher wages give more incentives for automation. The economist Alberto Alesina documented that machines are more likely to substitute low-skilled jobs in Europe than in the US, attributing it to their 'different labor market policies, like binding minimum wage laws, permanent unemployment subsidies, firing costs, etc. Such policies create incentives to develop and adopt labor-saving capital-intensive technologies at the low end of the skill distribution.' A recent paper from European researchers, *Automating Labor: Evidence from Firm-Level Patent Data*, is able to isolate the causal effect of higher wages on automation innovation. They quantify that a 1 per cent higher low-skilled wage increases innovation in automation by 2 to 4 per cent. The four-day working week is a similar force to foster technological adoption.

If you are a manager or the owner of a company, you should watch the TED Talk by Andrew Barnes on the four-day working week. Straight away, you will notice that he is not an ordinary manager. He is the CEO of Perpetual Guardian, the company that re-launched the media discussion on the four-day working week. He implemented it, asking different teams within the company to change their internal processes and their time management. The results were startling. Not only did output not decrease, it went up marginally. Like in Henry Ford's factories, productivity fully compensated for the fall in hours. This went along with a fall in stress of 15 per cent and an improvement in work–life balance of 24 per cent. Visits to Facebook and related sites fell by 40 per cent as workers were better able to separate work and personal lives.

Andrew Barnes became one of the most prominent advocates for the four-day week. He created a non-profit organisation, *4 Day Week Global*, to help other companies reducing their working week. *4 Day Week Global* has organised several international trials and was listed as one of *Time*'s 100 Most Influential Companies of 2023.

You can dismiss the example of this firm as unique, a unicorn, but it is not. It is the rule rather than the exception. I have already mentioned Microsoft Japan's trial over the summer of 2019, covering its 2,300 employees. Productivity was boosted by 40 per cent, electricity usage shrunk by 23 per cent, meetings lasted thirty minutes, workers took 25 per cent less time off and printed 60 per cent fewer pages. More than 90 per cent of workers were happy. The company CompareNewTyres had a problem with absenteeism, and its CEO decided to conduct a month-long experiment, dropping staff working hours from forty to thirty-five hours per week. He recalls: 'we were astounded that what we produced in that one month was near enough identical to months when staff had worked forty-hour weeks. I think, like many business owners, I fell into the trap of thinking the more hours we work, the more work we get done.' Alex Soojung-Kim Pang describes in his book, *Shorter*, how several companies – software developers, advertising or financial services providers, cosmetic producers or Michelin-starred restaurants – from around the world, led by entrepreneurs full of ambition, are implementing four-day working weeks or a six-hour day, boosting productivity and profits.

Pang illustrates a compelling case of a care home that successfully transitioned to a four-day week. Despite increasing spending needed to hire additional caregivers, it proved to be a cost-saving measure because of savings elsewhere. By reducing absenteeism, it eliminated the necessity for temporary workers or agency staff called in on short notice to cover shifts – a group compensated at a higher hourly rate. Curiously, spending on Alzheimer's medication also decreased, as the constant turnover of staff destabilised the elderly residents who required higher dosages. This example shows that productivity gains are often not just about worker efficiency. A company is a team, and the gains can be reflected in various areas, such as reducing legal, human resources, and operational costs.

As the four-day week gains momentum, many firms are coordinating the start of a trial in organised pilots, all over the world. Some firms only open for four days, but many have kept operating for five, six or seven days. These firms reported more improvements than expected. Production increased or was maintained in the majority of companies and production costs decreased. The biggest effects were found on labour factors, such as better incentives, morale, and conditions for workers, more applicants, easier recruitment, and reductions in absenteeism, stress and burnout, labour turnover, tardiness and overtime. One disadvantage cited was the difficulty in scheduling, which became more complex. A few firms reported a high workload for supervisors and managers – another reason for lazy managers to loathe the idea. These were the same benefits reported in the book *4 Days, 40 Hours* regarding the twenty-seven pioneer US firms that adopted a four-day week in the 1970s.

Myself, I have witnessed first-hand these positive effects on firms. After the translation of this book was published in Portugal in 2022, I was invited by the Portuguese Government to coordinate their four-day-week trial. Our goal was to study this management practice in the context of the Portuguese economy and evaluate its impacts on workers and companies. We offered companies technical support and research expertise, but no financial support. The ongoing study includes forty-one firms testing a four-day week, twenty-one of which coordinated the start of the pilot in June 2023. In total, more than 1,000 workers are involved. More important than the number of participants is their diversity: a nursery, a research centre, a stem cell bank, entities from the social sector, commerce, industry, and several training and management consulting companies. While the concrete format of the four-day week adopted was different, most companies used the four-day week to change internal processes, adopt new technology, and reorganise work. After six months, the majority of companies extended the trial.

The stubborn rise of productivity following a shorter working week only comes as a surprise because we have such a short memory. Similar productivity gains occurred with the implementation of the five-day working week in the 1930s and 1940s. The newspaper articles from the time are instructive. In May 1947, *The Times* reported that during the second five-day working week in the British coal industry, output increased by 100,000 tons relative to production in the same period in the previous year. The same newspaper reported in November 1934 on the 'success of a five-day week experience' at the chemist Boots. The experiment proved so successful that the directors made it permanent. For industry after industry, firm after firm, production did not decrease after a reduction in the working week. As more industries and more firms turned to the five-day week, during the 1940s and 1950s, there was ever increasing evidence of how painless the transition was because of the consequent productivity gains. That is why it seemed so evident to everyone that the four-day week would follow soon, not least to Vice President Richard Nixon. Why do you think the critics of the five-day week evaporated and gave rise to so many supporters and visionaries of the four-day week in late 1950s?

There is more international evidence. The change from a six- to a five-day working week in Japan occurred in the late 1960s and early '70s. In January 1973, the *Wall Street Journal* wrote:

> The Japanese five-day week could seem like good news for U.S. companies battling tough Japanese competition. After all, a shorter workweek should mean less production. It should – but it doesn't. For the Japanese are working harder than ever, and companies that have cut the workweek say that, if anything, production is rising.

The implementation of the five-day working week in Japan, like in China and the US, also preceded their golden age. A 2011 research article from the International Labour Organization provides a comprehensive survey of past research on the link between different aspects of working time and productivity and firm performance. They found that in manufacturing, production does not necessarily increase when hours are lengthened, and that in many industries, shorter hours are associated with higher productivity per hour.

We can also turn to indirect methods to measure the productivity gains of a shorter working week. I once asked a friend of mine, a typical mother of a stressed modern family, why she wouldn't go part-time, to a four-day week. Her answer was simple. She would be doing the same amount of work but being paid 20 per cent less, and missing out on career opportunities. She knows too well the examples of her colleagues. If my friend is right, firms are pocketing the extra benefits of having long-term part-time workers. Evidence supports this hypothesis. A study by researchers from the Paris School of Economics and Université Libre de Bruxelles analysed data of all Belgian firms during the period 1999 and 2006, looking at how the variation of part-time rate across firms affected their performance. They concluded that an increase in the share of part-time jobs that exceed twenty-five weekly hours 'has a positive effect on firm productivity'. They find that 'this group is paid below its marginal productivity' and speculate that they face effective full-time workloads, for instance due to management not considering working time reductions when establishing work plans. Another study on the same question, using data from Dutch pharmaceutical firms, finds that a larger part-time employment share leads to greater firm productivity because it enables firms to allocate work more efficiently.

When illustrating the concept of productivity, economists usually choose examples from manufacturing. A baker produces ten loaves of bread per hour and with a new oven he can produce twenty loaves of bread per hour, is an enlightening example of how to measure productivity. But nowadays in the UK, 85 per cent of employment is concentrated in the service sector, and there, productivity is much harder to measure. It is harder to measure the inputs and the output. Let me illustrate with some examples.

Imagine a chef and her restaurant. When she doesn't have any customers, she doesn't produce any services, but she still employs her workers – productivity is low. Suppose that with the four-day week, aggregate demand increases and more people go for dinner at her restaurant. The restaurant would have more customers and the same number of employees, so productivity would be higher. 'Demand shocks can look like productivity shocks,' says Victor Ríos-Rull, an economist from the University of Pennsylvania.

Imagine a stock trader – a would-be George Soros. If the stock market only trades four days a week, what would happen to his productivity? Well, the measured productivity would go up by 25 per cent, almost by default. Whatever money he would gain or lose on a Friday, it would be compounded with the money he would gain or lose on a Monday, without working on Friday. Isn't he a winner? Imagine a journalist who must write a feature article with a deadline on Friday. If his deadline were on Thursday, he would still meet it, because there is no source of inspiration like last-minute panic. His measured productivity would also go up by 25 per cent. Myself, I am a professor at Birkbeck College. As I do not have lectures scheduled on a Friday, nothing in my measured output would change if the four-day working week were implemented. 'It is a commonplace observation that work expands so as to fill the time available for its completion.' This adage from a 1955 essay in *The Economist*, known as Parkinson's Law, applies to many other office jobs.

These examples highlight several of the problems with measuring productivity in the service sector, and how measured productivity in many jobs would mechanically go up with a four-day week. This might satisfy some pundits who attach too much importance to statistics. But, more important than its effect on measured productivity, the four-day working week will truly boost the underlying productivity of our economy. If this is true, why don't all firms see it? I'll answer this question later.

The Fourth Reason: Because It Will Unleash Innovation (Schumpeter)

'Hence when all such inventions were already established, the sciences which do not aim at giving pleasure or at the necessities of life were discovered, and first in the places where men first began to have leisure. This is why the mathematical arts were founded in Egypt; for there the priestly caste was allowed to be at leisure.'

Aristotle, Metaphysics

The terms macroeconomics, microeconomics and econometrics were all coined by Ragnar Frisch. But where does the underlying word, economics, come from? The original word from Ancient Greece, *Oeconomicus*, means literally house rules – the wisdom of household management – put into words by Xenophon, a Greek historian and philosopher. The achievements of the Ancient Greeks in economic theory were significant, but they are minor when compared with all their other cultural and scientific achievements. As Schumpeter wrote, 'there is hardly an idea that does not descend from Greek sources'. Xenophon was just one of their many scholars.

Modern economics, with all its maths, owes a lot to Greek mathematicians. Euclid is the father of geometry. His book, *Elements*, is considered the most successful and influential text-book ever written and it was used until the twentieth century. Keynes studied it before he was 10. Pythagoras did more than just draw triangles. Diophantus wrote *Arithmetica*, the most prominent work on algebra in Greek mathematics. Hipparchus founded trigonometry. Other natural sciences also owe much to Ancient Greeks. Anaximander was the first cartographer to draw a map of the known world. Eratosthenes invented the system of longitude and latitude. Ancient Greeks named most of the stars, planets and constellations of the northern hemisphere. Theophrastus founded botany. Doctors everywhere swear the Hippocratic oath. The Greeks were the first to take a scientific approach to medicine by studying diseases. Much of what we know about the early history of humanity was recorded by Greek historians. They developed philosophy – the search for wisdom and truth – on which Western culture built its foundations. They developed the first democracy in history.

Playwrights wrote and produced the first tragedies, comedies and satires in outdoor theatres. Ancient Greeks wrote wonderful literature, poetry and mythology. Homer's *Iliad* and the *Odyssey* are still compulsory reading today. They modernised architecture; built glorious buildings and hypnotising sculptures. We owe them the Olympic Games that still bring the world together every four years to remind us that there are plenty of other cool sports besides football.

Some of their inventions were of practical use. They invented the water mill, a revolutionary invention that provided mechanical energy for 2,000 years, and is still used today. Plato is credited with the first alarm clock, which he used to herald the start of his lectures. The odometer, included in every car to measure distance, is believed to have been invented by Archimedes, another mathematical genius. Other inventions of the Ancient Greeks include the gear, screw, bronze casting techniques, torsion catapult and the use of steam to operate some primitive machines.

What was behind such an explosion of ideas, science, culture and innovation? The writings of one of the most famous Greek thinkers, Aristotle, can clarify why Ancient Greece was one of the most brilliant civilisations. The culprit is leisure! Aristotle saw it as the ultimate goal of human behaviour – every action should be taken with the purpose of having more leisure.

In Ancient Greece, all economic and non-economic activities were tightly regulated – people were organised into different castes: soldiers, farmers, artisans, traders, shopkeepers, slaves or rulers. This separation of castes was justified by some early notion of specialisation – a now common economic wisdom. There were limits to the accumulation of individual wealth. As soon as all the political duties of a financially independent free man are satisfied, then he is worthy of *noble leisure* – the freedom from obligations and the necessities of life.

Leisure did not mean idleness, lack of purpose or waste of time. It was primarily the exercise of the intellect, our highest faculty, but also of the body. The intellectual development was purposeful outside the realm of real life and the basic necessities. It wasn't to get rich or develop the next breakthrough technology. It was to let your mind wander off. Education was encouraged to enhance the development of the intellect. But amusement and entertainment were not frowned upon. Aristotle viewed them as a form of rest, needed 'because we are not able to go on working without a break, and therefore it is not an end, since we take it as a means to further activity'. In Ancient Greece not everyone was a citizen, but every citizen was a researcher. They had time to rest, time to study and time to let their brains take them wherever they wanted to go, whether it was abstract mathematics, philosophy, botany, engineering or poetry. Aristotle represents the opposite of how we have responded to the improvements of productivity over the last 100 years. While we chose to consume more and work the same, for Aristotle we should have consumed the same and worked less. He would have gone further than Keynes and had everyone working only five hours per week.

It is now easier to understand the explosion of deep basic science, innovation, inventions and culture that Ancient Greece gifted to humanity. They had free time. The Greek view of leisure leading to enlightenment never resurfaced with the same strength. The Romans, for instance, had already a different opinion of leisure, more related to entertainment – the coliseum and the gladiators, the circuses and the chariots. Remember the metaphor of the 1922 pocket bulletin by the National Association of Manufacturers against the five-day week: 'It would mean a trend toward the Arena. Rome did that and Rome died.' And, of course, we are just escaping this ethical view that leisure is perverse, and work is salvation, which has dominated us for hundreds of years. Now the question arises: does this Ancient Greek view of leisure have any meaning for innovation in the modern world? Are we like Calvin, or like his father?

Let me come back to Henry Ford one last time. No, I am not going back to his statement on the implementation of the five-day week in his factories. It is the young Henry Ford himself who is the best example. Ford was born in 1863 to a family of farmers, which was, in all likelihood, his destiny. His parents had a small workshop with some tools that were his toys. At the age of 12, he was mesmerised by the sight of a vehicle – a boiler mounted on wheels with a water tank and a coal cart trailing behind. And so his passion for mechanics and his dreams of cars began. He later

qualified as a machinist. At night, he would repair watches in a jewellery shop. At the age of 16, he drove one of those primitive vehicles, and started experimenting in his workshop when he was not cutting timber or helping his father. He built a steam car, but sitting on a high-pressure steam boiler is not, apparently, the most relaxing experience, so he turned his interest to a novelty coming from Europe: the combustion engine. Ford later wrote: 'I do not recall any one who thought that the internal combustion engine could ever have more than a limited use.' The next big thing was electricity.

In 1890 he was offered a job as an engineer and machinist at the Detroit Electric Company, later known as the Detroit Edison Company, and he left the farm life, taking his passion for cars with him. This is what he wrote in his memoirs:

> It was in 1890 that I began on a double-cylinder engine. [...] During the first several months I was in the night shift at the electric-light plant – which gave me very little time for experimenting – but after that I was in the day shift and every night and all of every Saturday night I worked on the new motor. I cannot say that it was hard work. No work with interest is ever hard. [...] In 1892, I completed my first motor car, but it was not until the spring of the following year that it ran to my satisfaction.

It took him three years to build his first proper car, while having a full-time six-day job. He became Henry Ford because of what he did in his leisure time. Working – and he worked a lot – was just the means to allow for his noble leisure, the personification of Aristotle's ideal. It is no surprise that Ford said, 'power and machinery, money and goods, are useful only as they set us free to live'.

Innovation is often framed as coming from special people in R&D departments. History is full of cases of innovation coming from passionate people tinkering in their own sheds. Let me tell you some stories of people, not more or less special than you and me, who are still remembered today by what they did after their day job – driven by their passion.

Born in 1880, William Harley worked in a Milwaukee bicycle factory from the age of 15. One day, to blow off some steam, he and a friend snuck into the Bijou Theatre to watch a cabaret show of Anna Held, a famous performer. Anna entered the stage on a small powered bicycle. William's mind was blown away, more because of the bike than because of Anna. The seed was planted. Together with his friend, they started dreaming of motorised bikes. By 1904, working in their spare time in his garage, they had built three identical motorbikes. His friend's name was Arthur Davidson and the brand that they created, more akin to a religion, is easy to guess.

Chester Carlson was born in 1906. He was a brilliant boy who, from an early age, had to work to support his family. His father had tuberculosis and his mother caught malaria. He began doing small jobs for money from the age of 8. By the time he was 13, he would work for two or three hours before going to school, then go back to work after classes. In high school, he was his family's breadwinner. He was admitted at Caltech and worked to support his studies. Carlson graduated at the onset of the Great Depression, so job prospects were anything but great. As a last resort, he began working as a research engineer for Bell Telephone Laboratories in New York. Finding the work tedious, he wrote over 400 ideas for new inventions in his personal notebooks. The one he pursued with passion was the idea of making a paper copy. He carried out his first experiments in his own kitchen, which were not too popular with his wife, so he rented another apartment. There he made the first ever electrophotograph – better known as a photocopy. Joseph Wilson, the founder of Xerox, saw the potential of Carlson's invention and, in 1946, signed an agreement to develop it as a commercial product.

In 1996, Sara Blakely was selling fax machines door-to-door. It was not the most glamorous of jobs, but she was good at it. One day she had an idea for a special type of leggings. She spent the next two years researching and developing her idea, and founded

Spanx. It turns out that her leggings are pretty good! It was only in 2000, after Oprah Winfrey named Spanx a 'Favorite Thing' and sales exploded, that Blakely resigned from her job. In 2014, *Forbes* estimated her net worth to be $1 billion and ranked her, as the youngest self-made billionaire, the 93rd most powerful woman in the world.

Phil Knight spent five years selling Japanese athletic shoes before leaving his full-time job in accounting. The company he founded? Nike. Daymond Garfield John, one of the sharks swimming in *Shark Tank*, hustled in a lobster restaurant while developing his clothes brand FUBU. Ina Garten was a civil servant but she really loved cooking. While a staff member at the White House Office of Management and Budget, she unrolled her own brand, Barefoot Contessa. She now has countless books and TV shows, and she makes a delicious Chicken Piccata.

The development of new products in leisure time is commonplace in new technologies. Steve Wozniak kept his job at HP for a year after inventing the Apple computer with Steve Jobs. Facebook started as a side project. Markus Persson, a computer programmer, developed *Minecraft* on the side, a computer game that he sold to Microsoft for $2.5 billion. Kevin Systrom was in Mexico with his girlfriend, on vacation from his job in a start-up, when he had the idea for Instagram. Many big tech firms, like Google, give 20 per cent of the time to employees to dedicate to their own projects. It was this practice that brought Google News, Gmail and AdSense.

I don't hide my interest in obstetrics. I guess it sank in after all those dinner talks with my wife, despite my best intentions. So I am a particular admirer of Jorge Odon, an Argentinian car mechanic and part-time inventor. Argentinians love *asado*; grilling meat is their national pastime. It was during a barbecue in 2005 that Odon had to pull a cork out from inside an empty wine bottle. He applied a virtuoso technique using a plastic bag. He then thought, why can't we use the same technique to deliver babies? Let me guess what is in everyone's mind – he had probably drunk the whole bottle, right? It turns out that he was onto something. He sketched the idea and brought it to a medical research centre, and together they developed the Odon Device. The device has already been tested in small-scale trials and it does work! He received several awards, including from the World Health Organization, because it could become a good alternative for deliveries in a non-medical environment. The device is already under a full-blown clinical trial and, if it succeeds, it will be the first major obstetrics innovation in over 150 years, adding a twenty-first-century cork extractor to my wife's toolkit.

How many art collections, in homes or in museums around the world, were built as a hobby? Azzedine Alaïa, a Tunisian couturier and shoe designer; Pilar Citoler, a Spanish professor in medicine specialising in odontology; Peter Herzog, a Swiss legal expert; André Jammes, a French bookdealer; Martin Parr, a British documentary photographer; Pádua Ramos, a Portuguese architect; Reiner Speck, a German urologist; and Bob Wilson, an American theatre and opera director, are all unfamiliar names that were among the most prominent global collectors at the beginning of this century. Their collections, now worth millions, were built in their leisure time.

Last summer I met Tito Fernandes, a Parisian art dealer in *ukiyo-e*, the traditional Japanese art representing the 'floating world' in prints and paintings, and I was fascinated by his story. In 1981, at the age of 19, he started working for Citroën, a French car manufacturer. He first worked in the assembly line, moved on to industrial computing, and then worked in the department designing prototypes of components for future models. He was happy with his job. In 2005, Tito visited the home of nineteenth-century French impressionist Claude Monet. Monet was one of the first European collectors of *ukiyo-e* and his collection is displayed on the walls of his house. Tito was spellbound and started collecting prints that he bought online or from auction houses and learning all about *ukiyo-e*. It became his hobby. As his collection grew, he started selling some of the cheaper prints online to finance more expensive ones. He realised that he could sell them very easily. In 2006 his hobby would occupy about six weekly hours. Without knowing, Tito was launching the foundation of his future business. In 2008, a victim of the Great Recession, Tito's department was shut down. He was given the option of either staying in the company with a less exciting job description, or leaving with an indemnity. After twenty-seven years working for Citroën he left, using the money to scale up his art business. He was certain that he would succeed. He already had his place in a small niche where there were few experts and even fewer sellers. Ten years later, his business flourishes and, besides his website where you can buy old prints from £50, he has his permanent gallery in the chic 17th arrondissement in Paris.

New businesses fail all the time. The high failure rates and the uncertainty about how good the business idea is frighten many potential entrepreneurs. Many of the most cautious people don't give it a go. In the article 'Should I quit my day job? A hybrid path to entrepreneurship', researchers from the University of Wisconsin–Madison argue that *hybrid entrepreneurship* – starting a business while keeping a 'day job' – can reduce this uncertainty and influence entrepreneurial entry and survival. They show that hybrid entrepreneurs who later quit their day job have much higher rates of survival relative to those who enter full-time self-employment directly from paid employment. Unknowingly, Tito was a hybrid entrepreneur. Kickstarter and eBay are full of stories of side-hustles that became successful businesses. No wonder that *Wired*, a technology magazine and bible of tech geeks and wannabe entrepreneurs, writes, 'Entrepreneurs, don't give up your day jobs (yet).'

Schumpeter would be thrilled with these case studies. They personify his ideal of entrepreneur. But beyond economics, Schumpeter loved arts and culture and he was an avid reader. So, I think he would also be excited by finding a never-ending list of writers who started writing alongside a day job, or even kept it throughout their literary careers. I didn't have to go very far in my quest for examples. Some of my favourite writers fit these criteria.

'Capital is dead labor, which, vampire-like, lives only by sucking living labor, and lives the more, the more labor it sucks,' Marx wrote in *Das Kapital*, referring to an obscure vampire literature that first appeared in eighteenth-century poetry. It was later that Bram Stoker popularised vampires with his masterpiece, *Dracula*. With a passion for the arts, Bram Stoker was, for twenty-seven years, manager at the Lyceum Theatre in London. It was during this time that he wrote *Dracula*, as well as other less popular novels. He recalled the role of an illness that kept him bedridden when young: 'I was naturally thoughtful, and the leisure of long illness gave opportunity for many thoughts which were fruitful according to their kind in later years.' We owe to Stoker all the vampire imaginary, from bestselling author Anne Rice, author of *Interview with a Vampire* and herself a former insurance claims examiner, to the *Twilight* novels, written by stay-at-home mum Stephenie Meyer, which sold more than 120 million copies and whose cinema adaptation made more than \$3 billion at the box office – and not forgetting *Buffy the Vampire Slayer*, which is priceless.

Dracula has featured in 239 films. In close second is *Sherlock Holmes*, with 226 film adaptations. Sir Arthur Conan Doyle had a remarkable career as medical doctor and wrote the Sherlock Holmes novels and short stories after work. If you, like Schumpeter, prefer something spicier, Henry Miller worked in the Western Union Telegraph Company, and Vladimir Nabokov, author of *Lolita*, was an English professor and butterfly researcher. Franz Kafka was an insurance clerk. Virginia Woolf, a close friend of Keynes, was a publisher. She also shared Aristotle's view of leisure: 'If you are losing your leisure, look out! – It may be you are losing your soul.' One of my favourite novels, *J'irai cracher sur vos tombes*, was written by Boris Vian while working during the day as an engineer at the French Association for Standardisation, and moonlighting as a jazz trumpeter at night.

T.S. Eliot, Keynes's friend and winner of the Nobel Prize in Literature in 1948, worked for Lloyds Bank as a clerk and later worked as a publisher. T.S. Eliot himself wrote the introduction to the book *Leisure, The Basis of Culture* by the philosopher Josef Pieper, which tried to revive the Greek view of leisure. Toni Morrison, winner of the 1993 Nobel Prize in Literature, was an editor and teacher and only left her job after her third novel. The winner three years later was the Portuguese José Saramago, who started his career as a mechanical locksmith.

Keynes loved poetry and he would surely know Lord Byron's first poetry book, *Hours of Idleness*. Translated poetry rarely has the same power, so I don't expect you to know either of my favourite poets, both Portuguese. José Regio was a high-school teacher and Fernando Pessoa, Portugal's unmatched poet, made a living as a freelance translator of business correspondence. Like T.S. Eliot, this is a common life story for many poets. Poetry rarely pays the bills.

Antoine de Saint-Exupéry was a commercial pilot who joined the French Air Force at the onset of the Second World War, working airmail routes in Europe, Africa and South America. He disappeared while on a reconnaissance mission over the Mediterranean in 1944, but not before gifting the world the most beautiful of gems, disguised as a children's book. *Le Petit Prince* has sold more than 140 million copies worldwide and is the world's most translated non-religious book.

When I was young, I devoured books by Isaac Asimov, from the *Robot* short stories to the *Foundation* series. I wasn't the only one. The dream of a mathematical social science capable of predicting the evolution of society 1,000 years into the future and saving civilization from chaos, as laid out in *Foundation*, was the reason why Nobel Laureates Paul Krugman and Roger Myerson studied economics in the first place. The genius of science fiction was a professor of biochemistry all his life, and he wrote close to 500 books in his spare time. With his knowledge of chemistry, he could have thought of alternative hobbies, like the fictional

Walter White, a high-school chemistry teacher from New Mexico who built a short-lived drug empire, estimated by *Forbes* to have been worth half a billion dollars. Turning to fantasy, Andrzej Sapkowski studied economics and was a sales representative for a multinational, before converting to writing. He is best known for his book series *The Witcher*, now turned into a Netflix production.

But probably the most successful cinematographic adaptation of a fantasy book is *Harry Potter*. After graduating, J.K. Rowling worked at the research desk for Amnesty International, doing translation work. On a delayed train from Manchester to London's King's Cross station, Rowling came up with the idea for Harry Potter. Over the next five years, she outlined the plots for the seven books of the series. Rowling then moved to Porto, Portugal, and taught English. There, she started writing the first Harry Potter book. *Forbes* ranked her as the highest paid novelist in the world in 2019, making $92 million.

I will avoid detailing examples from other arts at the same length. Until their big break, musicians and artists don't make much money out of their passion. They often get along doing something else. Freddie Mercury, together with Roger Taylor, sold second-hand clothes in Kensington Market, even as Queen's album charted in the US. Tom Waits was a cook in a pizzeria, Art Garfunkel was a high-school mathematics teacher, Ian Curtis from Joy Division was a civil servant. Madonna was a coat-check girl in a famous nightclub. In that same nightclub, the artist Keith Haring was a busboy. I won't even go into sports. If you google 'Olympians with Day Jobs', each hit will be a unique life story of someone who was at their best outside work.

I love board games. Unfortunately, no one ever wants to play with me. I am told I am too competitive, an accusation I strongly deny. My favourite board game is *Settlers of Catan*. I think this must be the favourite of every economist, because in the stage where players exchange resources, we see the law of supply and demand in action. This game was invented by Klaus Teuber, a German dentist, who loved playing board games and had a good idea for one. The game has sold more than 22 million copies in thirty languages around the world. Nowadays, the number one board game is *Pandemic*, a cooperative game developed by Matt Leacock while working for AOL and Yahoo. In fact, this is a common story of creators of board games. Take *Wingspan, Modern Art, Euphrates & Tigris, Scythe, Viticulture, Azul, Bohnanza, Rummikub* or *Tortoise and Hare* – all great board games that you can find in specialised shops and whose creators had 'serious' jobs.

These are good examples of innovation with a different origin – innovation by consumers. Charles Leadbeater, a prominent management thinker, argues in his book *We-Think: Mass Innovation not Mass Production* that consumers play a huge role in innovation that is often neglected. He argues that the common view that consumers are passive children, who just take on whatever products are designed by firms, is wrong. Passionate, engaged and knowledgeable consumers contribute as much to the development and improvement of products as firms themselves. Emerging new markets are magnets for passionate users. Leadbeater describes, for instance, how the mountain bike originated from young users who, frustrated with the usual bikes, decided to 'fix' their own. It took fifteen years for big companies to pay attention to this niche, which is now worth $58 billion in the US alone. Another example is rap music, which was developed by users, not by any corporation. Much innovation comes from consumers, particularly after a disruptive innovation. More often than not, the creator does not foresee all the possibilities of use, and only consumers, by using it, can realise and shape its full potential. Leadbeater calls them *Am-pros*, amateurs that take leisure seriously, have skills, learn and see 'consumption as the expression of their potential'.

Creativity is often collaborative. Take, for instance, the open-source model that brought us Wikipedia, Apache, Linux, Firefox, Bitcoin, Python: mostly developed by users. The most hardcore accountant would point out that Wikipedia has lowered

GDP, because it is free, and people have stopped buying the *Encyclopædia Britannica*. The most popular web server software is the open-source Apache. It is used by 57 per cent of the one million busiest websites, and it is valued at between $2 billion and $12 billion, but it contributes zero to GDP. But these are true innovations, nonetheless.

Economists place innovation at the very core of economic growth. Not even the most dogmatic Keynesian economist would argue that economic growth could be sustained for decades through Keynesian aggregate demand policies. The first main model that economists developed to think about growth is called the Solow model. The model shows that the accumulation of capital – building new machines – can sustain economic growth for some time; think how China has maintained growth rates of about 9 per cent in the past fifty years. Still, the Solow model shows that if only relying on investment and more machines, economic growth will eventually stop. Beyond the accumulation of capital, one needs innovation and technological improvements. This was emphasised by the *endogenous growth theory*, for which Paul Romer won the Nobel Prize in 2018. The endogenous growth theory thinks about technological progress as coming from either *process innovation* – ideas to produce the same good in a better way, often through automation – or *product innovation* – ideas that give rise to new or better products. Whatever the source of innovation, it is driven by the number of researchers and their research productivity.

Edmund Phelps, another Nobel Laureate, shares the view of mainstream economists that innovation is key for prosperity and economic growth, but disagrees that innovation is driven by scientists in universities or by the R&D departments of big corporations. In his book *Mass Flourishing: How Grassroots Innovation Created Jobs, Challenge, and Change*, he lays out his view that the true engine of modern economies is 'indigenous innovation', coming from the dynamism of regular people, exploring their ingenuity to solve problems in their everyday life. In modern economies 'even people with few and modest talents – barely enough talent to get a job – were given the experience of using their minds: to seize an opportunity, solve a problem, and think of a new way or a new thing'. In a roundtable organised by the magazine *Prospect*, the economic historian Robert Skidelsky, a prominent British thinker, replied, 'To you, mass flourishing depends on continuous grassroots innovation', adding:

> An important measure that you mention is job satisfaction. In my conception, there is a contrary view, in which mass flourishing depends on the continuous enlargement of leisure, which productivity growth makes possible of course. You mentioned Aristotle – Aristotle's idea of a good life was really one he called *eudaimonia*, which is a kind of active leisure.

Phelps does not mention leisure in his theory, but Skidelsky is spot-on. Leisure is one of the forces, if not *the* force, behind innovation by the grassroots.

Supply-side economists also offer their own explanation for the secular stagnation, our current malaise. They attribute it not to lack of aggregate demand like their fellow Keynesians, but to low productivity growth. They think of two potential culprits. The first is that the innovation engine is stalling. Four leading economists, in an article published in the *American Economic Review*, another prestigious economics journal, document a worrying trend: ideas are getting harder to find. Research effort is rising, but the productivity of researchers is declining faster. This theory is usually accompanied with a farming analogy. Think of innovation as fruit on a tree. The low-hanging fruit were easy to pick, but now only the high-hanging fruit are available, and these are harder to pick. The same number of researchers can pick fewer and fewer fruits. This echoes the economist Robert Gordon, who proclaims the death of innovation and the end of growth. Quite a depressing prospect!

This theory, however, seems hard to square with talk of the Fourth Industrial Revolution – automation, digital technology, the rise of robots, artificial intelligence or nanotechnology. Maybe the innovation engine is not failing per se, but is not being transmitted into productivity. 'You can see the computer age everywhere but in the productivity statistics,' said Robert Solow. Perhaps these technologies are not revolutionary enough to impact productivity, but most likely it takes time to uncover all the potential of the new technologies, and how to use them effectively. We just need to wait and see. But are there ways to speed up the dissemination of new technologies through the veins of the economy? The missing link is filled by Phelps's 'indigenous innovation'. The fruits of technology are not like apples in trees, they are blackberries in bushes growing in all corners of our economies. There are many fruits, but they are small and have to be picked one by one. These cannot be picked by scientists or by R&D departments of big multinationals. We need everyone, men and women, young and old, with or without higher education, in London or in Lancaster, in offices or in shops, in the private or the public sector, to reinvent their jobs or innovate through a new business. For this, we need to give everyone time, and that is precisely what the four-day working week brings.

Schumpeter said: 'Without innovations, no entrepreneurs; without entrepreneurial achievement, no capitalist returns and no capitalist propulsion. The atmosphere of industrial revolutions – of "progress" – is the only one in which capitalism can survive.' For capitalism to survive we must find other sources of ideas. The four-day week is the best solution because it will give time to everyone to develop their passion. You could argue that all the examples I documented were achievements of people who made it, even without the four-day week. This is true, but as Sherlock Holmes taught us, the key is not what you see, but what you don't see. How many people had to sacrifice their dreams for a job that pays the bills? How many inventions were not created, or how many new products were not developed, because people didn't have time to devote to their passion? I can't answer this question. No one can answer this question. These are stillbirths, ghosts carrying the blueprints of progress. How many of them can come into existence if we add another day to the weekend?

For the Ancient Greeks, it was easier to enjoy a long period of leisure when 40 per cent of society were slaves. Still, with only a population of 10 million, they achieved unimaginable progress. Today, the US and Europe have 500 million workers whose hidden potential can be unleashed with the four-day week. It would be a game changer for innovation, entrepreneurship, culture and progress. This argument, which has been absent from the debate around the four-day working week, was made very eloquently by Bertrand Russell, together with a gibe at academic economists who were blind to it. The close friend of Keynes, a member of his intellectual circle in Cambridge and his cultural Bloomsbury circle in London, wrote in his essay *In Praise of Idleness*:

> In the past, there was a small leisure class and a larger working class. The leisure class enjoyed advantages for which there was no basis in social justice; this necessarily made it oppressive, limited its sympathies, and caused it to invent theories by which to justify its privileges. These facts greatly diminished its excellence, but in spite of this drawback it contributed nearly the whole of what we call civilization. It cultivated the arts and discovered the sciences; it wrote the books, invented the philosophies, and refined social relations. Even the liberation of the oppressed has usually been inaugurated from above. Without the leisure class, mankind would never have emerged from barbarism.
>
> The method of a leisure class without duties was, however, extraordinarily wasteful. None of the members of the class had been taught to be industrious, and the class as a whole was not exceptionally intelligent. The class might produce one Darwin, but against him had to be set tens of thousands of country gentlemen who never thought of anything more intelligent than

117

fox-hunting and punishing poachers. At present, the universities are supposed to provide, in a more systematic way, what the leisure class provided accidentally and as a by-product. This is a great improvement, but it has certain drawbacks. University life is so different from life in the world at large that men who live in academic milieu tend to be unaware of the preoccupations and problems of ordinary men and women; moreover their ways of expressing themselves are usually such as to rob their opinions of the influence that they ought to have upon the general public. Another disadvantage is that in universities studies are organized, and the man who thinks of some original line of research is likely to be discouraged. Academic institutions, therefore, useful as they are, are not adequate guardians of the interests of civilization in a world where everyone outside their walls is too busy for unutilitarian pursuits.

In a world where no one is compelled to work more than four hours a day, every person possessed of scientific curiosity will be able to indulge it, and every painter will be able to paint without starving, however excellent his pictures may be. Young writers will not be obliged to draw attention to themselves by sensational pot-boilers, with a view to acquiring the economic independence needed for monumental works, for which, when the time at last comes, they will have lost the taste and capacity. Men who, in their professional work, have become interested in some phase of economics or government, will be able to develop their ideas without the academic detachment that makes the work of university economists often seem lacking in reality. Medical men will have the time to learn about the progress of medicine, teachers will not be exasperatedly struggling to teach by routine methods things which they learnt in their youth, which may, in the interval, have been proved to be untrue.

Russell brings up the role of universities, more professional and specialised, in substituting the leisure class in the development of new ideas. Certainly, they started as institutions where academics had time and freedom to think, and contributed much to innovation, but with the massification of higher education, they have become too structured. This is certainly true in the UK, where higher education has become a 'business of teaching', where students are the customers and each department has to be 'profitable' for the university, where professors have to devote too much time to teaching to avoid student complaints that would push the department down the rankings, or to endless administrative tasks that serve no purpose except to tick boxes. For free time to research, academics apply for grants that, no matter what is written in their charters, privilege status quo research instead of riskier ideas. The pressure to publish, to move forward in their careers, and ever bigger time constraints make riskless incremental research a safer bet than more innovative but much riskier research that possibly will never get anywhere. Universities cannot be substituted, but we should also look elsewhere for innovation – we should look everywhere for innovation.

Schumpeter viewed himself as a conservative. He planned to write a book on the meaning of conservatism, but he added: 'I am pretty sure that no conservative I have ever met would recognize himself in the picture I am going to draw.' Schumpeter's theories enjoyed a resurgence during the 1980s and were adopted by conservatives who designed economic policies to create conditions favourable to entrepreneurship. They revised the tax system by slashing taxes on corporations and abolishing inheritance taxes. They pushed for the development of financial and credit markets to allow for good entrepreneurs from poorer backgrounds to have access to finance to start their own business. They also strengthened intellectual property rights to guarantee larger returns from innovation. The development of a business does require money, but the seeds of the deepest innovation are not planted with money. They are planted with time. Give people time. A true conservative should see it. Schumpeter, the prophet of innovation, would.

Work-Sharing: A Weak Argument (Marx)

'Reason has always existed, but not always in a reasonable form.'

Karl Marx

In 2018, a 4.4m bronze statue of Karl Marx, gifted by China, was uncovered in his hometown of Trier, in Germany. The ceremony was occasionally interrupted by applause and boos from different groups of activists. Today, Karl Marx is still a polarising figure. For some, he is the Hulk of the working class. For others, he was the brain who gave communist regimes the intellectual backing to justify their atrocities. His understanding of the history of class struggle, laid down in *The Communist Manifesto*, still has a political and social appeal. Schumpeter preferred to admire the economist, calling him a 'genius', a 'prophet', and a 'learned man'. Marx's view of the dichotomy between *capital* and *labour*, detailed in the impenetrable *Das Kapital*, remains at the core of modern macroeconomics.

I take for granted that Marx would support the four-day working week, as much as today's unsullied Marxists do.

Marx would look for powerful arguments that would win over economists. Marxists, or at least most of them, have not. They have built their case on philosophical, social and environmental arguments. 'We should work to live, not live to work.' 'How much is enough for the good life?' 'The four-day week will even out the gender imbalance.' 'It will increase happiness.' 'It will clean the environment.' Fair enough. These are all good points. The problem is when they come to the economy. Many of the promoters of the four-day week repeat the same argument, claiming it will reduce unemployment through work-sharing. This was the main claim of the book *A Shorter Workweek in the 1980s*, by William McGaughey. 'The French government has legislated a shorter work-week for large enterprises. The arithmetic is simple: if existing workers work less, the same amount of work will be done by more workers,' wrote Arvind Ashta, a professor in accounting, finance and law when France implemented the thirty-five-hour week. The promise is breathtaking. Firms will see a fall of 20 per cent in their *labour input*, so they have to hire 25 per cent more workers to fully offset it (you read it correctly, percentages are tricky: there is a 20 per cent reduction from five to four, but a 25 per cent increase from four to five). New jobs will spring up like mushrooms, firms will absorb all of the unemployed, and workers will live happily ever after.

At the origin of this argument is the management practice with the same name. Work-sharing is sometimes used in recessions or in other situations where the demand for a particular firm falls. Instead of firing workers, the firm agrees with them to reduce the number of working days, usually one or two, for all workers, with a corresponding reduction in pay. Often enough, it looks like a four-day working week implemented with a proportional cut in wages. Work-sharing has been used since the nineteenth century. One prominent example is Volkswagen, who in the recession of 1993 saved 30,000 out of their 100,000 jobs in Germany. This practice is actively promoted by the International Labour Organization, a United Nations agency, as an alternative to layoffs at a firm level, sustained on research that has found it saved 400,000 jobs in Germany, 370,000 jobs in Japan and 100,000 in Turkey during the Great Recession. Sometimes, work-sharing is even subsidised, with a portion of the lost income replaced by social security, with specific policies such as Kurzarbeit in Germany, Chômage partiel in France, Cassa Integrazione in Italy, Short Time Compensation programs in the US or the Work Sharing program in Canada. While work-sharing as a management practice can help protect jobs when firms have temporarily fewer customers, it is a misjudgment to claim that the four-day week implemented across the entire economy will make all firms hire many more workers, especially when the proponents are adamant in ruling out wage cuts – a necessary condition for work-sharing as a management practice.

I feel frustrated when I hear this argument. Out of all the economic arguments that could have been picked – and I am giving eight – Marxists have chosen one that is scorned by most economists. They should be forgiven. This reasoning is so common and its allure so powerful that economists named it: the *lump-of-labour fallacy*. Wikipedia includes it in a list of common fallacies. We find this fallacy everywhere, but it is particularly common when people talk about migration or retirement: 'migrants are stealing our jobs' or 'older workers should retire to give their jobs to young workers'. We are back to an accounting view of the economy. In its essence, it is the false premise that the number of jobs or the total output in the economy is fixed, and that nothing else adjusts. Economists scorn this argument because economics is all about these adjustments. When migrants come into a country, they rent a house and buy goods like everybody else. Aggregate demand expands and firms hire more workers. Also, no company that I know of replaces all experienced workers that retire with young graduates fresh out of university. I will deconstruct the work-sharing argument before building a more powerful one in the next chapter.

In the context of the four-day week, the work-sharing argument is wrong in many ways. First, it is incompatible with Schumpeter's argument that the four-day week will raise productivity. Anyone who uses both arguments together doesn't understand economics. Suppose that the gains in productivity offset the reduction in hours, so that total production is maintained, as was the case with Ford Motor Company in the 1920s, and Perpetual Guardian in 2018. Firms would produce the same amount of goods, pay the same wages to their workers, charge the same prices to their customers, and keep the same number of workers and profits. If the productivity gains occur and output is the same, why would firms hire more workers? The productivity argument, which is very powerful, wipes out the work-sharing argument.

But let us abstract from the productivity argument. Consider a gardening firm owned by an Adam Smith businessman. When the four-day week is implemented, he puts no effort into improving productivity: no changes in processes, no new software or machines, no adaptation of the plants and flowers they grow. The manager still faces a dilemma. To maintain production, he must employ more workers. But increasing the workforce by one quarter raises the wage bill. Some firms might accept a cut in profits, but most likely the higher costs will be reflected in higher prices. Then again, higher prices will lower the demand for their gardening services. Customers will turn to cheaper firms that have dealt better with the transition to the four-day week, or give up on having their garden taken care of by professionals. The fall in demand implies that the firm will not hire 25 per cent more workers as initially predicted. The employment effects will be weaker.

There is a third way to dismantle the lump-of-labour fallacy in the context of the four-day week. Consider a consultancy company that operates for five days during the week and a restaurant that operates only on weekends, relying on part-time workers. According to the work-sharing argument, the consultancy company will hire 25 per cent more workers, because its current workforce will work one day less, and it must keep the same production. Now think about the symmetric problem of the weekend restaurant. If it is now open three days instead of two, will it hire more or fewer workers? According to the inverted work-sharing argument, the restaurant will get rid of one third of its workforce, because its workers will now work one more day but the number of meals served in two days will now be served in three days. Sounds ridiculous, no? It is ridiculous because you don't expect that the number of meals served in a three-day weekend will not be the same as in the two-day weekend. As I argued through Keynes, the demand for 'weekend' industries will increase, so we should expect exactly the opposite: more jobs for the weekend restaurant, rather than less. How about the consultancy? I would not bet on a significant increase in employment. Either it will compensate for the lost day by increasing productivity, or it will keep its workforce and scale down its output.

Although weaker than what the 'simple arithmetic' suggests, the lump-of-labour fallacy does not necessarily mean 'zero work-sharing'. Two of the most prestigious Italian labour economists, Pietro Garibaldi and Tito Boeri, have studied a policy reform that increased the retirement age by up to five years for some categories of workers in Italy. In the context of this *natural experiment*, they find that, for five workers locked in before retirement, the firm hires one fewer young worker – that is one fifth of the naive effect.

In the Portuguese four-day-week trial, one of our flagship participants was a nursery. Nurseries provide a direct service, need to maintain a certain ratio between staff and children, and must be open five days. I often hear that in this type of sector, firms reducing the working week must hire 25 per cent more workers to maintain service, but that was not the case: they only increased staff by 4.5 per cent (1 in 22). As most of the nursery's staff are women in their 20s and 30s with children, they often miss work. To deal with chronic absenteeism, the nursery had to overstaff. When implementing the four-day week, they set up a rota where workers have different days off during the week. If a worker cannot attend her shift, she swaps with a colleague off on that day. The nursery reduced the non-essential contact hours for parents, and the person who was previously in the office became an all-rounder. They also increased the length of the day from 7 to 7.30 hours to improve the service at the end of the day. The improvement in the service was also felt at the end of the week, with more energetic staff who had rested on Wednesday or Thursday. Summing up, with all the organisational changes adopted, the nursery reduced weekly hours by 14 per cent from 35 to 30 hours, with an increase of 4.5 per cent of workers, meaning that productivity per hour increased almost 10 per cent. They also saved on non-essential pilates classes and cut a transport allowance, which partly compensated the higher labour costs.

If we transpose the numbers to the implementation of the four-day week, we could expect, at most, an increase of 5 per cent in employment, sizeable but far from the 25 per cent that is naively promised.

The argument for work-sharing not only has weak theoretical foundations, it also has scant support in the data. One of the best papers quantifying the effects of the implementation of the thirty-five-hour week in France also contains a good review of other studies measuring the effects of a reduction in hours through legislation. These covered countries like France, Brazil, Germany, Canada and Portugal. All the studies established causal links by exploring the difference between firms or workers that were affected by the legislation and firms or workers that were not. Few of the papers reviewed found significant increases in employment for affected firms. In the French case, the research found no employment effects within affected firms. This does not mean there won't be positive employment effects (there will!), but simply that they won't come through work-sharing.

The idea of work-sharing is like a siren song that, on so many occasions, entraps the best of minds. What is the allure of this theory? I figured out the answer in the unlikeliest of places: back home with my parents! I started writing this book during a Christmas vacation in Portugal. Over lunch, I explained to my parents the eight arguments in favour of the four-day week. My dad was an economist, and my mum was for many years the headteacher of a high school. They are both retired. My mum is a doer; she never bothered much with intellectual, philosophical, and certainly not economics questions. That is my dad's turf. My dad and I are known to have long conversations over meals that are as passionate and profound to us as they are boring to everyone else. My mum usually listens attentively and rarely engages in counter-arguments. To my surprise, when I was explaining the lump-of-labour fallacy, my mum told me, with a conviction that shocked me, that I was wrong. When she was a headteacher, the government implemented legislation reducing working time. It did not affect teachers but it reduced the hours of all support staff. My mum faced gaps in the school's rota and she had to hire additional staff to cover them.

Thanks to my mum, I realised the one sphere where the lump-of-labour fallacy is not a fallacy – the public sector. Why? Because employment decisions in the public sector are taken for other motives than in the private sector. My mum didn't maximise profits because there were no profits to be maximised. She didn't charge a price for the school's services, nor did she fight for customers. She did have a budget and her objective as headteacher was to provide the service the school was supposed to provide, with the highest quality possible, within that budget. When the legislation came into force, her staff reduced their weekly hours and, to maintain the standards, my mum hired additional workers. She did change a few organisational aspects of the school but, mainly, the central government gave more money to accommodate the extra spending. The mindset of the private sector does not apply to the public sector.

A recent report by Autonomy, an independent and progressive think tank, and a strong promotor of the four-day working week, called for a thirty-two-hour week in the public sector to pave the way for the whole economy. Autonomy claims that the government would have to create 300,000 to 500,000 new full-time jobs in the UK. Can this angle partially rescue the work-sharing arguments for the four-day week? Partially, but at a cost. If we are to expect lower productivity improvements and a larger headcount in the public sector, this will come with a bigger price tag, which in turn implies more government spending and more taxes. While it would contribute to lowering unemployment, it could jeopardise the success of the four-day week, because it makes it non-neutral from a budgetary point of view. I will come back to this problem in the third part of the book, when I'll discuss the implementation of the four-day week in the public sector.

Unemployment is what economists call a *stock variable.* When you fill your bathtub, the water comes in through the tap and goes out through the drain. You can prevent it from overflowing even when the tap is on if the same volume of water keeps draining. You should think about unemployment in the same way: how many people are coming in and how many people are going out. Every quarter, there are workers who lose their job and there are unemployed people who find one. Over the past two decades in the UK, about 30 per cent of the unemployed find a job within one quarter. Out of an average of 1.7 million unemployed, every quarter there are 450,000 who become employed, but simultaneously 366,000 lose their jobs.

The argument that the four-day week would *take people out* of unemployment through work-sharing is weak – it is theoretically flawed and empirically contentious. The four-day week might boost hiring, but this is unlikely to come from affected private-sector companies operating over five days. They are more likely to come either from the public sector or from private-sector firms operating in leisure industries that will see a boom in their demand. Marx would have never pushed the argument formulated like this. He would have looked for a twist. We might not see more people finding jobs, but we will see fewer people losing theirs, for a different reason.

The Fifth Reason: Because It Will Reduce Technological Unemployment (Marx)

'My Lords: During the short time I recently passed in Nottinghamshire not twelve hours elapsed without some fresh act of violence; [...] I was informed that forty Frames had been broken the preceding evening. These machines [...] superseded the necessity of employing a number of workmen, who were left in consequence to starve. By the adoption of one species of Frame in particular, one man performed the work of many, and the superfluous labourers were thrown out of employment. [...] The rejected workmen in the blindness of their ignorance, instead of rejoicing at these improvements in art so beneficial to mankind, conceived themselves to be sacrificed to improvements in mechanism.'

Lord Byron

We are living in the era of the Fourth Industrial Revolution, proclaimed Klaus Schwab, the executive chairman of the World Economic Forum, in 2015. This industrial revolution could only have been imagined by Isaac Asimov. Progress in artificial intelligence, genome editing, biometrics, nanotechnology, 3D printing and the internet are merging the abilities of men and machine. Powered by renewable energy, *Terminators* are taking over production and, soon, *Transformers* will be driving on the highways.

The First Industrial Revolution took place between 1760 and 1820. Powered by coal and water, the steam engine replaced small-scale production with large-scale manufacturing of goods, such as textiles. The second revolution, between 1870 and 1914, followed the invention of electricity. Henry Ford, of course, played the important role of developing the internal combustion engine and the automobile, and pioneering mass production. We became dependent on oil for power. The Third Industrial Revolution started in the 1950s, bringing with it electronics, semiconductors, microprocessors, computers and automation, and adding nuclear energy to our power sources.

Through Keynes, we have already marvelled at the productivity gains and the rise in living standards that all these revolutions brought. But there was a dark side in all industrial revolutions, one side that Keynes warned us about – *technological unemployment*. Lord Byron, in his maiden speech in the House of Lords on 27 February 1812, described how machines were putting people out of work. The stories of workers, usually trained artisans, revolting and destroying the new mechanised knitting frames were all too common. In one of these stories, an apprentice artisan, Ned Ludd, destroyed one of these machines in 1779. His identity is not confirmed by historians, but the name gave rise to the word 'Luddites' to denote people who oppose new technology.

The loudest cry of upheaval during the Second Industrial Revolution was Karl Marx's *Das Kapital*. Its three volumes were published in 1867, 1885 and 1894. Marx understood that improvements in technology were the most powerful means to shorten the working hours, but they had been used, instead, to place workers – men, women and children – at the mercy of capitalists. According to Marx:

Machinery [...] supplants skilled labourers by unskilled, men by women, adults by children; where newly introduced, it throws workers upon the streets in great masses; and as it becomes more highly developed and more productive it discards them in additional though smaller numbers.

The economists tell us, to be sure, that those labourers who have been rendered superfluous by machinery find new venues of employment. They dare not assert directly that the same labourers that have been discharged find situations in new branches of labour. Facts cry out too loudly against this lie. Strictly speaking, they only maintain that new means of employment will be found for other sections of the working class; for example, for that portion of the young generation of labourers who were about to enter upon that branch of industry which had just been abolished. Of course, this is a great satisfaction to the disabled labourers. There will be no lack of fresh exploitable blood and muscle for the Messrs. Capitalists – the dead may bury their dead. [...] But even if we assume that all who are directly forced out of employment by machinery, as well as all of the rising generation who were waiting for a chance of employment in the same branch of industry, do actually find some new employment – are we to believe that this new employment will pay as high wages as did the one they have lost? If it did, it would be in contradiction to the laws of political economy. [...]

But capital not only lives upon labour. Like a master, at once distinguished and barbarous, it drags with it into its grave the corpses of its slaves, whole hecatombs of workers, who perish in the crises.

One has to love the power of Marx's metaphors. Capitalists are *vampires*, and now the technological unemployed are *corpses of slaves* and *hecatombs of perished workers*. Brilliant! Marx explains the labour market consequences of new labour-saving technology. Machines substitute workers who are thrown into unemployment, a word that was only added to the *Oxford English Dictionary* in 1888. This type of unemployment is what economists call *structural unemployment*, different from *cyclical unemployment*, the one that arises because of lack of aggregate demand that we have seen with Keynes. Marx also explains the typical response of economists, which has not changed in more than 100 years. Yes, after the introduction of a new technology we should expect technological unemployment *in the short run*, but these people will soon find other jobs, in other occupations or in other industries. *In the long run*, the economy will get back to employing all workers. Do you know of any stable boys or switchboard operators unemployed today?

Marx is right. Numerous studies over the past thirty years on the effects of job displacement document that workers who are laid off for reasons outside their control, like plant closures, face worse labour market outcomes: fewer re-employment opportunities, earnings losses, lower consumption, and even poorer health. Displaced workers with at least three years of job tenure face between 20 and 40 per cent loss in earnings, which persist for twenty years. These earnings losses are explained by the reduction in workers' re-employment probabilities – they face multiple spells of unemployment – and a stagnant growth in their re-employment wages.

Up until 1940, one way that was used to curtail the *corpses of slaves* was the reduction of the working day; first from sunrise to sunset, to twelve hours, then to ten hours, and finally to eight hours. Then, workers achieved a reduction of the working week to five days. The argument was that in a situation where firms are investing in labour-saving technologies, it reduces the incentive to lay off workers. Consider a firm that invests in automatic check-out machines and finds itself with less need of hours of labour, contemplating layoffs. Shortening the working week, by with-drawing hours from the current workforce, will put down such thoughts for a while. While it might not be enough for firms to hire more workers, it can reduce displacements.

These achievements in working time reductions were settled by governments after intense pressure from the unions inspired by Marx, but not without bloodshed. We celebrate International Workers' Day on 1 May, the starting date of a strike in 1886 in Chicago in favour of an eight-hour working day, where several workers were killed and wounded. Six years later, in one of Andrew Carnegie's steel plants, Homestead, where production and prices were increasing, workers demanded wage increases while man-agement offered them a 22 per cent wage cut. A 143-day strike ended with a private army being hired, resulting in a fight killing ten men. The public outrage led to Carnegie – falsely, according to several accounts – shifting the blame to the plant manager.

During the Third Industrial Revolution, another major econ-omist worried about technological unemployment. Wassily Leontief was a Russian-American economist who had joined Harvard University in the same year as Schumpeter. The two were Samuelson's PhD supervisors. Rumour has it that, at the end of Samuelson's dissertation defence, Schumpeter asked Leontief with irony, 'Well, Wassily, have we passed?' Samuelson later wrote: 'The whole world appreciated the genius of Wassily W. Leontief. But we his disciples knew the full measure of his inspiration and potential.' It was not by chance that, beside Paul Samuelson, three others of his students got the Nobel Prize: Robert Solow, Vernon Smith and Thomas Schelling. A further seven of his students' students got one. Leontief himself won it in 1973, for developing input–output tables, a method to ana-lyse the interdependence between industries, by calculating a

network based on how much of the production in one industry is used in all other industries. Leontief was a strong advocate of the use of data in economics, campaigned against a science based on 'theoretical assumptions and non-observed facts' and embarked on a large-scale project of processing US industrial data for the years prior to the Great Depression.

Later in his career, in 1982, Leontief wrote an article, 'The distribution of Work and Income', with the following lead: 'When workers are displaced by machines, the economy can suffer from the loss of their purchasing power. Historically the problem has been eased by shortening the work week, a trend currently at a standstill.' He explained:

Over the past two centuries technological innovation has brought an exponential growth of total output in the industrial economies, accompanied by rising per capita consumption. At the same time, until the middle 1940s the easing of man's labor was enjoyed in the progressive shortening of the working day, working week and working year. Increased leisure (and for that matter cleaner air and purer water) is not counted in the official adding up of goods and services in the gross national product. It has nonetheless contributed greatly to the well-being of blue-collar workers and salaried employees. Without increase in leisure time the popularization of education and cultural advantages that has distinguished the industrial societies in the first 80 years of this century would not have been possible.

The reduction of the average work week in manufacturing from 67 hours in 1870 to somewhat less than 42 hours must also be recognized as the withdrawal of many millions of working hours from the labor market. Since the end of World War II, however, the work week has remained almost constant. Waves of technological innovation have continued to overtake each other as before. The real wage rate, discounted for inflation, has continued to go up. Yet the length of the normal work week today is practically the same as it was 35 years ago. In 1977 the work week in the U.S. manufacturing industries, adjusted for the growth in vacations and holidays, was still 41.8 hours.

Concurrently the U.S. economy has seen a chronic increase in unemployment from one oscillation of the business cycle to the next. The 2 per cent accepted as the irreducible unemployment rate by proponents of full-employment legislation in 1945 became the 4 per cent of New Frontier economic managers in the 1960's. The country's unemployment problem today exceeds 9 per cent. How can this be explained?

Without technological change there could, of course, be no technological unemployment. Nor would there be such unemployment if the total population and the labor force, instead of growing, were to shrink. Workers might also hang on to their jobs if they would agree to accept lower wages. Those who are concerned with population growth are likely to proclaim that 'too many workers' is the actual cause of unemployment. Libertarians of the 'Keep your hands off the free market' school urge the remedy of wage cuts brought about by the systematic curtailment of the power of trade unions and the reduction of unemployment and welfare benefits. Advocates of full employment have been heard to propose that labor intensive technologies be given preference over labor-saving ones.

A more familiar medicine is prescribed by those who advocate stepped-up investment in accelerated economic growth.

Each of these diagnoses has its shortcomings, and the remedies they prescribe can be no more than palliative at best. A drastic general wage cut might temporarily arrest the adoption of labor saving technology, even though dirt cheap labor could not compete in many operations with very powerful or very sophisticated machines. The old trend would be bound to resume, however, unless special barriers were erected against labor saving devices. Even the most principled libertarian must hesitate to have wage questions settled by cutthroat competition among workers under the pressure of steadily advancing technology. The erection of Luddite barriers to technological progress would, on the other hand, bring more menace to the health of the economic and social system than the disease it is intended to cure. [...]

There remains the alternative of direct action to promote a progressive shortening of the work week combined with income policies designed to maintain and to increase, as increases in total output allow, the real family income of wage earners and salaried employees.

This passage could have been written today. Leontief praises the waves of technological improvements responsible for the rise in living standards, but worries about their collateral damage in the form of technological unemployment. He explains how the reduction of the working day, working week and working year was the main tool to limit this collateral damage, until 1940. Coincidently, since the trend to limit working hours stopped, the US economy has seen a chronic increase in unemployment. He dismisses many of the stereotypical prescriptions from different schools of thought, from both liberals and Keynesians, and warns against trying to reverse the technological adoption with Luddite barriers – an even bigger mistake. Leontief argues for direct action to promote a progressive shortening of the working week, a better solution than shortening of the working day. Being a quantitative economist by nature, Leontief presented several calculations based on input–output tables for Austria, predicting that within fifteen years, under full mechanisation, there would be 386,000 unemployed on the streets, but with a 'shorter work week' there would only be 76,000.

Coming back to the present day, the Fourth Industrial Revolution has not yet brought the economic fruits in terms of productivity growth, but it has the potential to drive us out of the *secular stagnation*. We had robots and automation before, during the Third Industrial Revolution, but now they are autonomous in movement, and they can make decisions by analysing large quantities of data. In contrast with the First Industrial Revolution, where most jobs destroyed belonged to skilled workers, and the third one, where the jobs destroyed were more unskilled, the current revolution is replacing jobs in the middle of the pack. Technology is replacing routine jobs. The top non-routine abstract jobs are benefiting from technology, and the bottom non-routine manual jobs have not been substituted by technology, but they haven't benefited from it either. If the promises of the Fourth Industrial Revolution are true, studies foresee that artificial intelligence will replace jobs with predictable environments like telemarketers, cashiers, loan officers, taxi drivers, legal assistants and fast-food cooks.

'History repeats itself, first as tragedy, second as farce,' famously said Karl Marx. We have been here before and we should learn from the past. Technology has been the source of progress during the last 300 years. We should not reject it; we should embrace it. But we can't ignore the trail of unemployed that it leaves behind. The technological unemployed have been hidden for many years and are not reflected in the official unemployment rate. Some are masked as *inactive*. By December 2019, for the 1.3 million unemployed in the UK, there were 1.8 million people who *wanted a job*, but, often discouraged, *did not actively search* for one, so they were out of the unemployment statistic. Others are *underemployed*. Out of the 45 per cent of workers who have a college degree, one third of them are employed in occupations that are majority done by workers without a college degree. These add up to about 4.4 million workers. The US has the same statistic – one out of three workers with a college degree are working in unskilled occupations. Out of the 2.5 million waiters and waitresses, half a million have a college degree. One quarter of taxi drivers or telephone operators and 30 per cent of door-to-door sales workers, news and street vendors have higher education. Finally, some just have precarious jobs, zero-hour contracts or gigs. The Covid-19 pandemic has exposed many of them. In two months in the UK about 600,000 people lost their jobs, even with a supportive furlough scheme in place. Many of them did not find work again in their occupation.

These statistics also incorporate *cyclical unemployment*. In practice, it is hard to disentangle how much of unemployment is driven by lack of aggregate demand, and how much is due to long-term structural reasons, like technological unemployment. This remains another source of contention between Keynesians and supply-side economists who take unemployment seriously. If most unemployment is cyclical, the solution is to stimulate demand. If most unemployment is structural, stimulating demand will not bring back the jobs lost to technology.

Supply-side economists say jobs will be created elsewhere. This is true. Firms will invent new tasks. Loan officers will disappear, but relationship banking will spread. The industries developing new technologies will create new jobs – in the peak of the pandemic, Google had 132 open vacancies for its London office – and so will other sectors of the economy. The question is how long it takes to rearrange the economy. Some economists say not to worry because the unemployed will disappear quickly. This is both heartless and untrue. Don't listen to them. It takes a whole generation to bury the corpses, and the transition is painful and full of other perils for the economy in the form of social unrest.

The four-day working week will reduce *technological unemployment,* not only by withdrawing many hours from the labour market, but also by giving time and fostering retraining. I am a Professor of Economics at Birkbeck College. I have been there for four years and it is impossible not to admire the institution. Initially named the London Mechanical Institute, it was founded in 1823 by George Birkbeck alongside Jeremy Bentham, a philosopher and political economist, as a school for the working class to access 'the universal benefits of the blessings of knowledge'. Seven years later, the college admitted women as students, forty years before Oxford or Cambridge. Birkbeck College has kept its mission for 200 years. All lectures are in the evening between 18.00 and 21.00. Most students work during the day and come to us for further training to advance their careers or to change them altogether. The students compensate the lack of available time with motivation and hard work. It is rare for a professor to admire their students. At Birkbeck, it is unusual not to admire them. The last class in each of the modules I teach always ends in the pub on the fourth floor, where students share the inspiring stories of why they are continuing to study. The stories only finish when the bell signals closing time.

I teach Applied Statistics and Econometrics in the Graduate Diploma in Economics, a one-year programme at undergraduate level, directed to people with a BSc or a BA in other fields who want to convert to economics. The students this year are no different from any other. Jonathan is an in-house lawyer at a technology company. When he reached 30 he realised how much he enjoyed reading about economics and what drives behaviour and distribution of resources, but he did not have the quantitative skills to pursue this formally. He sees our graduate diploma as a means to plug a skills gap and fulfil a dream of pursuing an MSc in Economics at a top university and making a career change from law. Jonathan works a four-day week. Ginette has a degree in Modern Languages and an MA in International Business. She has worked as a freelance translator and interpreter and now is a consultant in digital marketing, but she wants to change to an organisation that focuses on social issues or public policy. She wants to spend her energy improving society. David also has an undergraduate degree in Modern Languages. He worked in teaching, translation and for an airline. He hopes this qualification will put him on course to a career in finance. Debbie is a freelance make-up artist for television commercials. She is seeking a career with greater stability, and she loves economics. Thomas is a political analyst providing strategic advice to clients on complex regulatory, political, and policy issues like international trade and Brexit. Four years out of university, he realised that what he truly enjoys is investigating public policy challenges through in-depth research, and he is hoping the degree will develop sharper quantitative skills and open the doors to pursue a PhD. Isabel studied engineering but soon realised she didn't want to become an engineer. She then studied public health and fell in love with economics after an introductory course. She balances her studies with full-time employment at the UN Refugee Agency.

The spirit of Birkbeck represents the opportunity that the four-day working week provides for people to retrain, opening new prospects in more promising occupations. The book *4 Days, 40 Hours* documents how 6 per cent of the workers who switch to a four-day working week enrolled in further education. In the Portuguese trial, 16 per cent of participant workers devoted more time to training or went back to the classroom. We don't need everyone to keep studying; a small margin is enough to feel the macroeconomic effects of retraining.

The four-day week is our best solution to deal with technological unemployment because it will withdraw hours from the labour market, and it will foster retraining. Shortening the working week was an option between the 1950s and '70s, but it was always set aside in favour of other Keynesian policies that are expensive and only effective when aggregate demand is temporarily lower. They are a disaster when dealing with structural problems. Perhaps, the four-day week was not implemented then because it was too soon after the big step of introducing the five-day week, but now eighty years have passed.

For decades, during which new technologies have been introduced, workers have faced the stick in the form of unemployment, and firms have enjoyed the carrot in the form of higher profits from new machines. With the four-day working week, they will swap places – the workers will get more leisure and the firms will face the pressure to adapt. The right set of incentives for everyone will still be there and will work even better.

11

The Sixth Reason: Because It Will Raise Wages and Reduce Inequality (Marx)

'To the militant trade unionist, the move towards a 4-day week is one more skirmish in the continuing battle for higher standard wage rates, improved work conditions on the job, and improved fringe benefits for retirement and health needs. Particularly in declining industries.'

Paul Samuelson

In 1977, the Nobel committee awarded its prize to a British and Swedish pair, James Meade and Bertil Ohlin, 'for their path-breaking contribution to the theory of international trade and international capital movements'. The focus on international economics, the study of economic interactions between countries, was the common aspect between the two economists, but James Meade's contribution to economics theory and policy was far more wide-reaching. He worked on income and wealth distribution, poverty and social security, unemployment, monetary and fiscal policy, taxation, co-operatives and economic growth.

The Independent wrote in his obituary: 'James Meade was one of the greatest economists of his generation. He, more than anyone since John Maynard Keynes, influenced the way in which economic policy is now discussed in Britain.'

Born in 1907, James Meade trained in Oxford. He taught in Cambridge, alongside Keynes in the early 1930s, and later at the London School of Economics. Former Bank of England governor Mervyn King wrote with admiration: 'More than any other of his contemporaries, he used rigorous economic theory to show how an efficient market economy could be combined with an intense concern about inequality of income and wealth. He produced many schemes for public policy initiatives to promote equality while retaining the benefits of competition.' Samuelson called him a 'Don with a Heart' who 'would give his cloak to a shivering beggar, not only because he feels it is right and fair to do so, but also for the reason that the beggar will receive more pleasure from it than a well-off professor of political economy.'

Meade worried about inequality. Like Frisch, he was horrified by the heavy unemployment in the inter-war period, considering it 'both stupid and wicked'. He thought that government policies should aim to achieve both *efficiency* and *equity*. Scarce resources should be used to produce something that is wanted, and they should be used efficiently. Unemployment was a pure waste of resources. But besides efficiency, it is not desirable that income and wealth are unequally shared between the citizens in the community. The reason is that an extra £10, like a cloak, brings more well-being to a poor person than to a rich person.

Reassessing the fundamental implication of technological progress that Keynes analysed in 'Economic Possibilities for our Grandchildren', Meade, in 1964, shared a different view of its side-effects, more worried about the implications for income distribution than for technological unemployment:

> What, we ask, shall we all do with our leisure when we need to work only an hour or two a day to obtain the total output of real goods and services needed to satisfy our wants? But the problem is really much more difficult than that. The question which we should ask is: What shall we all do when output per man-hour of work is extremely high but practically the whole of the output goes to a few property owners, while the mass of the workers are relatively (or even absolutely) worse off than before? [...]
>
> But what of the future? Suppose that automation should drastically reduce [the proportion of the national income that accrues to wages]. The country would tend to become a wealthy edition of Mauritius. There would be a limited number of exceedingly wealthy property owners; the proportion of the working population required to man the extremely profitable automated industries would be small; wage-rates would thus be depressed; there would have to be a large expansion of the production of the labour-intensive goods and services which were in high demand by the few multi-multi-multi-millionaires; we would be back in a super-world of an immiserised proletariat and of butlers, footmen, kitchen maids, and other hangers-on. Let us call this the Brave New Capitalists' Paradise.

These worries about unequal division of the gains of technological progress were shared with Leontief when he wrote, almost twenty years later, that: 'Sooner or later, and quite probably sooner, the

increasingly mechanized society must face another problem: the problem of income distribution.' Marx had also warned a century earlier: 'are we to believe that this new employment will pay as high wages as did the one they lost?'

During the Fourth Industrial Revolution, the economist picking up the torch from Meade and Leontief is Christopher Pissarides, a British-Cypriot economist who spent his career at the London School of Economics. Together with Peter Diamond and Dale Mortensen, they received the Nobel Prize in 2010 'for their analysis of markets with search frictions'. Pissarides developed a new theory to study unemployment, called *Search and Matching Theory*. Receiving the Nobel Prize was the second best thing that happened to him that year. A few months before that, he got rid of one of his annoying PhD students (yes, Pissarides was my supervisor).

Since 2006, Pissarides has been interested in the future of work in the age of robots and artificial intelligence. He is more optimistic than Leontief regarding technological unemployment:

> A lot of jobs will no doubt be taken over by robots but many more will be created, ranging from software engineers who will develop and feed the robots with data and instructions to carers who will look after the children and ageing parents of men and women engaged in the new economy.

This is a restatement of the conventional position of economists. Technological developments are not uniform throughout the economy. They vary by sector and by industry; some expand while others shed jobs. Pissarides, together with the economist Rachel Ngai from the London School of Economics, has studied what economists call *structural transformation*, the progressive reduction of workers in manufacturing, and their increase in services. But the ever-so-optimistic Pissarides warns us: 'inequality and the question of who will get the rewards from the robots' work is a big unresolved issue; governments need to work hard to come up with credible policies for how to reduce poverty and achieve more equality if the optimistic scenario is to materialise'.

The worry of Meade, Leontief and Pissarides is not misplaced: income and wealth inequality has risen since 1980. According to the World Inequality Database, the top 10 per cent of the UK's highest earners pocketed 29 per cent of total income in 1980 and 36 per cent in 2017. The 10 per cent wealthiest individuals, in 2012, held half of total wealth, up 5 percentage points since 1984. The 'Brave New Capitalists' Paradise' is here. Jeff Bezos has a fortune estimated to be $150 billion – $150,000,000,000. His fortune is thirty times larger than the richest man in the world in 1955. It was always hard for me to have a perspective on very large numbers. My mind cannot grasp them. To accumulate as much wealth, I would need to work 2 million years and save every penny of my salary. That is the time that separates us from our ancestors *Homo habilis* and *Homo erectus*. A worker with the median income in the UK would need to work 3.7 million years. Lucy, the Australopithecus, lived 3.5 million years ago. Even spending all that money is *mission impossible*. If I spent £1 million every day, it would take me 310 years to squander Bezos's fortune.

To evaluate the consequences of the four-day week for income inequality, we must first understand the two main sources of income. The payment to labour is called *wages*. The payment to capital is called *rental rate* or *return on capital*, often associated with interest rate and profits.

We already covered how economists view the output of production from the *optic of spending*. Whatever goods and services are produced, they are bought by households, firms or governments. But there is another side of production. All the goods sold generate income used to pay the *factors of production*. The income generated by a restaurant pays the cooks, the waiters and the sommelier, the rental of the space, and whatever is left makes up the owner's profit. When we look at production from the *optic of income*, the diligent statisticians divide it into labour income and capital income. The labour income measures the payments in the form of wages and bonuses to workers. Everything else, from rents to operating surplus, is considered capital income. There are grey areas which are hard to separate. For instance, should executive pay and share options be included in labour income?

What do you think is the share of income going to workers? This is called *labour share*. Because of the complexity of the grey areas, different institutions calculate different numbers. The UK Office for National Statistics says it is 60 per cent, while the OECD, an international organisation, says it is 70 per cent. Whatever the method used, the labour share has been falling since the 1970s, and more noticeably since the 2000s. In the UK, the fall was about 10 percentage points. Half a century ago, British workers received 70 per cent of income, now they only receive 60. Behind this is the fact that *real wages* – not the pounds that you get at the end of the month, but how many goods you can buy with them – have been stagnant for most of the population. According to the Office for

National Statistics, the average real wage only grew by 17 per cent in twenty years, while GDP per capita grew by 40 per cent. Between 2022 and 2023, high inflation has eroded real wages even further.

Do you remember the 1964 testimony of Mr Nunn, representative of the National Restaurant Association, where he claimed that the great increase in labour productivity was passed on to workers in the form of higher wages? He wasn't lying. Between 1950 and 1970, according to the US Bureau of Labor Statistics, labour productivity increased by 79 per cent and real wages (after accounting for inflation) increased by 76 per cent, close, just like a mainstream economic model predicts. However, between 1980 and 2019, while labour productivity increased by 113 per cent, real wages only increased by 50 per cent. The link between labour productivity and real wages is broken. Workers are no longer reaping the benefits of economic growth.

What does economic theory say about what determines the wage rate? The most conventional theory of the labour market, taught in Labour Economics 101, views labour as any other good, and its market as any other market. Firms demand labour. Workers supply labour. The wage rate is adjusted by the law of supply and demand. We have seen this before. So, the wage rate depends on the scarcity or abundance of labour relative to capital. More people wanting to work lowers the wages. Conversely, spare capital and many firms looking for workers would raise their wage. Technology and automation might tilt this relation against workers, which could explain the divergence between wages and productivity.

Other economists think that the labour market is fundamentally different from other markets. It takes time for someone to find a job and often unemployment coexists with firms not being able to find suitable workers. That is the idea behind the Search and Matching Theory of unemployment, pioneered by Pissarides. In his theory, the wage rate is the outcome of *bargaining* between workers and firms, which depends on the *bargaining power* of workers, and their *outside option*. Stronger unions threatening strikes are a show of force that pushes wages up. Higher unemployment and lower unemployment benefits mean that workers who lose their jobs will struggle with less compensation and more difficult job searches, which pushes wages down. For Marx, the wages were the result of an uneven war between capitalists and workers. Capitalists could live longer without workers than workers without a job, so workers were always disadvantaged. There was an *industrial reserve army* desperate for a job, so the wage rate would be the lowest possible, just enough to provide for the subsistence of the worker and his family during his work. One can interpret Marx's view as a bargaining problem, where the capitalists have all the bargaining power, and the workers have none.

Many macroeconomists have proposed explanations for the decline of the labour share. The leading explanation is, of course, technological change with automation and the change towards using more machinery in the production process, as predicted by Leontief and Meade. Globalisation has also contributed, as I will discuss later. But other explanations also have some traction. One explanation, supported by Larry Summers, relates to the loss of power of the labour unions, which together with a deregulation of the labour market have raised the monopsony power of firms, and left workers' jugulars at the mercy of vampires. During the Thatcher years, 50 per cent of UK workers were members of a trade union. Now, a bit more than 20 per cent are. In the US private sector, unionisation rates came down from 25 to 5 per cent.

Another explanation is the rising market power of companies that are facing less competition and setting higher prices and lower wages, helping themselves to 'unnatural' profits. Nowadays, there are fewer Fords and more of Adam Smith's businessmen. Do you think that having a hard time choosing which beer to drink in the pub is a sign of competition? Think again. After a joint venture between two brewing giants, MillerCoors – producer of more than 100 brands of beer and cider including Fosters, Grolsch, Staropramen and Aspall – and Anheuser-Busch InBev

SA/NV – producer of Budweiser, Corona, Stella Artois and Becks – their beer prices went up by at least 6 per cent. A study of mergers between competing manufacturing firms between 1998 and 2006 finds that they systematically increased profit margins without reducing costs, suggesting that the loss of competition raised prices. New technology firms are running amok. Microsoft ran unchallenged for years. Facebook buys any potential competitor before they learn how to walk. Apple had a €13 billion fine from the European Commission because of tax avoidance.

Sometimes, lack of competition is well hidden. Large institutional investors, such as BlackRock or The Vanguard Group Inc., collectively own two thirds of the shares of publicly traded US firms. Their weight doubled over the last forty years. It is now usual that competitor firms have a common shareowner, which is ignored by regulators. What does this spell for competition? The research on shared ownership, carried out by José Azar and Martin Schmalz, two economists with a PhD from Princeton University, is among the most interesting I have seen in the last few years. In one article, they describe how the top seven shareholders of American Airlines are among the top ten investors of Southwest Airlines. The top six shareholders of Southwest Airlines are among the top ten shareholders of American and Delta Airlines, and so on. Following the merger of asset management companies that owned different portfolios of airline companies, the ownership of airlines became more concentrated, and the airlines started charging higher prices on competing routes. Azar and Schmalz find that due to shared ownership, ticket prices are 3 to 7 per cent higher than under separate ownership. Newer research found that share ownership also squeezes wages.

Inequality is a deep and complex issue, and this is not the book to go over all its causes, implications and antidotes. Besides the decline of the labour share and the decoupling between labour productivity and real wages, it also reflects the fact that wages themselves became more unequal. To learn more about it you can read *Capital in the Twenty-First Century* by the French economist Thomas Piketty or *The Price of Inequality* by Nobel Laureate Joseph Stiglitz. To some extent it is a moral question: how much inequality are we, as a society, willing to accept? There is no right or wrong answer; serious people with a heart like James Meade could give different ones. But beyond the moral problem, inequality can bring negative economic consequences, starting with political instability and the rise of populism, which I'll look at in a subsequent chapter.

There are no simple solutions and achieving a less unequal society requires many measures. Some were pointed to by James Meade in 1964: heavily progressive taxes that should also depend on wealth, corporate taxes, inheritance taxes, the encouragement of financial intermediaries to allow small savings to be pooled for investment in high-earning risky assets, and financing and expanding education. Furthermore, although not one of his front-line measures, Meade proposed reducing the working week. He explained that a:

> possibility is that an effective arrangement for the universal application of a minimum real wage should be combined with an effective limitation of the amount of work which any one individual citizen might do. Such work-sharing – or might one not more appropriately call it such unemployment-sharing? – might be effected partly by preventing some potential workers (e.g. the young, the old, and the married women) from working at all, partly by limiting the number of hours which any worker might work.

Also according to Pissarides, one of the responses to get to the optimistic scenario is 'taking more leisure', which is already happening but in an uncoordinated and asymmetric fashion. Of course, inequality is one of the main problems affecting modern societies and there are plenty of other proposals to deal with it: expand education and retraining policies, encourage cooperation between top universities and industries, maintain generous unemployment insurance schemes, promote job creation, create more jobs to absorb the less qualified workers, give a universal basic income. There is no shortage of proposals, but it is hard turning them into concrete policies.

The four-day week is one concrete policy that will contribute to raise wages and reduce inequality. Whatever angle one looks at the determination of wages from, and whatever is the source of the decline of labour share and wage stagnation, the four-day week would contribute to a reversal. For a start, it would raise hourly wages. If you think about Schumpeter's productivity increases, the workers will see it fully reflected in their wage. This, in itself, would not raise the labour share. But the effect on wages is likely to be stronger. The reduction in unemployment due to the higher demand for leisure industries explained in the previous chapter will be reflected in higher wage growth. On the one hand, from the perspective of labour supply–labour demand theory, by withdrawing hours from the workforce, making labour less abundant, the natural consequence is a rise in wages. On the other hand, under the bargaining theory of wages, the four-day week will increase the bargaining power of workers, who would get a larger share of the pie. This was put more poetically by Senator Eugene McCarthy:

> The more the economy consists of wasteful pursuits, however, the less needed a particular piece of work becomes, and the more precarious the livelihood obtained from it. The shorter work week would push the balance back from the political toward the economics. With a leaner economy – where work was more necessary – production workers would have more leverage as suppliers of a labouring service. They would command more income and enjoy more real economic security.

The three decades following the Fair Labor Standards Act of 1938 saw the strongest wage growth in the US economy: 27, 33 and

27 per cent, per decade. Since then, wages have never grown much past 10 per cent in any one decade. 'The end of cheap Chinese labour' came after their implementation of the five-day working week. Between 1978 and 1995, real wages in China grew at a meagre 0.1 per cent yearly. Between 1998 and 2010, the average annual growth rate of real wages was 14 per cent, well above the growth rate of GDP. Are we to assume this once-in-a-century policy had no part in the extraordinary development of the Chinese economy in the last quarter of a century? Adding to this evidence, studies that measured the causal effects of the implementation of the thirty-five-hour week in France and similar legislation elsewhere found little impact on employment, but strong increases in hourly wages. The positive effect on wages is beyond debate.

Joseph Stiglitz calls for 'social innovations' to fight inequality. The four-day week is the social invention we are looking for. Compare it with other measures, like offering a universal basic income, increasing corporate tax or fully funding higher education. These are likely to be more partisan. Either they are expensive, or they reduce efficiency or both. The four-day week would not fall into either category. The measure won't have a direct cost to the government, except perhaps as an employer, and will affect all companies – large and small – in the same way. James Meade showed us that policies should aim at *efficiency* and *equity* – the four-day working week passes the test.

12

The Seventh Reason: Because It Will Give People More Freedom to Choose How to Spend Their Time (Hayek)

'If in a thousand years the artefacts of our civilization are unearthed and examined, we would want to have left something more than storage boxes filled with legal, medical, and accounting records. We could use our economic surplus instead to colonize space, increase historical or scientific knowledge, feed the world's hungry, provide education for the sake of its own experience, or rebuild the cities and farms. Or else, we could give people the opportunity, in the form of leisure, to create their own kind of waste. Why make people pay for someone else's waste – give them a blank page to fill with the expressions of their own. That is another meaning of freedom, the ability to choose one's own form of waste.'

Eugene McCarthy and William McGaughey,
Nonfinancial Economics: The Case for
Shorter Hours of Work

Friedrich August von Hayek was born at the end of the nineteenth century. He was the last of the great old political economists, who lived long enough to be given the Nobel Prize. He received it, in 1974, jointly with Gunnar Myrdal 'for their penetrating analysis of the interdependence of economic, social and institutional phenomena'. Hayek and Myrdal made an unlikely pair for a Nobel. Myrdal stood in for Keynes, who was long dead and whose ideas were about to be dethroned. Myrdal was a strong supporter of Keynes's theory and had anticipated much of it in his book *Monetary Economics*, published four years prior to Keynes's *General Theory*. He had also been a Member of Parliament for the Social Democratic Workers' Party of Sweden. Hayek, as is well known, was a fierce critic of the Keynesian ideology that dominated macroeconomics since the 1940s. Hayek placed individual freedom above everything else. For him, Keynesian policies that intervene too often and too deeply in the economy are downright dangerous. Samuelson joked that 'the election committee must have known that they were making two opposite ideologues furious over their being ironically paired'. It wasn't the last time the Nobel committee played such as trick. In 2013, Eugene Fama and Robert Shiller both won, jointly with Lars Hansen, for having developed contradicting theories about financial markets.

Hayek had much in common with Schumpeter. They were both Austrian. They both believed in the rules of the pure capitalism of the nineteenth century: free trade, stable money and balanced budgets. They were both embraced by conservatives and liberals as their torchbearers in the second half of the twentieth century. Hayek met with President Reagan at the White House and had a fan in Margaret Thatcher. She said, 'the most powerful critique of socialist planning and the socialist state which I read at this time [the late 1940s], and to which I have returned so often since [is] F.A. Hayek's *The Road to Serfdom*'. But Hayek, unlike Schumpeter, never commanded the same respect within the economics profession and was marginalised for three decades. He was much more

critical of adopting mathematical methods than Keynes ever was. He shunned what he viewed as the blind belief that these methods are of universal application in economics, in what he labelled as *scientism*. Samuelson wrote, 'So you might say Hayek as an economist fell into what physicists call a black hole. Wisely, libertarian Hayek turned away to weighty constitutional and philosophical interests. And from his pen came commendable items on history of economics doctrines.' The consistency of his opinions was rewarded. After thirty years of Keynesian domination of macroeconomic theory, the tables turned, and liberalism came out on top.

The 1974 Nobel symbolically celebrates the change in dominant macroeconomic paradigm, from the Keynesian interventionism to the economic liberalism that has taken over since. As with the previous paradigm shift, it followed a major economic crisis. The consecutive oil crises of the 1970s and 1980s proved too difficult for the Keynesian theory. Rising oil prices created simultaneous inflationary pressures and higher unemployment. The main Keynesian instrument – government spending – was a small blanket for a large bed. Spending more would reduce unemployment but worsen inflation, which was getting out of hand. Spending less would curtail inflation but shed more jobs. Keynesians could not explain what was going on, nor could they deal with it. Inflation reached 25 per cent in the UK and 18 per cent in the US. Simultaneously, the unemployment rate reached about 12 per cent in both countries. As Keynesian tools failed, the rise of new macroeconomic models that emphasised the role of expectations and dynamics in the economy seduced economists. Milton Friedman and Robert Lucas, two economists from the University of Chicago, were the preachers who converted economists from government intervention to more free market ideology. Hayek was the messiah who converted everyone else.

The Economist wrote in his obituary that 'like Maynard Keynes, Friedrich von Hayek achieved fame less for what he wrote than for what others said he wrote'. The instinctive response to the four-day working week of some liberal ideologues is that the government should not tell people how much they can or cannot work. The contract between firms and workers is a private matter, and if they agree to work 100 hours per week, that is freedom. 'Why should politicians tell you how long to spend in the office?' wrote Daniel Hannan, a conservative former Member of the European Parliament, in *The Telegraph*. Anyone who makes this argument should spend more time re-reading Hayek. These are the words that the messiah wrote in chapter three of *The Road to Serfdom*:

> It is important not to confuse opposition against this kind of planning with a dogmatic laissez faire attitude. The liberal argument is in favour of making the best possible use of the forces of competition as a means of coordinating human efforts, not an argument for leaving things just as they are. [...]
>
> This [referring to undesirability of government intervention] is not necessarily true, however, of measures merely restricting the allowed methods of production, so long as these restrictions affect all potential producers equally and are not used as an indirect way of controlling prices and quantities. Though all such controls of the methods of production impose extra costs (i.e. make it necessary to use more resources to produce a given

output), they may be well worth while. To prohibit the use of certain poisonous substances or to require special precautions in their use, to limit working hours or to require certain sanitary arrangements, is fully compatible with the preservation of competition.

If you still have doubts interpreting his words, the following was taken from a radio interview in April 1945, part of his auto-biography *Hayek on Hayek*:

MR KRUEGER: What about limitation of working hours—a maximum-hour's act? Is that compatible with your notions of proper planning?

MR HAYEK: Yes, if it is not carried too far. It is one of these regulations which create equal conditions throughout the system. But, of course, if it goes beyond the point where it accords with the general situation of the country, it may indeed interfere very much. If today you dictate that nobody is to work more than four hours, it may completely upset the competitive system.

MR MERRIAM: Would any limitation on the hours of labor be objectionable in your judgment?

MR HAYEK: Not 'any,' but they can be. There you have one of the instances where my objection is not one of principle but one of degree. It is one of the things which cannot be made to fit the question of the cost involved in that particular measure.

For Hayek, legislation on working hours does not interfere with competition, because it places all firms on an equal footing. He might object to the degree, but he did not oppose the principle. Today, it is possible that Hayek would consider Keynes's fifteen-hour week excessive. But what would he think about a four-day week, seventy-five years on, when living standards have increased fivefold, when it has already been chosen at a hefty cost, by 25 per cent of the workforce, and when it is desired by 40 per cent of full-time workers? It can hardly be considered excessive.

I have mentioned another typical response of liberals to the four-day working week: people have chosen to work forty hours. 'The reason we don't have a four-day week is that most of us don't really want one,' continued Daniel Hannan, echoing the words of Mr Nunn in 1964 that workers prefer wage increases to a reduction of working hours. My original answer was that societies can change their minds and I am trying to persuade them. But let me dissect this argument further. Are people really free to choose?

To answer whether people are free to choose, we must return to labour market theory to understand how people decide how much to work. The conventional theory takes the liberal view that workers are free to choose any number of hours of work for a given hourly wage. We do not distinguish between hours per day and days per week. The worker chooses the most convenient number of weekly hours.

Consider Joey and her decision of how many hours to work. The more she works, the fatter her pay cheque will be at the end of the month. One extra hour means that she can buy an extra pair of leggings, go to the restaurant by the park, or get a subscription to *The Economist*. But there is a downside to working more hours. They are tiring and prevent her from enjoying leisure. Her decision depends on her preferences – how she values the extra consumption she can afford by working, against the missing leisure. This is what economists call *opportunity cost* – working one extra hour means that you won't enjoy an hour in the gym, a coffee with a friend or an episode of *Game of Thrones*.

Economists don't expect everyone to have the same preferences and choose the same hours, but they find it convenient to think in terms of a *representative agent*, the average Joey in the economy. What will the average Joey, currently working forty hours per week, do if a new technology doubles her productivity? For an extra hour of work, she now gets two extra pairs of leggings, goes twice to the restaurant, or gets a subscription to *The Economist* and *Fashion Doll Quarterly*. Will the average Joey work more or less? Notice the similarities with the problem of the cab drivers in New York, analysed by Richard Thaler. Can you spot the difference? While for the cab drivers, the extra customers will disappear with the clouds – they reflect a *temporary* increase in productivity – Joey encounters a *permanent* increase in her productivity.

The answer to whether Joey will work more or less is not obvious, because there are two conflicting effects, what economists call *income* and *substitution effects*; two magnets, each pulling in opposite directions. If Joey keeps working the same number of hours, her pay cheque doubles, affording her twice as many goods, so to keep a balance between buying new leggings and time at the gym, she will want to enjoy more leisure. This is the income effect, and it pushes Joey to work less. On the other hand, that extra hour – which has the same opportunity cost – now pays double. Economists say it changed the *relative price* of leisure. It makes leisure relatively more expensive, because to enjoy the episode of *Game of Thrones*, Joey must sacrifice twice as many pairs of leggings. The substitution effect pushes Joey to work more. Which of the two magnets is stronger? It depends on how strong the substitution effect is.

Now, here comes the final assumption. Macroeconomists studying long-run growth, *for convenience*, assumed that Joey's preferences are such that the two effects exactly offset each other. By a divine coincidence, the two magnets are equally strong, meaning that with higher productivity Joey will keep working the same hours. This was assumed for pure mathematical convenience. If the substitution effect is weaker, with time, Joey will progressively work less, following Keynes's instructions. When she gets old, very old (the average Joey lives forever), she will work closer and closer to zero hours. And zero gives headaches to mathematicians. Just try to divide any number by zero on your calculator.

This assumption raised some eyebrows. Does the data support it? The empirical justification relied on the fact that since the 1940s, weekly working hours have been roughly constant. It was quite suspect to start in the 1940s. As we have seen, if we start in the nineteenth century, we observe a clear downward trend in working hours. But the justification convinced for a while; it was better than upsetting the calculator.

Some economists interested in predicting the effects of income taxes on labour supply started estimating the substitution effect in the population. Is it as strong as macroeconomists were assuming? When the government alters the tax system, bank statements at the end of the month are different, allowing researchers to measure how people adjust their hours. Whatever the empirical strategy used, better or worse, the timeframe used – in the 1990s or in the 2000s – or the country inspected – in the US or in Europe – the numbers are never the same, but the substitution effect is nowhere near as high as it is assumed in macro models. One magnet is weak, but most models studying long-run trends in economics kept assuming these unrealistic *steady state preferences*. Now the justification was not empirical or mathematical convenience. They were simply following renowned economists who have done so.

The most mainstream economic growth model, when you feed in the right characterisation of Joey's preferences, predicts what Keynes and Schumpeter already knew: as the economy grows we should expect people to both work less and consume more. The model does not tell us that we are still working forty hours because we want to; it assumes that we want to keep working forty hours because hours haven't declined in the last seventy years. It doesn't offer a justification against the four-day week. It simply confirms Keynes's argument for it. But don't start bashing economics! The nature of a model, as Frisch explained, is to help us think. There were plenty of assumptions, some more innocuous than others, but the model is still useful. It tells us what we should be doing, as societies, if we were free to choose. The fact that we haven't done it poses the natural question: why? There are two answers. One is that workers are not free to choose. The second is that even if they are free to choose, the dice are loaded.

In the real world, we find a labour market with two sides: workers and firms. Workers supply labour. Firms demand labour. They negotiate a contract specifying hours of work and wages. In theory, these contracts are flexible, but in practice, most workers cannot set the number of hours. The status quo matters. Most jobs have a stipulated schedule, normally the benchmark forty-hour, five-day week. Schumpeter explained why many macroeconomists, including Keynes, didn't think people were free to choose: 'the individual worker must accept the regulation [of the] working day and cannot vary the quantity of labor he is willing to offer,' adding that the 'labourer accepts a fixed working day which he is powerless to alter, he must accept it or die'. Research on 3.5 million UK job vacancies ads, cited in *The Guardian*, found that only 6.5 per cent of vacancies of jobs that paid above £20,000 offered flexible working conditions. Firms do not offer flexible contracts to newcomers. The starting condition of most new jobs is a forty-hour week, an example of what economists call *institutions* – the social, legal, or political constructs that organise economic relations. Workers can go part-time, but this is often negotiated in an ongoing job, usually with wage cuts larger than 20 per cent, pension penalties and loss of promotion opportunities.

This is a *puzzle*. If people want to work less, as our economic model predicts, and firms would see gains in productivity, as I argued through Schumpeter's voice, why aren't firms jumping on it? Why do we need the government?

The answer has been known for a long time, thanks to one of Keynes's most famous followers, John Hicks. An Englishman, Hicks studied labour history at Oxford. He then taught at the

London School of Economics with Hayek, and at Cambridge with Keynes, before returning to Oxford. On the Nobel timeline, Hicks came two years after Samuelson, and one year before Leontief. The committee recognised him, together with the American economist Kenneth Arrow, 'for their pioneering contributions to general economic equilibrium theory and welfare theory'. Samuelson did not hide his admiration for Hicks:

> I went over his contributions with a powerful microscope, a much more intensive analysis than he ever gave either to my own work or to that of any other economist. That was the way Hicks was. Always he preferred to do things his way. And that was the source both of his creative originality and prolific scientific productivity. [...] Hicks' works are immortal.

Hicks *translated* Keynes's *General Theory* into equations in one of the most famous models in economics – the IS-LM model – that is still taught today. His first book, *Theory of Wages*, published when he was 28, gave him the reputation of being the best young economist. At the time, in 1932, John Hicks was at the London School of Economics, which was dominated by Hayek's 'liberal' line, so the book was viewed as having an anti-union stance. The following passage shows that Samuelson was right, and Hicks's works are indeed immortal:

As industry develops, the strain to which workpeople are exposed probably increases; rest and recreation become more necessary; and thus the output optimum length of day probably falls. If output is to be maintained at the maximum possible, hours ought to be reduced. On the other hand, the development of industry brings with it higher wages and a raised standard of living. The desire for leisure and the willingness to sacrifice income for leisure almost certainly increase too; for without leisure the advantages which can be derived from a higher income are very limited. If the equilibrium length of working day is to be found, hours ought to be reduced below the output optimum.

History gives us no ground for supposing that the reduction takes place at all easily. The long hours worked in the early days of the Industrial Revolution are notorious; they were reduced, it is well known, mainly by State regulation and Trade Union action. It was found, after they had been reduced, that 'the output of eleven hours' work might be greater than that of twelve. Employers had been working at more than the output optimum, without realising it.

Probably it had never entered the heads of most employers that it was at all conceivable that hours could be shortened and output maintained. But it is clear that there were a few who had realised it. Why did they not reduce hours by their competition, just as enterprising firms force up wages by their competition?

By now, you should be familiar with these ideas. Hicks states that for employees, freedom to choose how many hours to work is limited and subject to the will of the employer. He mentions the length of the day, because people were still working six days and the policy debate until then was whether to reduce the daily hours to eight. He explains what we have learned from Henry Ford, that excessive hours might reduce output. Rest will increase alertness of workers, reduce their mistakes and raise their efficiency. This implies that beyond a certain point more hours hurt production.

With technological progress the ideal length of the day is likely to fall, for two reasons. First, to deal with more complex technology, workers need more rest. Second, with higher wages, workers would want more leisure.

Hicks claims that, by looking at history, we should not expect the reduction in hours to be driven by firms. It was always driven by legislation and unions. And only after it was imposed did firms realise that the productivity of the last hours was much lower than the average productivity. He is dismissive of employers who could not *enter in their heads* that hours could be reduced, and output maintained. This hasn't changed in a century. Why don't firms compete by reducing hours, as some naive economists argue? Hicks explains:

> One reason [...] lies in the technical considerations which usually make it necessary for a change in hours to apply to a whole establishment at once. [...] A reduction in hours must therefore come from the initiative of employers (if it is not imposed from outside). And there is a good reason why they should be rather slow to take it. The immediate effect of reduced hours must be to reduce output and increase costs, unless the reduced hours are accompanied by reduced wages [...] But a reduction of wages in the period of adjustment has to meet all the objections against temporary wage-reductions which have been discussed in previous chapters. [...] But if he does not reduce wages, he has to bear the cost of the transitional period himself. His losses during this period are a form of investment, from which he hopes to gain later. But they are a very risky investment, since it must always be extremely uncertain whether additional leisure really will improve output in the end, and if so to what extent. It is not surprising that the number of employers who are willing to undertake investments of this kind is limited. They can only be undertaken by those who are possessed of adequate capital (no one could raise a loan for such purposes) and they are at least only

likely to be begun by people of a certain kind of temperament. Though doubtless when these have pointed the way, others will slowly follow.

There is, in addition to this, a further difficulty. When the transitional period is over, an employer has no guarantee that those men whose efficiency he has improved will stay with him.

Hicks highlights three reasons why firms will be slow in adjusting the hours. First, shorter hours must be implemented to the whole establishment, so it must come from the employer's initiative. The organisation of teamwork requires the coordination of hours between all workers. Increasing wages, on the other hand, can be driven by individual workers looking for other jobs. The second, and more important, reason is that shortening working hours is like an investment. It has an immediate restructuring cost, but the gains (in terms of productivity) are not expected straight away. Plus, the gains from this investment are uncertain and firms must bear the cost of transition. As explained by Andrew Barnes from Perpetual Guardian: 'That fear – "What will it cost us if it goes wrong?" – is probably the four-day week's biggest obstacle.' Henry Ford experimented with the five-day week for three years, back and forth, so he was confident about the productivity gains of the move. A third problem is that, in a way, the shorter working week is also an investment in the workers themselves. If a worker leaves for unexpected reasons, firms will have to bear the additional cost of hiring and training new workers to a novel form of organising production.

There are other reasons to be pessimistic about the change coming from the bottom. Even Schumpeterian managers who recognise the operational benefits of shorter working hours might have their hands tied by short-sighted shareholders. In 1919, Ford Motor Company was sued by two of its shareholders, who accused Henry Ford of running the company as a charity, rather than to the benefit of its shareholders. They argued that Ford was paying too high wages and selling the cars too cheaply, instead of distributing dividends. This famous court case, Dodge *v.* Ford Motor Company, was decided by the Michigan Supreme Court ... against Henry Ford. The court ordered Ford to pay close to $20 million in extra dividends and instructed him not to lower consumer prices or raises his employees' salaries. Following this judgment, Ford threatened to abandon the company and start a competitor to force the dissident shareholders to sell their shares, and he regained authority. If he hadn't recovered control over the board of directors, I doubt the five-day working week in Ford's factories would ever have passed a shareholders' meeting. Andrew Barnes didn't inform the independent board of directors of his four-day working week trial for a reason.

Recently, economists have argued that high unemployment and monopsony power of firms is giving employers the power to exploit workers, leading hours to depart from the ideal hours–wage package. After all, finding another suitable job is not as easy as exchanging a defective product. Alternatively, your boss might be like Elon Musk, who pulls eighty- to ninety-hour work weeks because that is what you need to 'change the world', and imposes those hours on his subordinates even if they don't share his god-like aspirations.

Hicks didn't think that 'a purely competitive system is powerless to reduce the hours of labour'. He was hopeful that some visionaries would adopt it and show the way to other entrepreneurs. 'Even the darkest days of the Industrial Revolution had their Robert Owen'; an allusion to a prominent Welsh textile manufacturer who supported the passage of child labour laws and free

co-educational schools, the union movement and the eight-hour day. Henry Ford was another of these visionaries. But visionaries can only go so far. In the end, it must be the government implementing it. Both Hayek and Hicks accepted it.

Suppose you ignore these arguments and maintain that people are working the hours they want to. Could they still be overworking? Men and women are social animals and are constantly comparing themselves to others. I consider myself quite immune to external comparisons, but I still swim faster when someone around me is swimming at a similar pace. We can't avoid it. Already Adam Smith, in the *Wealth of Nations*, said that 'mutual emulation and desire of greater gain frequently prompted them [workers] to over-work themselves, and to hurt their health by excessive labour'. This is a classic case of what economists call *externalities*. A tap dance company that moves just above a yoga studio is an example of a negative externality. Instead, if a vegetarian restaurant moves next door to the studio, it is a positive externality because they will bring each other customers. Either way, positive or negative, these are textbook situations where the *invisible hand* fails to achieve the best outcome, and government action is justified. Externalities occur in the labour market when workers work longer to prove their worth. When I decide to stay until 17.30 instead of 17.00, I put psychological pressure on my colleagues also to work longer. No one wants to be the first to leave the office. Because they keep working, I'll also keep working, and soon everyone is staying until 19.00. In the words of Marx: 'for this simple reason: the more he works, the more he competes against his fellow workmen, the more he compels them to compete against him'. The economist Daniel Hamermesh, when promoting his book *Spending Time: The Most Valuable Resource*, explained:

> It's a rat race. If I don't work on a Sunday and other people do, I'm not going to get ahead. Therefore, I have no incentive to

get off that gerbil tube, get out of it and try to behave in a more rational way. Again, it's a wonderful example of what economists call externalities. I do it. You do it. The only way it's going to be solved is if somehow some external force, which in the U.S. and other rich countries is the government, imposes a mandate that forces us to behave differently. No individual can do it.

A particular example of the *rat race* is what economists call *tournaments*. Who gets the promotion? Research tells us that workers who put in the longest hours are more likely to get promoted. ABBA knew 'the winner takes it all, the loser's standing small'. Bosses view long hours as a measure of commitment to the firm, pushing everyone to work too much. Researchers, using data on the population of Danish workers, observed a positive association between working hours and career success that is consistent with the two distinct theories: the rat race and tournaments. For managers, working long hours improves their chances of top management appointments in the same firm, but not in a different one. The chances of top management appointments rise significantly by becoming the longest working-hour person among your peers. The positive correlation between working hours and subsequent promotion has been documented in various studies on large Japanese manufacturing firms, large law firms and among MBA students.

We are currently shackled, working more hours than we want to. But wouldn't a four-day week, imposing that people work less,

shackle us to another master? Suppose half of the workers prefer a four-day week and the other half want to keep working five days. With the shortening of the working week, the slaves become the masters, and the masters become slaves. Is this any better?

For most people, nothing needs to change with the four-day week. Whoever wants to keep working is welcome to do so, and opportunities will be plenty. The self-employed will keep taking ownership of their choices. Workers in high-end services could keep putting hours in over the weekend. A partner in a large law firm will still prepare cases over the weekend, but the administrators will not be expected to be there. Other white-collar workers could set up their own company to do consultancy projects on the side.

Blue-collar workers can think of driving an Uber during the weekend, or just moonlight with a second job in a restaurant or a pub. In the US, moonlighting was common in a small fringe of workers after the transition to the five-day week. Currently, in the UK, about 1 million workers already hold a second job. The catch is that the extra hours would be with a different employer. But this brings more competition which, in the eyes of Hayek, can only be positive. Having a second job weakens the *monopsony* power of employers. A waitress who also teaches in a dance school has a better exit strategy if one of the bosses is exploiting her. And, of course, people can also agree extra hours with their employer that should be paid at a premium. In the Portuguese trial, 9 per cent of workers devoted more time to other sources of income.

In other words, it will be easier to monetise the free time under a four-day week than 'buy' free time under a five-day week.

Whoever wants to work more, can work more. The current trend of the *gig economy* brings many dangers. In particular, it hides the true dimension of technological unemployment. But the gig economy can also be part of the solution. It can offer thousands of the people at the bottom of the distribution an easy opportunity to work additional hours for the extra income, and at the same time strengthen their power relative to their main employer.

Marx said that the limitation of working hours 'has never been settled except by legislative interference'. One doesn't need to be a Marxist to agree. Even Hayek, the most fervent, but thoughtful, supporter of liberalism, and John Hicks accepted the role of the government in legislating working hours. It does not threaten competition because it keeps a level playing field. It does not limit individual freedom. On the contrary, under the four-day week workers would have more freedom to decide how much to work.

Myself, I love my work. One of my colleagues jokes that I have been working six days a week on my four-day week book. It is true. I researched for this book and wrote it during holidays, weekends and hours of darkness, with as much pleasure as I get from gardening, swimming, playing chess or dancing salsa. With a three-day weekend, I will still bring academic papers to read at home. You might accuse me of being disingenuous. I don't think I am. I don't pretend to know what people will do with their extra day, nor do I want to tell them what to do. Like Hayek, I just want everyone to have the freedom to choose; is there anything more liberal?

13

The Eighth Reason: Because It Will Reconcile a Polarised Society (Hayek)

'Modern capitalism is absolutely irreligious, without internal union, without much public spirit, often though not always, a mere congeries of possessors and pursuers. Such a system has to be immensely, not merely moderately, successful to survive.'

John Maynard Keynes

Before Samuelson and Frisch, economics was called *political economy*, a name that reflected the conviction that economics could not stand outside politics. Nowadays, political economy denotes a specific field of economics, like labour economics, development economics or health economics, that looks at the interaction between politics and economics. How does the political process affect economic outcomes? How do the incentives of politicians shape economic policies?

'To be a good economist, you must be a good political economist,' advocated Samuelson, 'it's not enough to know the diagrams of supply and demand and the mathematics of econometric regressions. You have to be able to understand social tensions and conflicts.' There is a symbiotic, or perhaps parasitic, relation between economics and politics. Their roots are profoundly intertwined. Economics studies the effects of different government policies and determines which ones promote the highest well-being. It abstracts from political and institutional factors. Winners and losers are but a footnote. Politics, on the other hand, is about the struggle for power and authority, and the nature of decision-making. Economists might know what is best for society, but they cannot simply raise their economist's voice with conviction and expect everyone to bow in admiration and rush to implement the brilliant idea they saw in their crystal ball, disguised as a differential equation. 'Macroeconomic policy can never be devoid of politics: it involves fundamental trade-offs and affects different groups differently,' says Joseph Stiglitz. In a world with opposing interests between actors in society, implementing a policy requires bringing people together and building coalitions, and this is the job of politicians.

Typically, economists don't worry about political constraints. They won't have their way entirely, but in between a stable centre-right or centre-left government and the need for consensus, politicians will get things about right. Economists had their way with globalisation, intellectual property rights regimes, financial development and financial integration between nations, the European common market, central bank independence and budgetary responsibility. The problem is when politics go sideways, and the foundations of the political system get wobbly.

Barry Eichengreen, an economist from Berkeley and author of *The Populist Temptation*, defines populism as a movement with authoritarian and nativist tendencies that builds a simple narrative, one of the pure people against the corrupt elite. This 'thin' ideology can take cover in other 'thick' ideologies, such as socialism, anarchism, nationalism, ultranationalism, religious nationalism, secular nationalism, anti-imperialism, antisemitism, Islamophobia or racism, to justify particular agendas. I must confess I am not a good sommelier of radical political ideologies, but I can smell a populist from afar. In the US, Trump rode the Tea Party with style, aiming to 'drain the swamp', but all he has done is degrade the US political institutions in a way that would mortify Abraham Lincoln, trivialising racism and sexism and belittling the English language. In the UK, Brexiteers, currently in power, denounced experts and referred to themselves as 'the people', as if they had not been educated at Eton, Cambridge or Oxford. At least *they* preserve a superior mastery of their mother tongue. Jair Bolsonaro in Brazil, Viktor Orbán in Hungary, and the puppets of Jarosław Kaczyński in Poland are dismantling liberal democracy in their countries. In Europe, far-right nationalistic parties are gaining ground. They account for more than 25 per cent of votes in Austria, Switzerland and Belgium; about 18 per cent in Italy, Sweden, Estonia and Finland; and close to 15 per cent in France, the Netherlands, Germany, Portugal and Spain. The lack of substance of populists is hidden in their catchy slogans and nostalgia for past achievements. Instead of a vision for the future, they want to turn back the clock, returning to life as it was fifty years ago. They are charlatans, and charlatans always find their victims. The problem is not the charlatans; they have always existed, and will go on existing. The problem is not the people who vote for them. Most of them are not racist nor stupid; they are people who believe that progress should been better lives for themselves and their communities. The problem is with the system that is not working for the majority and is having trouble reinventing itself.

We should analyse the problem from two angles: the economic origins of populism, and the economic consequences of populism. First, unemployment, hardship or downright misery, if ignored or minimised, creates social and political instability that can take the form of rising populism. James Meade and Wassily Leontief warned us. Second, populists are likely to adopt popular but damaging economic policies that can undo much of the progress that we have achieved. Beyond the negative economic consequences, populist regimes might easily descend into authoritarian regimes, bringing a loss of political or individual freedom, as we are already observing in the heart of the European Union. Forget taxes or bureaucracy, this was Hayek's worst nightmare.

Whatever the guise of the populists, their rise reflects a frustration over the decline in economic status. There are social and political causes of the rise in populism but it is undeniable that technological change, globalisation and growing inequality combined have made people feel left behind. They have lost faith in the system. Are economists to blame? Mostly, we are messengers. It is not because we say people are greedy that people are greedy. But economists do have to take some responsibility. They are guilty of one cardinal sin.

Bertil Ohlin is an oddity in the world of economics. He is probably the only economist who understood parliamentary procedures as well as equations. Born in Sweden in 1899, the same year as Hayek, he was not only a Nobel Laureate – another pioneer in the development of modern macroeconomics – but also a successful politician. He was leader of the Liberal Party from 1944 until 1967, sitting opposite Gunnar Myrdal. During the war he was in the coalition government, as Minister of Trade.

In the economics textbooks, 'Ohlin will live forever as one of the great innovators in the theory of international trade.' In 1933 he published the work that won him world renown, *Interregional and International Trade*. Developed in his doctoral thesis, it builds upon earlier work by Eli Heckscher, Ohlin's former professor at the Stockholm Business School. The theory, now known as the Heckscher–Ohlin model, became one of the standard mathematical models of international trade, taught to undergraduate students. Ohlin had sent a version to the *Economic Journal*, but it was returned by the editor-in-chief with these words: 'This amounts to nothing and should be refused. J.M. Keynes.' More than forty years later, in 1977, he was awarded the Nobel Prize, together with James Meade. I remember this story whenever I get a rejection letter for my own papers, to overcome the disappointment. It is my mental pot of ice cream.

Before Ohlin, economists viewed international trade through the lens of David Ricardo's theory of comparative advantage, a fascinating theory. Often economic theories are either obvious or irrelevant. The theory of comparative advantage is neither. Ricardo, a nineteenth-century political economist, showed that two countries gain from free trade, if each specialises in the production of goods in which they have a *comparative advantage*. In the UK, a case of wine was twice as expensive as a pair of trousers. In Portugal, a case of wine was cheaper than a pair of trousers. Both wine and trousers were cheaper in Portugal. Ricardo concluded that, even if Portugal had the *absolute advantage* in both goods, it should specialise in the production of wine and the UK in textiles, and by trading, both countries can consume more of both goods. International trade is not a *zero-sum game*; both sides win. The example with Portugal and the UK, wine and textiles, was not random. One century before, the two countries signed the Methuen Treaty, one of the earliest international commercial treaties, where Portuguese wine would have preferable tax treatment in England and English textiles would not be charged taxes in Portugal. The ritual of high-table dinners in Oxford and Cambridge being followed by a glass of Port wine in the common room has its origins in a trade agreement. The theory of comparative advantage set the view of economists on trade for more than 100 years.

Ohlin's contribution was to step back and ask what determines a country's comparative advantage. The answer is the endowments of the factors of production, *capital* and *labour*. Let me generalise his theory, by also distinguishing *skilled* and *unskilled labour* as factors of production. Ohlin's model predicts that countries export products that use in their production the most abundant factors, and import products that use the countries' scarce factors. Western countries specialise in the production of capital and skill-intensive goods, like machinery, aeroplanes and higher education, while developing countries specialise in the production of goods that require more (unskilled) labour, like toys, clothes or coffee beans. Will everyone benefit if countries open up to trade? The average Joey will certainly be better off, but not all Joeys in the economy will benefit. Samuelson, in one of his countless contributions, studied the distributional implications of free trade. 'Free trade need not help everybody everywhere.' The owners of the least abundant factor of production will be worse off. Western countries, by specialising in capital and skill-intensive goods, will have higher returns on capital and skilled wages, but unskilled workers will be worse off. Understanding this, the economists wrapped up the argument for free trade: *there will be winners and losers but if there are mechanisms to share the gains of free trade with the losers, everyone will be better off.* Economists were aware of the distributional problems but thought they shouldn't stand in the way of free trade. To mitigate them, they listed policies to compensate the losers: funding retraining, generous unemployment benefits, minimum wages, the availability of public-sector jobs or free public services. This was a minor detail in a very powerful argument for free trade, and it was pushed into a footnote.

Economists got their way and international trade flourished. Since the Second World War, the value of exported goods as a fraction of world GDP has increased from 5 per cent to 30 per cent. With the decisive impulse of James Meade, we created the General Agreement on Tariffs and Trade, precursor of the World Trade Organization, and we built the European Union, the most ambitious economic integration and political project in world history. We owe to free trade a significant share of growth in income and productivity in the Western economies. Ohlin was right: the average Joey is much better off thanks to free trade.

But the mechanisms to compensate the losers and share the gains from free trade, written in fine print, turned out to be expensive and inefficient to run. They put in place the wrong incentives. Generous unemployment benefits make the unemployed too complacent and not so active in searching for a new job. Free universal health care and primary, secondary and tertiary education are very expensive to run by a government and required their citizens or firms to face higher tax rates, which discourages work and investment. The promises were made during one paradigm that accepted state intervention, but when globalisation was on course, the paradigm changed, and Hayek was on top. Most of those 'promises' were broken.

We never have much faith in politicians. Politicians who never break their promises don't go far. But economists should have known better. They were victims of a problem they know too well. *Time inconsistent problems* arise when policymakers prefer one policy in advance, but later prefer a different one. I always promise my daughter she won't watch cartoons if she misbehaves. Often, she misbehaves. After the deed is done, she gazes at me with innocent eyes, and I will say, 'Okay, but next time you'll have to behave.' I can promise all I want, but when the time comes, it is not in my best interest. My promise is time inconsistent. These problems arise repeatedly in economics, because of its dynamic nature. They were first pointed out by Nobel Prize winners Finn Kydland and Edward Prescott. The government promises multinationals zero taxes to attract foreign investment, but when the factories are installed, it would prefer to tax more because they are locked in. Latin American politicians promise low inflation in the future, but when they must trade low inflation for higher unemployment today, they don't even try it. We will always quit smoking tomorrow, not today. These dynamic problems are the reason why credibility for economic actors is so important. That is why we gave independence to central banks, so they are able of holding to their promise to keep inflation low. That is why we sign contracts and have the institutions to enforce them. But we didn't sign any contract accepting free trade only with compensation mechanisms in place. And with no contract signed, we just broke the promises. This is the economists' cardinal sin, and it is recurrent. When countries joined the euro and surrendered control of their monetary and exchange rate policy, they were assured that, while the European Central Bank would deal with symmetric shocks to the euro area, the rules restricting their fiscal policy were flexible enough for them to use Keynesian policies to deal with asymmetric shocks. But when the Great Recession hit the periphery countries, they were forced into austerity.

Keynes showed us how technological progress brought a tremendous rise in living standards. Marx showed us that it comes at a cost of short-run technological unemployment and lower wages, even though they will go away in the long run. Technological progress is not so much a responsibility of economists, when compared to globalisation, but we also failed in acknowledging its side-effects. Another mistake of economists was thinking that the short run is only a few years and the long run is just around the corner. For technological unemployment, the short run is one generation. Some economists, like James Meade, argued that societies should set in place compensation mechanisms, but we defaulted once they became too expensive or inefficient.

The increasing wage inequality of recent decades was in part a consequence of technological progress that privileged machines and non-routine abstract occupations, but also globalisation, the loss of union power, and the withdrawal of the state. Leontief and Meade warned about technological progress and inequality. Samuelson warned about globalisation and inequality. But since the 1980s, economists and politicians haven't listened. Promises were broken and the rise of inequality was ignored. The financial crisis of 2007, with the bailout of the banks and financial institutions, compounded by austerity in Europe, sending the bill to those who haven't benefited from technology or globalisation, together with corporate scandals like the Libor manipulation, the Volkswagen emissions and the Wirecard accounting scandal, and the high-end corruption exposed by the Panama papers, were the straws that broke the camel's back.

The paper 'Did austerity cause Brexit?' published in the *American Economic Review* provides convincing *causal* evidence of the political consequences of these effects. The author, Thiemo Fetzer, shows that regions with a larger initial share of residents in 'routine jobs', a larger share of 'low-educated' residents, and higher employment shares in retail and manufacturing, all experienced an increase in support for UKIP, the Eurosceptic, right-wing populist political party, yet only after 2010. What was the trigger? Austerity. The fiscal contraction starting in 2010 was sizeable but varied across districts. Spending on welfare and social protection was cut, in some districts by 46 per cent, and in others by only 6 per cent. Using government estimates of the predicted effects of austerity in the local budget cuts as *instruments*, Feltzer shows that support for UKIP grew in districts more exposed to benefit cuts after these became effective. He estimates that UKIP vote shares increased by 4 to 12 as a consequence and concludes that the 'EU referendum could have well resulted in a victory for Remain had it not been for austerity'. Complementary research has found that British regions more exposed to trade with China voted more for Brexit. Another paper published in the *American Economic Review*, by David Autor, an economist from MIT, looks at the effects of competition from China on political polarisation in the US. Congressional districts exposed to larger increases in import competition disproportionately removed moderate representatives from office throughout the 2000s. In presidential elections, counties with greater exposure shifted towards Republican candidates. If the Chinese import penetration had grown by half of its actual growth, the states of Michigan, Wisconsin and Pennsylvania would not have voted for Trump in the 2016 elections and he would not have won the electoral colleges. This adds to evidence from the European Union. Using similar empirical strategies, research has found that European regions more exposed to trade with low-wage countries and to the Great Recession saw larger increases in vote shares for extreme-right populist parties.

All these studies show strong causal links between globalisation, austerity and the rise of populism: 'It is the economy, stupid!' Now, the *gilets jaunes* are invading the Champs-Elysees and the populists are taking over European parliaments. What is the problem with that? It is impossible to list *all* the economic blunders of populist leaders once in power. Most populists are incompetent and don't bring new ideas to the table. They simply propose running back the clock, undoing technological progress and globalisation. Reversing globalisation is easier than reversing technological progress. Brexit took the UK out of the single market. Trump implemented protectionist measures, raising tariffs on targeted imports from an average of 3 to 17 per cent. Of course, trade partners retaliated by raising tariffs on US exports. Technological progress can't be undone, but it can be slowed with Luddite barriers. Trump introduced measure after measure to subsidise the coal industry, artificially protecting jobs, but mainly profits. *The Economist* reports that each steel-industry job saved by the Trump administration cost $900,000 to the US consumer. In a paper published recently in the *American Economic Review*, German researchers identified fifty-one populist leaders since 1900 and calculated that, after fifteen years, GDP per capita in the country was 10 per cent lower compared to a plausible non-populist counterfactual.

Populists can degrade institutions that brought years of stability. Trump constantly tried to influence the Federal Reserve, in an unprecedented move that jeopardised the independence of monetary policy which has given us low and stable inflation. Recep Erdoğan, the Turkish President, said that interest rates were 'the mother of all evil' and that higher inflation was a consequence of higher interest rates, a contradiction of everything economists know about monetary theory. And if you think that populists will keep the budget in line, think again. They will spend. In the UK, Brexiteers campaigned on opening the tap. The US deficit increased from 2.5 to 4.5 per cent of GDP under Trump, even before the pandemic. One could argue for more government spending to fund schools or research, but don't expect populists to spend the money wisely. How productive is a wall between the US and Mexico? Or spending money on dying industries? To finance them, Trump cut funding to the Department of Education and the Department of Health and Human Services. This was *The Economist*'s damning verdict on Trump's four years in the White House:

> Our bigger dispute with Mr Trump is over something more fundamental. In the past four years he has repeatedly des-ecrated the values, principles and practices that made America a haven for its own people and a beacon to the world. [...] Those who breezily dismiss Mr Trump's bullying and lies as so much tweeting are ignoring the harm he has wrought. It starts with America's democratic culture. Tribal politics predated Mr Trump [...] Yet, whereas most recent presidents have seen toxic partisanship as bad for America, Mr Trump made it cen-tral to his office. [...] Today 40% of the electorate believes the other side is not just misguided but evil.
>
> The most head-spinning feature of the Trump presidency is his contempt for the truth. All politicians prevaricate, but his administration has given America 'alternative facts'. Nothing Mr Trump says can be believed. [...] Partisanship and lying undermine norms and institutions. That may sound fussy – Trump voters, after all, like his willingness to offend. But America's system of checks and balances suffers. This president calls for his opponents to be locked up; he uses the Department of Justice to conduct vendettas; he commutes the sentences of supporters convicted of serious crimes; he gives his family plum jobs in the White House; and he offers foreign governments protection in exchange for dirt on a rival. When a president casts doubt on the integrity of an election just because it might help him win, he undermines the democracy he has sworn to defend.

'Conservatism had died and been born again, a lower animal,' condemned Keynes in 1903, when conservatives changed their stance on free trade to support protectionism, betraying their liberal soul. We could say the same today. Republicans have dropped all their principles, their codes and their policies to ride alongside Mr Trump. Instead of searching for conservative solutions to rekindle the economy, conservative parties in Europe are adopting the rhetoric of right-wing nationalists, and in several countries, like Spain and Portugal, they are considering parliamentary alliances with populists to get into power. The European People's Party took too many years to distance itself from Fidesz, the illiberal party of Hungarian leader Viktor Orbán.

Republicans argue that the economy did very well under Trump's administration: stock markets boomed and unemployment plummeted before the pandemic. This is what they repeat to themselves to be able to sleep at night. The economy benefited from Trump in the same way a wrestler benefits from taking steroids. It grows his muscles and improves his performance for the next fight while entertaining the crowd, but he won't live long past fifty. It is easy to get short-term gains at the expense of the long-term costs. Just cancel your health insurance policy and stop spending on small car repairs, and you will have more money to spend at the end of the month. For a little while you will look like an economic genius because of all the other things you can buy, but the cost will come at some point, with a bang, when you are diagnosed with a disease, or when your car breaks down. Removing environmental and safety regulations is an easy way to fuel the economy, but when accidents like the Exxon oil spill happen again, their costs will become visible. Why spend money on stockpiling protective personal equipment, when pandemics rarely happen? Trump's policy was never one of increasing the size of the pie. It was one of borrowing from the future and giving a larger share to his entourage.

The economic dangers of populism are real, and they are bigger than having a narcissistic buffoon starting a trade war, or a Churchill-aspiring Hop-Frog taking the UK out of the single market. There is a risk of a real war, with real blood, real death and real destruction. The parallels with the conditions prior to the First World War are disturbing. The liberalism of the nineteenth century, so admired by Hayek and Schumpeter, saw an increasing pace of globalisation like today's. Technological advances displaced workers who saw their skills become worthless. Inequalities were visible. Significant acts of terrorism, then perpetrated by anarchists, were common. But the defining parallel is the complacent conviction that economic interdependence and prosperity had made war unthinkable. In 1913, *The Economist* reassured its readers that 'War Becomes Impossible in Civilized World', explaining how 'The powerful bonds of commercial interest between ourselves and Germany, have been immensely strengthened in recent years [...] removing Germany from the list of our possible foes.' *The Economist* also didn't see that one coming! The invasion of Ukraine by Putin and the conflict in the Middle East are worrying warning signs.

Hayek's biggest nightmare, expressed in *The Road to Serfdom*, was the limitation of individual and political freedom. Hayek was against economic planning by the government, not because of any loss of efficiency or higher taxes, but because he saw it as a first step towards an authoritarian regime. The loss of economic freedom was the start of a slippery slope towards the loss of political and individual freedom, as had happened in Nazi Germany and later in the Eastern bloc. These were the same worries that Keynes expressed in *The Economic Consequences of the Peace*, ten years earlier. In fact, Keynes wrote directly to Hayek about *The Road to Serfdom*:

In my opinion it is a grand book. [...] morally and philo-sophically I find myself in agreement with virtually the whole of it: and not only in agreement with it, but in deeply moved agreement. [...]

I come finally to what is really my only serious criticism of the book. You admit here and there that it is a question of knowing where to draw the line [between free-enterprise and planning]. You agree that the line has to be drawn somewhere, and that the logical extreme is not possible. But you give us no guidance whatever as to where to draw it. In a sense this is shirking the practical issue. It is true that you and I would probably draw it in different places. I should guess that according to my ideas you greatly underestimate the practicability of the middle course. But as soon as you admit that the extreme is not possible, and that a line has to be drawn, you are, on your own argument, done for since you are trying to persuade us that as soon as one moves an inch in the planned direction you are necessarily launched on the slippery path which will lead you in due course over the precipice.

Unlike the vision of popular culture, the distinction between Keynes and Hayek was not one between a socialist and a liberal; it was one between a pragmatist and an idealist. Keynes was always a liberal and he shared Hayek's worry, but he disagreed with the argument that any state intervention would forcefully send the country over the precipice. On the contrary, he believed that some intervention was needed *precisely* to save us from that very precipice. Robert Skidelsky, Keynes's master-biographer, named his philosophy, which 'deliberately aimed to surrender some of the "outworks" of the individualist system to collectivism in order to protect its "central structure"', as the *intelligent way.*

Hindsight disproves Hayek's view. Scandinavian countries, much influenced by Ragnar Frisch and Gunnar Myrdal's view of active interventionism, are the best counter-examples. Samuelson wrote that the Scandinavian countries 'are the most "socialistic" by Hayek's crude definition. Where are their horror camps? Have the vilest elements risen there to absolute power? When reports are compiled on "measurable unhappiness," do places like Sweden, Denmark, Finland and Norway best epitomize serfdoms? No. Of course not.'

Neither Keynes nor Hayek was infallible. Keynes got his prediction on working hours wrong. Hayek also missed his. Government economic intervention did not throw countries onto a slippery slope. Instead, economists, without intent but with the naivety of a 5-year-old child, together with politicians and the elite, have thrown us all into a shit-show of a slippery slope, a *shittery slope*. I won't apologise for the term. Trump, the President of the United States of America, the man in charge of 5,000 nuclear weapons, suggested that injecting bleach could cure Covid and believes it is fine to 'grab women by the pussy'. He lied more than 30,000 times in office, bluntly tried to overturn an election, and incentivised an attack on the Capitol. And he is running again for office! We cannot accept this as normal. We might think it was temporary and that the economic costs were low because the stock markets didn't seem unhappy, but this is pure wishful thinking. Populists are setting the narrative and history shows we can end up in a nasty place. There were many valid arguments for Brexit, including the lack of transparency of the EU and the weight of its bureaucracy. But populists don't restrict themselves to these arguments. They lie, deceive and incite racism. When in power, they undermine democracy, they attack the free press, they limit freedom, they break the law or pressure it, undoing what has taken decades to build.

Barry Eichengreen's book, *The Populist Temptation*, traces the history of populist movements over the past two centuries in the US and Europe. He discusses their roots in 'the combination of economic insecurity, threats to national identity, and an unresponsive political system'. He argues, more cheerfully, that such movements 'can be quelled by economic and political reforms that address the concerns of the disaffected'. The classic example was Roosevelt's New Deal, which brought us the five-day working week and suppressed populists for half a century. In Europe, the average vote share of far-right parties between 1950 and 1975 was less than 2 per cent.

How can we defeat the current wave of populism? Taking a step backward, with less globalisation, less integration and a budgetary open bar, is the worst possible way because it just plays into the hands of populists and condemns our economies to a worst fate. On the other hand, we cannot propose the same solutions

and expect a different outcome for the disenchanted. Doubling down, asking for more globalisation, more integration, less regulation and more budgetary rigour, will not work. Fool me once, shame on you; fool me twice, shame on me. That will just accelerate populism. Eugene McCarthy once said, 'Vote against anything introduced with a "re" in it, especially reforms, reorganizations, and recodifications. This usually means going back to something that failed once and is likely to do so again.' None of these will fix the collateral damage that they created in the first place.

As Roberto Unger, a philosopher at Harvard Law School, puts it: 'we need to have the imagination of the post-war, before the war'. The four-day week is the imaginative and courageous solution that is a step forward, rather than backward. It brings everyone the benefits of progress and technology. It is universal – every worker will benefit. In today's world what do rich and poor, men and women, black and white, Christians, Muslims and Jews, left and right, Brexiteers and Remainers, have in common? Everyone loves a bank holiday weekend. People will be happier, and happy people don't vote for charlatans. The four-day week is a simple solution that is supported by economic theory. It has all the pure economic advantages that Keynes, Schumpeter and Marx have argued. Although it is not completely neutral from a budgetary perspective because the government is itself an employer, it does not require direct financing and the price tag would be lower than other measures such as a universal basic income. It does not hinder competition; on the contrary, it will enhance it, rewarding good firms that better adapt. It does not twist incentives – the playing field will be levelled. It won't fix all the problems modern economies face, but it will take us in the right direction and protect our economy from the risk of populism. The four-day week is both Left and Right and it can become the most powerful flag of a system that people have come to disdain. Bring the four-day week to reconcile society with capitalism.

Conservatives and liberals throughout the world now face an unavoidable and defining choice. They can sacrifice their principles and their policies, like most American Republicans, and align themselves with the populists for the sake of winning elections and staying in power, condemning the economy. Or they can stay true to their values and work hard for real solutions to make capitalism 'immensely successful' again. That should start by accepting the four-day working week and sitting at the table with politicians across the aisle to discuss the best way to implement it. If they accept the marriage, then they will have a say on which flowers they will have at the wedding.

PART THREE

Making it Happen

14

An Adjustment Protocol

'If to do were as easy as to know what were good to do, chapels
had been churches, and poor men's cottages princes' palaces.'
William Shakespeare, The Merchant of Venice

Robert Lucas Jr was a history student when he read Karl Marx
and Friedrich Engels' *Communist Manifesto*. The power of Marx's
writing convinced the young mind that economics was the most
powerful driver of history and Lucas decided to study economics
instead. He cared about how normal people lived and he wanted
to improve their lives, and that is the goal of economics. 'I am not
a Marxist, but I would have been in 1848,' he says, perhaps with
the aim of shocking his admirers. The image of Lucas couldn't
be further from a Marxist. He led the revolution that swiped
macroeconomics in the 1970s and overturned the Keynesian
paradigm. Hayek provided the philosophical foundations of
liberalism. Milton Friedman persuaded economists and policymakers with his passionate speeches and pungent op-eds in

Newsweek, alternated with Paul Samuelson in fierce ideological battles. Lucas never liked the attention that followed Friedman and preferred the comfort of academia. He received the Nobel Prize in 1995 'for having developed and applied the hypothesis of rational expectations, and thereby having transformed macroeconomic analysis and deepened our understanding of economic policy'. His contribution was methodological; he created a new type of economic model whose complexity and mathematical elegance, allied to a powerful message for economic policy, seduced most macroeconomists.

The basic Keynesian IS-LM model, the mathematical formulation of Keynes's ideas by John Hicks, is *static* in nature. It has no notion of time, past or future, only present – everything happens simultaneously, taking no time for economic policies to affect the economy. There were dynamic models of the economy with a notion of time, with today and tomorrow linked because today's decisions affected the future. For instance, in the Solow model, the simplest model of growth, how much an economy invests today determines the number of machines and factories operating in the future.

Lucas envisioned that causality between present and future runs both ways. Today's decisions determine the future, but what families and firms expect for the future also affects today's actions. When you think about it, most economic decisions depend on expectations about the future. When an entrepreneur decides to set up a firm, he thinks about expected profits. When a young couple buy a house, they calculate how long they will stay and the future house prices. Later in their lives, when they advise their kids on which college to go to or which courses to follow, they compare the career prospects. When a publishing house offers a book contract, they project the book sales. The idea that the future affects today's decisions was not new. If you recall, Keynes attributed a crucial role to 'animal spirits' as a driver of economic decisions. Lucas's contribution was to take this idea seriously. Most economists thought of expectations about the future as *exogenous*, a thunderbolt coming from outside the economic system, impossible to explain. But for Lucas, expectations are part of the economic system: they are *endogenous*. As today's decisions determine the future economic conditions, when people, firms or the government change their behaviour, their future is bound to change and so will everyone's expectations about it, creating a complex interaction between present and future. Sometimes the interdependence creates serious problems. At the beginning of the Covid-19 pandemic, the rumour that there wouldn't be enough toilet paper drove people to binge buy, effectively leading to empty shelves in the supermarkets and fuelling the rumour for longer. The toilet paper run was the result of a *self-fulfilling prophecy*, an example of how expectations can be crucial drivers of the economy.

Lucas's new theory completely overhauled the models macroeconomists used. Modelling seriously the interaction of present and future – actions and expectations – was a huge mathematical challenge. If a simple macroeconomic model included income, consumption, government consumption and investment, each one became a Matryoshka doll, with infinitely many future dolls inside, all connected through an arc of coherence. Think about a classic time-travel movie, like *Terminator* or *Back to the Future*. Suppose a time-traveller describes your future and, knowing it, you make decisions and life will unfold as you had been told it would, in one coherent time loop. The maths becomes very complicated, but Lucas figured out how to deal with it, with what is called rational expectations. If you think Samuelson's models taught to undergraduates are complicated, wait until you see one of Lucas's *Real Business Cycle* models, the simplest of the *Dynamic Stochastic General Equilibrium* models that now populate central banks and academic journals. Their complexity is such that they are only taught at a postgraduate level, and are agonising to solve without a computer. They are as beautiful as they are impenetrable to outsiders, and to many economists themselves.

Hidden within the beautiful mathematics, Lucas made a powerful critique that revolutionised our understanding of economic policy: the *Lucas critique*. Let me explain it with a mundane example, familiar to any dog lover. Sometimes, I take my neighbour's dog, Figgy, to the park. I throw a small ball and watch her running after it, coming back happily wagging her (very small) tail. The second time, I pretend to throw a ball but I hide it behind my back and watch Figgy running in search of a ghost ball. Then I reveal my trick and try it again. Figgy is not particularly clever, so she falls for it once more. But even Figgy eventually learns, and after a while, she doesn't get fooled any more – she adjusts her expectations, and she doesn't budge. In this analogy, I represent the policymakers, and Figgy represents the actors in the economy. Lucas argued that when economic policies change, so will the expectations of families and firms, so their fundamental response to a new economic policy will be different. If Figgy can figure out my trick, why can't everyone in the economy? Lucas's assumption of rational expectations meant that actors use all the available information to make the best possible forecast of the future. For Lucas, humans making economic decisions have super-human brains that, in the absence of any unexpected events, thunderbolts hitting the economy, will get their prediction right. They will still make mistakes in their forecast, but they won't make the same mistake time after time. Many social scientists criticise this assumption, as regular people don't have super-brains and their behaviour is everything but rational. But the theory of rational expectations is just an abstraction to get a grip on a jelly-like reality. It is a simplification, one benchmark to help economists understand the economy and the role of policy; it is not a sanctity. More recent macroeconomic models have considered actors less brilliant in forecasting. They are *learning*, faster or slower, just like different dogs.

At the beginning of the 1970s, when oil price hikes hit the economy and unemployment escalated, policymakers used Keynesian stimulus policies, but all they were getting was ever-increasing inflation without getting a hold on unemployment. Lucas argued that government policies drove inflation expectations. Suppose people expect zero inflation, but the government overheats the economy by spending too much and inflation is 2 per cent. The following year, the same happens: people expect zero inflation, government overspends, and inflation is 2 per cent. How long can the government trick the economy? Lucas said that people will see the trick coming and adjust their (rational) expectations beforehand. They will expect an inflation rate of 2 per cent, adjusting all the lending and labour contracts in advance, and the government stimulus will end up causing an inflation rate of 4 per cent. This became the accepted explanation as to why inflation quickly got out of hand in the 1980s, and why Keynesians were dethroned.

Lucas was the winner of the methodological debate, and soon Keynesians were breaking up into two camps: the *New Keynesians* – those who adopted these new models, adding Keynesian concepts like slowly adjusting prices, giving rise to the models now used by central banks – and the *Post-Keynesians*, who kept rejecting these models and were marginalised in the profession. Whatever one assumes about the quality of banks, firms and workers' forecasts, the idea that expectations about the future determine today's decisions took over macroeconomics and will never go away.

Lucas's theory teaches us the main principle to guide the implementation of the four-day working week: we must give it time. Giving it time is not making a hollow promise of a four-day working week in the not-too-distant future, like Richard Nixon made. To be credible, the four-day working week must be announced and approved in parliament, several years before it legally comes into effect. Don't expect an elected government to implement it in the first 100 days in office. We shouldn't shoot the starting pistol for a marathon when people haven't trained for it. Instead, we should set the date for the marathon, to give people the time to prepare. Everyone will begin adjusting to pre-empt the day when Friday will become the new Saturday. Firms that better adapt will switch before the deadline, paving the way for other firms. Instead of a bang-bang painful adjustment, the longer the transition, the smoother it will be. The Fair Labor Standards Act allowed two years for the implementation of the five-day week. Today, I think a window of four to six years is better for all the actors – firms, families and government – to plan the transition and adjust to the new reality. After all, coming down from five to four days is a bigger step than coming down from six to five days.

How can firms adjust to the loss of one day of work per week? Let me start with the accounting view that wages must be cut by 20 per cent for the firm to be viable. This is the fundamental principle of work-sharing as a management practice to prevent layoffs during downturns. It is also similar to the deal many part-time workers, including my wife, have. However, in the context of government legislation, this agreement is an undesirable start to be avoided for the majority of workers. How can firms adjust, then, if not by cutting wages by 20 per cent? There are several alternatives.

First and foremost, the time between the announcement of the four-day week and its implementation is in itself an adjustment mechanism – a Lucas adjustment. If firms anticipate the change, they can restrain the wage growth during the adjustment period, to avoid wage cuts when the implementation takes place. Wages in the UK grew in the six years prior to the pandemic at a rate of 4 per cent a year. If firms and workers agree on no wage rises in the year prior and the year after the implementation, this would take care of 8 percentage points, out of the 20 per cent necessary adjustment. This simple adjustment mechanism tells us why the 'four-day week without loss in pay' is an empty (but effective) slogan. The economy is essentially dynamic and forward-looking.

Even the need for this channel might be limited. Second, the four-day working week will raise productivity on the remaining days. Henry Ford made the argument, and firms that have implemented a shorter working week have shown, that the productivity gains will be large. On top of it, we should add the productivity gains that occur naturally in growing economies. Since 1947 in the US, labour productivity per hour has increased by 2.5 per cent every year; so if the adjustment lasts for four to six years, we can count on a 10 to 15 per cent increase in productivity, even in the absence of any improvement linked to the four-day working week.

Third, and related to increases in productivity, firms will have lower production costs, for instance with fixed costs such as electricity , and operational costs with recruitment and training of workers, absenteeism, or errors. Many companies or public-sector institutions that experimented with compressed work weeks did so to reduce their operating costs. While the gains of productivity and the reduction in costs will be significant, they will be different in a restaurant, in a newspaper or in the oil-extraction industry, so in some industries or some occupations, one might need further adjustments to avoid wage cuts.

Fourth, hours worked per day and days worked per year can adjust. The 4/40 proposal in 1970 contemplated only this adjustment, by adding two hours in each of the four working days. That seems too much for an economy-wide adjustment. It puts a heavy burden on workers over the four days and it fails to achieve the essential goal of reducing hours. However, in some occupations, if workers put in one extra hour in the remaining four days, it would already compensate half of the 20 per cent adjustment in wages. When Wall Street stopped trading on Saturday mornings in 1952, it extended the remaining daily sessions by 30 minutes. Some additional compensation could come from reducing vacations or bank holidays; after all, from the moment of implementation, every weekend will be a bank holiday weekend.

The Indian government is currently preparing a major reform of the labour law, giving more freedom for firms and workers to mutually agree whether they prefer the current 6/48 system, a 5/48 or a 4/48. The labour secretary Apurva Chandra said: 'We have tried to give flexibility in working days. It is entirely possible that some employers may want to provide a five-day week. We have also come across employers who said they are keen to provide a four-day working week.' This law illustrates how the length of the working day could be adjusted to facilitate the implementation of the four-day working week to the entire economy.

Fifth, in capital-intensive industries, such as mining, goods manufacturing, and oil or gas extraction, where wages represent a small fraction of operating costs – about 20 per cent – part of the adjustment could be reflected in higher relative prices. Even if the four-day week translated fully into an increase of 25 per cent in wages (no wage cuts and no increase in productivity, so firms increase their workforce by 25 per cent, to the glee of Marxists who would prove the lump-of-labour fallacy wrong), it would only bring about an increase of 5 per cent in total costs, which could be compensated by a similar increase in prices, affecting all firms in the industry equally.

Sixth, in some industries, like big tech, where firms have enjoyed abnormally high profit rates, indicative of market power, part of the adjustment can be absorbed by lower profits. In 2019, Apple reported about $55 billion in profits with a workforce of about 137,000 employees. According to some reports, the average Apple worker earns $125,000. If this is the case, then a 25 per cent increase in the wage bill would only dent Apple's annual profits by 8 per cent.

Seventh, the government can temporarily subsidise the implementation in some industries or for some workers through tax credits, allowing the firms to cut pay but compensating part of it for workers. These subsidies are the core of government programmes to support and encourage the work-sharing management practice during recessions like the Chômage partiel in France or the Kurzarbeit in Germany. They might be used for specific industries, such as producers of green energy, research activities or vegan restaurants, but not for the entire economy. That would defeat the purpose of being a neutral measure from the budgetary perspective.

When we look carefully at most of the criticisms of the four-day working week, behind them is the assumption of only one specific form of adjustment. 'If workers have a 20 per cent cut, no one would accept it,' assumes an adjustment only through wage cuts. 'Firms will go bankrupt,' assumes an adjustment only through loss of profits. 'The four-day week will let inflation spiral out of control,' assumes only price increases. 'The four-day working week will be too expensive for the government budget,' assumes the government will subsidise the difference.

These eight possible adjustments, including wage cuts, together with the specifics of the legislation on overtime, exemptions (for instance in agriculture or in small businesses) and the legislation restricting economic activity on particular days, known as Blue laws or Sunday laws, allow plenty of flexibility to tailor the four-day working week to the requirements of different countries, industries, occupations and firms. One size does not fit all. Economic activity in real life varies: some processes are continuous and some production is in batches. Industries have different shipping, sales or maintenance requirements, utility costs per day, personnel advertising and training costs and personnel turnover. Some have lengthy start-up and shut-down procedures. This implies that the organisation of work across occupations and sectors is already very different in a five-day week and, naturally, they would also be different in a four-day week. Industries and occupation associations, together with unions, should study the impacts of the four-day week in their own trade. They should draw out the dangers and difficulties of implementation, as well as the opportunities it brings and the combination of adjustments that is best suited. What would it look like?

Let us think of a specific industry. In the 1964 US Congress hearings, Mr Ira Nunn, representing the National Restaurant Association, said, 'The restaurant industry has its own unique economic characteristics which make the shorter workweek all the more devastating.' Is that still the case, more than five decades later? What are the dangers and difficulties for restaurants? Like other service industries that rely more on labour – cooks, waiters and bartenders – the biggest difficulty seems to be the impact on costs. However, wages now represent only one third of the operating costs of a restaurant. Even if the four-day week translated into an increase of 25 per cent in the wage bill, total costs would increase by 8 per cent, which could be compensated by an increase in prices of the same magnitude, affecting all restaurants equally. Would someone going to a fancy restaurant worry about £16 extra on a £200 bill, or would a student be upset with a 40p increase on his £5 sandwich? Furthermore, the wage bill would likely increase by less than 25 per cent, given that most workers are part-time and paid by the hour.

Unlike office jobs, where productivity gains might completely compensate for the reduction of hours, in restaurants they might be more difficult to achieve. Still, several restaurants will reinforce the trend of getting self-order machines or start substituting cooks for robots. On the other hand, most restaurants can expect more customers on Thursday night and Friday. A study by Womply, a local commerce platform, finds that restaurants in the US have about 40 per cent more transactions at the weekend compared to a weekday. The number is in line with the rule of thumb in the restaurant business that you can expect 40 to 60 per cent more revenue at a weekend relative to a weekday. If Friday becomes the new Saturday, we could expect an increase in demand of up to 5 per cent.

These initial studies for each industry should analyse and draw lessons from pioneer cases of implementation of the four-day working week. María Álvares is a pioneer businesswoman in Spain. Co-owner of a chain of restaurants in Madrid, La Francachela, she implemented the four-day week without having to hire more workers or cutting her existing employees' pay. She altered her menu to make meal preparation faster and made small organisational changes. For example, customers started ordering through an app, thus preventing waiters from wasting time going to tables and waiting for orders. This change made the workday more intense, but more productive. In 2018, Paul Kitching's 21212, a ten-time Michelin star award-winning restaurant in Edinburgh, introduced a four-day working week. Kitching said, 'This is a tough industry and we thrive on the energy and passion behind our chefs,' adding, 'throughout my years in the industry, I have seen the effects that the pressure of the kitchen can have on an individual. I believe that this stress is not conducive to a thriving and creative environment.' There is as much stress in the kitchens of the best restaurants as in top law firms or consultancies. The same reasons were pointed to by Sat Bains, another UK chef, proprietor of a two-Michelin star restaurant in Nottingham that implemented a four-day working week. His restaurant is only open four days, from Wednesday to Saturday. After a six-month trial in 2015, he made it permanent. These are just three examples of restaurants. They do not help in predicting the gains in terms of customers, but illustrate the organisational changes involved. Beside the existing blueprints for successful implementation, during the transition period as more firms adopt the four-day working week more blueprints will become available.

A preliminary analysis performed constructively by industry or occupation associations is the first step to identify industries where the transition will be easier, the ones where it will be harder, and the suitable adjustment mechanisms. After, firms must experiment with the four-day week. Four to six years gives plenty of time. This was one of the main lessons from Henry Ford: 'Now we know from our experience in changing from 6 to 5 days and back again that we can get at least as great production in 5 days as we can in 6.' Experimentation was also key for Sat Bains and Andrew Barnes of Perpetual Guardian. Barnes proposes an initial four- to eight-week trial and he gives several pieces of advice. Firms should prepare the ground and define the benchmark to which the trial is going to be compared. CEOs must build trust so that everyone, managers and workers, is swimming in the same direction. Some workers will jump straight away into the mindset and others will oppose it. Everyone should be looking for ways to shorten processes. These trials should be informative of the challenges and the opportunities brought by the legislation. They should give an idea of the productivity gains and the cost reduction, and identify the potential problems. The problems with customer relations or with suppliers that some firms have found should disappear as the whole economy adjusts. The trials should also give management an estimate of the extra adjustment needed. Then, together with the workers, and following benchmarks set by industries and occupation associations, they should decide how to implement it. Will management ask workers to stay one extra hour on the remaining days? Can part of the effect be reflected in prices? Can the profit margins be temporarily squeezed? Would workers accept a two-year wage freeze during the implementation period?

Experimentation is crucial to find out the best way to implement a four-day week in a particular sector. While it is part of the DNA of the best companies to experiment with everything – new products, new suppliers, new technology, new publicity campaigns – most companies, especially the large ones, do not experiment with different forms of organising work. The Covid-19 pandemic offers the best example. The technology to work remotely existed for a long time and it had been shown to increase productivity by Nick Bloom, a renowned academic from Stanford University. But the practice never gained popularity among firms, which viewed it with suspicion without even trying it. It was the pandemic that forced all firms to experiment with remote working and find the positive and negative aspects in their own context. This aversion of companies to trying new forms of organising work makes the current pilots throughout the world so important.

Schumpeter wrote that 'Economic progress, in capitalist society, means turmoil.' The implementation of the four-day week will indeed bring turmoil. It will be disruptive because it will change our life patterns, and it will take time to reach a new normal. Many events are disruptive and we deal with them. Blizzards are disruptive. Brexit is disruptive. Pandemics are disruptive. They come without warning, without bringing economic progress. The four-day working week does not and should not come as a surprise, so, although it will profoundly change our societies and our economies, we will have time to adapt. The status quo arguments for the four-day working week can scare some people eager for stability, but they can easily be addressed if we work together to implement it.

15

A Four-Day Working Week in the Public Sector

'Change is the law of life. And those who look only to the past or present are certain to miss the future.'

John F. Kennedy

So far, I have based my arguments on current and historical academic literature, descriptive data, and the authority of Nobel Prize winners. Myself, I have never sketched a mathematical model to support the four-day working week (no one has), nor have I measured the effects of shorter working hours. If I embarked on that journey now – to promote the four-day working week within the circle of academic economists – I would waste my career before being heard.

When it comes to the public sector, I can add a new dimension, having spent fifteen years studying the macroeconomics of public employment. I have published in top journals and received awards for my work. I have written mathematical models to understand the effects of government employment and wage policies on unemployment and other labour market outcomes. I have analysed detailed survey data of many European countries. I have visited policy-oriented institutions like the World Bank, the OECD and the European Commission to present my work. I know all the most important – and most of the less important – papers on the topic, and there is hardly a new paper that I am not asked to review. My contribution to economic science is meek compared to any of the great economists in this book – a small brushstroke on a big canvas – but although I don't have the brains or the grit for a Nobel Prize, you won't find a macroeconomist better placed to discuss public-sector employment.

In advanced economies, about 18 per cent of workers are employed in the public sector, reaching over 30 per cent in Scandinavian countries. Even in the free-market-loving US, the government hires 16 per cent of workers. Adam Smith's invisible hand, powerful in the private sector, loses its touch in the public sector. As in my mum's high school, the goods and services produced by the public sector are not sold – you don't go to a market and order 500g of bureaucracy together with your vegetables. They are provided to citizens for free and are financed by taxes. Therefore, we can rule out an adjustment towards the four-day working week based on increasing prices or reducing profits and, given the lack of competition, one might fear lower productivity gains. The implementation of the four-day working week might be harder in the public sector unless combined with a well-thought-out reform. But the blueprint for such reform, one that involves a change in how public-sector wages are set, already exists.

Behind this reform lies the principle of the optimal wage: it should be neither too low, creating recruitment and retaining problems, nor too high, so that the government is overpaying, which generates long queues for its jobs and an inflated wage bill. The principle to balance these two effects is to align the wages of public-sector workers with their private-sector equivalent. Aligning them does not mean they should be equal. If a public-sector job offers additional benefits to a worker over and above its wage – job security, better work–life balance, a better health plan, or higher pension – these *compensating differentials* should be properly valued and reflected in lower relative pay.

This principle is not satisfied in practice. In most countries, wages in the public sector are far from aligned with those in the private. The details matter a lot. The average wage in the public sector is much larger than in the private sector, but to a large extent this is due to a different workforce composition. The government hires more educated workers. The US government hires about one third of all workers with an MSc, a PhD or a professional degree. The UK public sector hires 37 per cent of workers with higher education – bureaucrats, doctors and teachers – but only 17 per cent of workers with lower qualifications. Governments also hire more women and workers with more experience. To have a better sense of relative pay, economists measure the *public-sector wage premium*, using survey data. They go to specific occupations and compare earnings of similar workers in the public and private sectors (think of twin brothers with the same education, doing the same job in different sectors), using econometric formulas that would make Ragnar Frisch proud.

Without entering the alpha and the omega of the econometrics, I can give a few examples from Italy and the UK, using the 2014 Structure of Earnings Survey, a European survey from which official statistics regarding pay are drawn. Let's start with 'Domestic, Hotel and Office Cleaners and Helpers', an 'elementary occupation' of workers who clean and tidy the interiors of hotels, offices and other establishments, as well as aircraft, trains, buses and other vehicles. In Italy, private-sector full-time workers in this occupation earned €1,460 per month, while their public-sector counterparts earned €1,585, a *wage premium* of 9 per cent. In the UK, private-sector workers earned £1,336, and public-sector workers £1,492, a 12 per cent premium. In both countries, the public sector respected the legal forty hours, but the private sector surpassed it by up to five hours.

Not all occupations are alike. The public-sector premium goes down as we move up the scale of jobs. Italian 'General Office Clerks' and 'Secretaries' earned €2,294 in the private sector and €2,239 in the public sector. In the UK, they earned £1,962 in the private and £1,940 in the public. In both countries the wages seem better aligned, but again, private-sector workers toiled up to six more hours per week. In top occupations such as 'Administration Professionals', the logic is reversed. Italian workers in this occupation earned €5,243 in the private sector, but only €3,074 in the public sector, 40 per cent less. In the UK, they earned £3,385 in the private and £3,128 in the public, 7 per cent less.

These are just particular examples. The econometric methodology to pin down the wage premium attributed to the sector accounts for the education of workers, gender, experience, the region where they live, and other characteristics. Studies find that, in most countries and years, the public sector pays *on average* higher wages for equivalent workers. Workers in unskilled occupations in poorer regions earn much more in the public sector, while some workers, usually in the better occupations in richer regions, earn less than in the private. Of course, the public-sector wage premium varies across countries and over time. Scandinavian countries pay less in the public sector respecting the principle of the optimal wage, but south European countries pay large premia. In Portugal, in 2009, a year of economic crisis and three elections, public-sector pay increased by 3 per cent. The following year, austerity packages brought progressive pay cuts, starting at zero for the lowest-paid and rising to 10 per cent for the highest-paid public-sector workers. In two years, the lowest earners in the public sector got a 3 per cent rise and the highest earners a 7 per cent cut, amplifying the misalignment.

Still, we should not aim for the exact same pay as the private sector, because of other characteristics of public-sector jobs. On the one hand, they offer more job security. The probability of private-sector workers finding themselves unemployed in the following quarter is two to three times higher than that of public-sector workers. In some countries, it is illegal to fire civil servants. The job security is especially valuable in recessions, when the private sector sheds many jobs. The public sector also offers better work–life balance. In both Italy and the UK, public-sector full-time workers worked forty weekly hours, but their private-sector brothers and sisters worked three more hours in the UK and five more hours in Italy. Besides fewer hours, they are more regular, making it easier to go to a dentist appointment, watch your team's Champions League away match in Russia, or pick up your children from school. After a first child, many women try to switch into the public sector. Adding in the better public-sector pensions, which, according to the OECD, can be twice as generous as in the private sector, and better health care plans, particularly important in the US, most jobs in the public sector, apart from the top ones, offer a better compensation package than the private.

Better compensation in the public sector, particularly for unskilled jobs, seems a very equitable thing – inequality is such a serious problem – but it does more harm than good. The idea that the government can deal with inequality only by protecting a minority of workers, rather than having comprehensive policies to deal with the problem for all workers, is short-sighted and self-defeating. It is like giving paracetamol to treat a patient with cancer.

There are many negative consequences of offering jobs that are too attractive, besides higher spending and higher taxes. For a start, many people queue for these jobs, shunning the private sector. When I was an assistant professor at the University Carlos III in Madrid, Spain, I supervised a very bright undergraduate student. Diego wanted to become *economista de estado* – an economist civil servant. He explained to me that he would face a tough examination called *oposición*, for which the average selected candidate spent two years studying full-time. To become a state legal clerk, the typical candidate spent five years preparing for the *oposición*. This is a pure waste of resources – the time of very bright people – and is often unfair because people who can afford to take so much time to prepare are necessarily the wealthiest.

There are further problems. In 2017 the Italian Central Bank advertised thirty job openings, for unskilled positions. The number of applicants was a whopping 85,000. This is a quote from a newspaper describing the process:

> Italy's chronic unemployment problem has been thrown into sharp relief after 85,000 people applied for 30 jobs at a bank [...] The work is not glamorous – one duty is feeding cash into machines that can distinguish banknotes that are counterfeit or so worn out that they should no longer be in circulation. The Bank of Italy whittled down the applicants to a 'shortlist' of 8,000, all of them first-class graduates with a solid academic record behind them. They will have to sit a gruelling examination in which they will be tested on statistics, mathematics, economics and English [...] The high level of interest was a reflection of the state of the economy but also of the Italian obsession with securing 'un posto fisso' – a permanent job.

This quote explains the problem with long queues for public-sector jobs and the waste of resources involved in the hiring procedure. It shows the importance of job security, particularly in times of high unemployment, and it hints at another problem. When unskilled public-sector jobs are so desirable, they attract people too qualified for the job and, given the hiring procedure based on ranking of candidates, they will naturally get it. They might be the best person for the job, but they won't be the right person for the job. The public sector will be wasting the skills of people who could be setting up their own business or creating value in a private firm. There is evidence that this *underemployment* is more perverse in the public sector. Furthermore, any government department with a limited budget will shy away from opening lower positions. Paying an extra £400 to open a position at a higher level, or outsourcing jobs to private-sector companies that hire workers at the minimum wage, will give more bang for the buck.

When public-sector jobs are too desirable, they encourage the use of unconventional channels to 'jump the queue'. Nepotism – using personal or political connection to get a job – is more salient in the public sector. In Spain, the press exposed that in the 'Tribunal de Cuentas', the institution in charge of invigilating economic and financial irregularities in the public sector, 100 of its 700 workers were family members or friends of the directors or of important politicians – irony doesn't get any better than this. François Fillon, a former French presidential candidate, was found to have put his wife, son and daughter on public payroll – a common practice in French politics. He was convicted of embezzlement only because his wife had admitted to a British magazine that she did not do any work.

This side trip into my own work illustrates the scope to improve the public-sector pay structure. These gains are independent of any legislation on the working week – governments should do it regardless. But a reform of the pay structure is politically hard to implement on its own and it could be made easier if it comes hand-in-hand with the shortening of the working week. Not only would the four-day working week help reform public-sector pay, but also the gains of reform would help implement it without increasing government spending. Governments can use the transition period to overturn the public–private wage differentials, without unpopular wage cuts, accumulating savings to hire more workers if need be. Using time to operate the wage readjustment can play a more important role in the public sector, but other adjustments are possible.

Despite the lack of profit motive, don't rule out productivity improvements. In most countries it is hard to fire public-sector workers. Many (right-wing) politicians and economists believe that this inability to downsize inflates the public sector with too many workers, rendering it unproductive. If there is truth in this argument, the four-day working week offers an opportunity to put everyone to use, avoiding additional hiring, while maintaining services. Also, the shortening of the working week might be done alongside a reduction of bureaucracy, freeing workers and citizens of useless red tape. A win-win!

The American politician Jon Huntsman Jr is a proud Republican. He worked as a White House staff assistant for Ronald Reagan, holding positions under George H.W. Bush and his son George W. Bush. Between 2005 and 2009, he was the governor of the state of Utah. He won a re-election with 78 per cent of the vote in 2008, winning in every county, but resigned the following year to become US ambassador to China, nominated by President Barack Obama. He ran an unsuccessful campaign in the Republican primary for the 2012 presidential election. He was not forgiven for having supported Obama's Keynesian economic stimulus, civil unions for gay couples, or a cap-and-trade scheme to reduce emissions of greenhouse gases. Plus, he was hurt by his ability to speak fluent Mandarin; instead of an asset, it was a liability mocked by his opponents – realpolitik at its best. In 2017 he served under Donald Trump as an ambassador to Russia. Huntsman always believed in crossing the aisle. Besides having served under President Obama, he headed a bipartisan political group called No Labels. Crossing the aisle does not mean sacrificing one's convictions. Huntsman defines himself as a centre-right, fiscal conservative, and he presided over the biggest tax cuts in Utah's history. He ran in the primaries speaking of his desire to revive the economy through a new 'industrial revolution', reducing debt, lowering and simplifying taxes, and cutting regulation, a plan out of the best supply-side economics playbook.

Huntsman is the son of Jon Huntsman Sr, a billionaire founder of the Huntsman Corporation, a petrochemical company that hit gold by manufacturing Styrofoam cartons for McDonald's. Huntsman grew up between the worlds of business and politics, and while governor of Utah he brought a business mentality to the job. In 2008, Huntsman implemented a mandatory four-day week for Utah's state workers, covering about 18,000 out of the 25,000 employees. Huntsman listed four objectives: lowering costs, in particular the energy costs that were at an all-time high; improving the state's poor air quality; service delivery; and recruiting and retaining of employees. Initially a pilot, the four-day working week's implementation was through the 4/40 practice, increasing the number of hours worked on the remaining weekdays. All nonessential services closed on Friday. Two state holidays were taken out to partially compensate for the move.

The initial objective of cutting energy consumption by 20 per cent turned out to be naive. Most buildings closed on Fridays, but power couldn't be cut entirely because of sensitive equipment. Still, energy use came down by 10 per cent, mainly through savings on natural gas. The final report on the pilot documented that annual gasoline consumption fell by 744,000 gallons, saving $1.4 million on the state fleet. Carbon emissions cuts were equivalent to taking 1,000 cars from the roads. Were services affected? Among participants in a state-wide survey, 66 per cent thought it should continue, against 20 per cent who thought it should be discontinued. More than 80 per cent of workers were happy with the new schedule, believing they were more productive during four days. Before the implementation, many expressed concern about childcare and transportation, but after, few workers complained. They benefited from lower commuting costs and having more time for themselves. Overtime pay decreased, providing savings of about $4.1 million. Fewer workers resigned and absenteeism was reduced. The findings mimic those of the 4/40 in the private sector.

In 2011, a new audit found that the savings were lower than expected. The audit recognised some benefits, like reductions in overtime and maintenance costs. It didn't find evidence of lower standards, but it also didn't find evidence of higher standards, which was ammunition enough for a Republican state legislator to sponsor a bill requiring state agencies to be open at least nine hours per day, five days a week. He cited public opinion polls showing that 20 per cent of Utah residents didn't like the 4/40 schedule, never mind the 66 per cent who did. When the bill passed, the governor vetoed it, but the bill was forced through, putting an end to Utah's four-day working week. Still, the experiment of Utah shows that it can be implemented in the public sector, while reducing spending.

Utah is not the only example of compressed working weeks in public-sector institutions. In the Philippines, the discussion around the four-day working week started in the early 2000s, and companies were given the discretion to implement it, much like the current proposal in India. The main reason was to reduce traffic; Manila was one of the most congested cities in the world. In 2011, the president commissioned an official report on the four-day working week and, by 2019, most government agencies, including the central bank, had adopted it through the 4/40 schedule. During the pandemic, it was extended to court officials. Another example comes from Iceland. A series of trials, pushed by a confederation of public-sector unions in the Reykjavík City Council between 2014 and 2019, have also been successful. They reduced weekly working hours by five. Initially set in two small departments, covering seventy workers, the results have been so positive that the trials have been extended, now covering more than 2,000 workers. The causal effects, drawn by comparison with a control group that kept their working hours, are the same as elsewhere: less stress and burnout, fewer sick days, better work–life balance, same amount of services provided, positive impact on other family members and men doing more activities at home. Inspired by Iceland, the South Cambridgeshire council started a trial in 2023 and the Scottish government started one in the public sector in 2024.

One alternative strategy, instead of implementing the four-day working week to the whole economy, is to restrict it to the public sector, hoping the private sector will follow suit by its own initiative. This idea springs from another recent book, *The Case for a Four Day Week*, by Anna Coote, Aidan Harper and Alfie Stirling from the New Economics Foundation. The book lays out the philosophical, environmental and social case for the four-day working week, and calls for the pioneering role of the public sector as an employer. This proposal might look like a good compromise, but it is a strategic mistake that must be avoided. Restricting it to the public sector will exacerbate the asymmetry between sectors, increase the grievances between factions of society, and risk the success of the four-day working week. This is a lesson from the Utah experience. The four-day working week should be implemented through legislation across the whole economy, and the transition period used to correct the existing imbalances between the public and private sectors. Concessions can be made on the length of the transition period, exemptions and the adjustments available to firms, but the two sectors should go hand-in-hand.

Another strategic mistake, in my view, is to push for the four-day working week alongside an extensive progressive wish list. The four-day working week is a once-in-a-century policy. It will change how we organise the economy and it will need much preparation. As you can probably see by now, I view it as a social innovation capable of bringing together different groups in society. Bundling the four-day working week with other partisan policies, like universal basic income or nationalisation of whole industries, will just alienate large parts of society that must be involved and should have a say in how it is implemented.

Three other aspects related to the public sector deserve some attention: education, health and social security. Although we are used to schooling five days per week, the four-day school week is not a new concept. The practice gained ground in rural schools in the US when energy costs increased in the 1970s. The budgetary pressures on public schools since the financial crisis have propelled it even more. Today, about 7 per cent of school districts have one or more schools with a four-day week. In Colorado, where the practice is more widespread, half of the school districts use it. The four-day school week is also in use in France, Canada and the UK.

The implementation varies by schools. In most cases, the remaining school days are extended by one hour. Friday is the most common day off, but some schools close on Wednesdays. Teachers work the same hours, sometimes devoting the fifth day to professional development. On the day off, students are assigned projects, are directed to online resources, attend study halls, enrol in extracurricular activities provided by the community, go on field trips or practise interschool sports.

Studies have found that the financial savings amounted to 5 per cent. Teachers and administrative staff worked the same hours and several buildings were kept open on Fridays. The savings came from reduced transportation, fuel and maintenance of school buses, cafeteria costs and other operating costs that are outsourced. There were other advantages besides cutting costs. Rural school districts struggle to keep and attract teachers. The four-day school week improved the ability to attract and retain teachers, increased student and staff attendance rates, and provided additional time for professional development.

What about the outcome for students? Some studies find that students benefited from the four-day school week, but others find detrimental effects. Causal evidence is hard to get because of *selection* – the schools or the school districts that have implemented it did it for a specific reason. Still, the lack of a strong negative association between the four-day week and student outcomes suggests there is nothing intrinsically bad about it. Critics argued that students become more tired by the end of the school day, they lose some of their learning over the long weekend, and those from a disadvantaged background are pushed towards criminal activities or gangs during their day off. Minimising these problems is possible if the four-day school week is operationalised in the right way. Some teachers argue that longer classes allow better teaching, with the use of multimedia activities after the regular sessions. Teachers can assign projects for the weekend, encouraging independent work. In some poorer areas, schools can open on Friday for students lagging behind or coming from disadvantaged families, supported by trainee teachers on the last year of their university degree.

The students would get some additional support and school meals, and would-be teachers would gain first-hand experience in a less formal environment.

The school curricula could include weekly online lectures and activities, developed centrally, for students to complete over the weekend. Such a system would complement students' learning and give them feedback on their progress. It would also allow schools to track the progress of students and flag problems, and allow the Department for Education to gather data on the progress of different schools, or even use it to reward teachers. My 5-year-old daughter is learning chess through Chesskid.com, a platform that teaches kids how to play, with a series of engaging lecture-videos followed by puzzles. The pandemic gave us much experience with online learning, and we can use this know-how to complement the four-day school week with top-quality online resources.

If schools close on Friday, the community can come together to keep children busy on their extra day off, creating a Friday enrichment programme in community centres, coordinated with schoolteachers to build on concepts they are learning. Sports clubs can boom with Friday and Saturday programmes, forming a new generation of Olympian athletes. This is the concept behind France's recent four-day school week in primary schools. France has alternated between the five- and the four-day school week for many decades, and is now moving again towards the four days. It was in place in 32 per cent of schools in 2017 and in 80 per cent of schools in 2018. This move came together with the *Plan Mercredi* – Wednesday Plan – which supports local municipalities financially and involves libraries, museums, conservatories and planetariums, sports federations, natural parks and farms in encouraging children to grow with a wider knowledge of the world, rather than a narrow view from the classroom.

Another possibility worth considering is to increase the length of the school year. The summer holiday lasts six weeks in the UK, Germany and the Netherlands, eight weeks in Norway and France, between nine and thirteen weeks in Eastern Europe, and fourteen weeks in Italy and Russia. Long summer breaks are very detrimental to learning, so many countries can compensate the loss of one school day per week, with fewer weeks in the summer break. The bottom line is that the four-day school week is not uncharted territory, it is not detrimental to students and, if we give time for education experts to plan, there is enough flexibility to make it a success.

In many countries the government oversees the health system. How would hospitals cope with the four-day week? All hospitals are open 24/7, so in terms of organisation, it would not be much different from what it already is. The book *4 Days, 40 Hours* devoted one chapter to the example of the Roger Williams General Hospital, a hospital in Rhode Island that implemented the 4/40. Take my wife's obstetric service. To maintain the key services, doctors, nurses and midwives work twelve-hour on-call shifts, day or night. These come in two packages: Monday to Thursday, and Friday to Sunday. Nothing would change under the four-day working week. The question is whether four days are enough to do the non-urgent procedures, or if more staff would have to be recruited.

Effectively, the four-day week will require hiring more personnel, but this is not incompatible with a more efficient system. Think of the nursery in the Portuguese trial that only had to hire 4.5 per cent additional workers, saved on other costs and improved service. The question is not 'can doctors treat the same number of patients in four days as they are now treating in five?', but rather 'can the health system work better and with lower costs, organised around a four-day week?' To answer this question, it is necessary to have a global vision of all the synergies generated. While the costs with permanent staff will increase, there will be savings in at least four areas: reduced absenteeism, reduced medical errors, improved worker retention and reduced costs of training physicians.

British hospitals often rely on locum work, where agency workers are hired to cover for absent workers, usually paid at a premium. They cost £6 billion to NHS England. Legal expenses and compensation for medical malpractice cost another £6 billion. Together they represent 25 per cent of the total wage bill, so the potential savings of a four-day week are high. After the pandemic, many countries are facing difficulties attracting doctors to the public system. This problem can only be solved by improving the compensation. The four-day week is a better alternative to salary increases. A final aspect is the cost of training doctors. High rates of 'attrition' in the profession, with doctors giving up their careers, moving to the private sector, or emigrating, mean that training each new specialist is becoming much more expensive. In the UK, the percentage of junior doctors continuing into a specialty has decreased from 80 to 40 percent between 2007 and 2017. This fall implies that the cost of training of each new doctor beginning her specialty has doubled in ten years. All these costs will be reduced if the public health system is organised around a four-day week.

The health benefits of the shorter working week won't come immediately, but they will be sizeable. For a start, there will be a reduction in stress, burnout and other mental illnesses. I have already mentioned their links with longer working hours and their costs for the economy. Reducing them will take pressure off the health system. A study on the effects of France's thirty-five-hour week found that it decreased smoking by 16 per cent, especially among blue-collar workers. The Framingham Heart Study, one of the world's longest-running studies on the risk factors for heart attacks, has found that having more social contact and more exercise, both likely to increase under the four-day working week, lowers the risk of heart disease. According to the US time use survey in 2009 to 2015, Americans spend 25 per cent more time doing sports and exercising on a weekend day compared to a weekday. The effects of regular exercise are far reaching. They have been proven to reduce depression and stress, increase happiness, help with weight loss, to be good for the muscles and bones, increase energy, reduce the risk of chronic diseases, keep the skin healthy and the brain active, help sleep, reduce pain and improve sex life. There is also evidence that it reduces hospitalisations. One survey of Australians over 45 found that, controlling for existing co-morbidities, doing a minimum of 150 minutes of moderate physical activity per week reduced the spending on hospital admissions by $255. The authors concluded that if the population doing the minimum level of exercise doubled from 50 to 100 per cent, Australia could save $415 million per year in hospital payments. The four-day working week will contribute to a more active society. If we give people time, they will take better care of themselves.

The government savings from an economy-wide adoption of the four-day working week have an additional dimension. The reduction in unemployment, because of a slower pace of job destruction, more retraining, and more job opportunities in the leisure industries and the government, will spell a sizeable reduction in unemployment benefits and other subsidies. Furthermore, in an economy with low unemployment, it will be easier to reform the welfare state to become more efficient, cheaper to run, and more focused on supporting people to return to employment.

Also related to social security are the benefits of the four-day working week with respect to an ageing population. Economic growth comes with longer lives. Since the year when Samuelson expressed his support for the four-day working week, life expectancy in the UK has increased from 71 to 81 years. In Japan, it has increased from 73 to 84. A ten-year increase in life expectancy is common in developed countries. This trend comes together with a decline in fertility. In the UK, the number of babies per woman fell from 2.3 to less than 1.9. In Japan it fell from 2.1 to 1.5. Longer lives and fewer babies puts pressure on the social security system. There are fewer young people to support a growing older generation, a problem that is bound to continue. To solve it, western economies have used a combination of increasing the retirement age, reducing pensions and increasing taxes. Increasing the retirement age is a penalty for poorer workers who have tougher jobs, cannot spend as much on preventive health and have lower life expectancy. A study from 1997 showed that in the US, the mortality risk is three times larger for people in households earning less than $15,000 compared to people in households earning $70,000. These asymmetries have only increased. The shorter working week will make a longer working life fairer.

From society's point of view, we can shift part of the burden of a shorter working week into a longer working life. The Mexican millionaire Carlos Slim thinks that we need bold plans to fight unemployment and protect the economy. He supports a 3/33, three-day week of eleven hours, combined with an increase in the retirement age to 72. Consider a 25-year-old worker starting his career, expecting to retire at the age of 65. If you add the days he will not work under the four-day working week – about fifty-two days per year – to the end of his working life, he would retire instead at 75. I am not calling for an increase in the retirement age, but as we live longer, it is a possible scenario. If this happens, wouldn't you prefer to enjoy leisure when you have the energy? Wouldn't it be fairer if people had only worked four days per week during their working life?

Regarding the other side of the problem – the fall in fertility rates – just as people do more sports over the weekend, they also have more sex. A baby boom followed the Fair Labor Standards Act. According to Google Trends, the keyword searches for 'morning after pill' are 50 per cent higher on weekends than on weekdays. With or without contraception, more sex will not harm the economy.

16

Shifting Gears

'Material wellbeing, and measures of it – GDP, personal
income, and consumption – have recently received a bad
press. Spending more, we are often told, does not bring us
better lives, and religious authorities regularly warn against
materialism. Even among those of us who endorse economic growth, there are many critics of GDP as it is currently
defined and measured. GDP excludes important activities,
such as services by homemakers; it takes no account of leisure; and it often does a poor job of measuring those things
that are included.'

Angus Deaton

When you drive a car, you notice the two main instruments displayed on your dashboard: the speedometer and the tachometer.
The first measures the speed of the vehicle and the second the
number of rotations per minute of the motor. We care about the
speed at which we are travelling more than the revolutions per

minute. When we step on the accelerator, the motor runs faster and so does the car. But there is another way to gain speed. Changing the gear allows you to go faster but with lower revolutions per minute. If you look at the tachometer, it might appear that you are going more slowly, when in fact you are gaining efficiency.

When policymakers 'drive' the economy, they only have one instrument: Gross Domestic Product (GDP). This measure was developed by Simon Kuznets and was one of the reasons he was awarded the 1971 Nobel Prize. For Samuelson, 'Simon Kuznets was a giant in 20th-Century economics', the founder of national income measurement and creator of quantitative economic history. In the 1930s, Kuznets spent two years working with the US government agency that provides official macroeconomic and industry statistics, deciding how the national income should be measured. His work, 'National Income and Its Composition, 1919 to 1938', was published in 1941.

When government officials and Kuznets embarked on this challenge, they had different objectives. The bureaucrats wanted to build a tachometer to measure the speed of the economic motor – the value of production. Kuznets, instead, wanted to build a speedometer to measure the *welfare* (well-being) of the economy. Welfare is a concept that is well grounded in economic theory. I have never heard an economist arguing we should maximise GDP; we always talk about maximising welfare. The theoretical foundation of the invisible hand that underlies the economists' fetish with free markets is called the *First Fundamental Welfare Theorem*, not the *First Fundamental GDP Theorem*. Kuznets said in 1934, 'the welfare of a nation can scarcely be inferred from a measurement of national income'. Here is one crucial distinction:

It would be of great value to have national income estimates that would remove from the total the elements which, from the standpoint of a more enlightened social philosophy than that of an acquisitive society, represent dis-service rather than service. Such estimates would subtract from the present national income totals all expenses on armament, most of the outlays on advertising, a great many of the expenses involved in financial and speculative activities, and what is perhaps most important, the outlays that have been made necessary in order to overcome difficulties that are, properly speaking, costs implicit in our economic civilization. All the gigantic outlays on our urban civilization, subways, expensive housing, etc., which in our usual estimates we include at the value of the net product they yield on the market, do not really represent net services to the individuals comprising the nation but are, from their viewpoint, an evil necessary in order to be able to make a living (i.e., they are largely business expenses rather than living expenses).

GDP turned out to be the tachometer in your car. It measures how fast the economic engine is running, the production of goods and services. Welfare is not about how many goods and services the economy produces. Welfare is about the goods and services that people consume, but it is also about inequality, leisure, environment and even happiness. Consumption increases welfare, spending on advertisements does not. Leisure increases welfare, expenses in speculative activities do not. Better environment increases welfare, bureaucracy does not. If hardly any economist understands all the details behind GDP, every economist understands it is not a measure of welfare. For Kuznets, to create a speedometer, we should take out of GDP 'evil' expenditures, such as spending on tanks, bombs and machine guns, but also the 'necessary' expenditures to run a country. Most government activities are an implicit cost of modern societies, and bring no direct benefit to their citizens. Knowing exactly which government activities improve welfare was not obvious to Kuznets, but he was certain that a measure of welfare must include the value of leisure.

Kuznets's objective of measuring welfare clashed with the views of government officials. First, a government on the verge of war needs to know whether the economy can sustain it, so measuring production capacity is more useful. Second, at the time of the New Deal, officials embraced Keynesianism, so they wanted an instrument that agreed with it and valued government spending, not one that ignored most of it. A welfare measure would only count the multiplier effect through private consumption, but not the direct effect of government spending. One of these US government officials, George Jaszi, later wrote: 'I resisted the will-of-the-wisp of forging national output into a measure of economic welfare, which required an independent point of view. I was a minority of one in a company that included such mental giants as the late Professor Kuznets and Professor Hicks.' Jaszi found support in one of the president's economic advisers, Richard Gilbert, who was trying to convince the politicians to invest in war capacity. In this battle between tachometer and speedometer, realpolitik won.

Kuznets lost the battle in the corridors of governmental buildings, but the quest for a speedometer continued in the pages of academic journals. In 1973, William Nordhaus and James Tobin, Nobel Prize winners, tired of the growing adulation of GDP by politicians, journalists and policymakers, proposed a new *Measure of Economic Welfare*. They started with GDP and made different adjustments, adding some elements, and taking out others.

Like Kuznets, Nordhaus and Tobin believed welfare should measure consumption rather than production, so they first needed to change the classification of *intermediate inputs*. Suppose you own a beach bar that serves tequila. In one month, you sell £10,000 in tequila shots. That is not the economic contribution of your activity. You must take out the cost of intermediate inputs – everything you bought to run your business – in our example, the bottles of Jose Cuervo. For each firm in the economy, the cost of intermediate inputs is taken out of GDP, so its contribution is its *added value* – the economic value created above the cost of inputs. But from society's point of view, as Kuznets argued, GDP counts many activities that are only instrumental overhead costs needed to maintain a complex society and are not consumed by its citizens. Nordhaus and Tobin take out a fraction of government expenditure, for instance on defence, police services or road maintenance, but they also remove several private activities, like commuting, and the services offered by lawyers, accountants, experts in high finance or real estate agents. Some represent what Senator McCarthy called waste, and none bring pleasure to consumers.

A second source of adjustment is called imputations. GDP measures the market economy – everything that is bought and sold. But ignoring activities that occur outside the market creates many paradoxes. If you live in a rented house, paying rent is a market transaction. However, if you own your house, you don't pay rent but you still benefit from it. If we only measured the market economy, an economy where everyone rented would have a far larger GDP than one where everyone owned their house. Homeownership would lower GDP. To avoid this paradox, when calculating GDP, the office of statistics imputes a rent – an imaginary number – to approximate the value of the services that owner-occupied housing provides. According to Nordhaus and Tobin, at least two other imputations are just as necessary, and these are crucial to understand the welfare gains of the four-day working week. They wrote:

> The omission of leisure and of nonmarket productive activity from measures of production conveys the impression that economists are blindly materialistic. Economic theory teaches that welfare could rise even while GDP falls, as the result of voluntary choices to work for pay fewer hours per week, weeks per year, years per lifetime.

One of the omissions is ignoring non-market activities, meaning things that people do that have an economic value, but which, because they are not bought or sold, are kept out of GDP. This gives rise to another paradox pointed out by Samuelson, who once said that if he married his maid, GDP would go down. In the words of Kuznets:

An individual spends most of his time producing scarce and disposable sources of satisfaction. In accordance with the above definition, most acts that might be called 'personal', such as washing, shaving, and playing for amusement on the piano would be treated as economic activity and their results as economic goods, since, when judged by the attributes of satisfaction-yielding, scarcity, and disposability, they do not differ from the same activities carried on for money as services to other people (nursing, barbering, and giving concerts).

The second necessary imputation was to value leisure like other consumption goods. But how can a monetary value be attributed to leisure? One could do different imputations, but the most natural is to value each hour of leisure at the ongoing hourly wage. After all, if people choose leisure, it is because they value it more than the wage they would receive if they worked instead. Another Nobel Laureate, Angus Deaton, reflected:

Leisure time is not counted at all; if people decide to work less, and take more time for things they value more than work, national income and consumers' expenditure will fall. One reason that French GDP per capita is lower than American GDP per capita is because the French take longer holidays, but it is hard to argue that they are worse off as a result. Nor do we count services that are not sold in the market, so that if a woman works at home to care for her family, it is not counted, but if she works in someone else's home to care for their family, it is counted, and national income will be higher.

Nordhaus and Tobin incorporate the different corrections in their Measure of Economic Welfare. The biggest correction is for leisure, whose economic value was twice the value of consumption. The value of leisure increased by about 80 per cent between 1929 and 1965, when working hours were pushed down by the Fair Labor Standards Act. In the same period, the Measure of Economic

Welfare increased by 120 per cent, mainly due to a large increase in consumption of about 180 per cent, the same as GDP.

In 2008, French President Nicholas Sarkozy created 'The Commission on the Measurement of Economic Performance and Social Progress' led by Joseph Stiglitz, Amartya Sen and the French economist Jean-Paul Fitoussi. Their task was to identify the limits of GDP as an indicator of economic performance and social progress and to propose alternatives. The commission included top economists, including other Nobel Laureates Kenneth Arrow, Angus Deaton, James Heckman and Daniel Kahneman. Their first recommendation was to improve GDP as a tachometer, particularly how it accounts for the quality of goods. If a computer twice as fast is sold for the same price as last year's model, it is not necessarily reflected in GDP. There are many products whose quality is complex, multidimensional, and advances rapidly. The national statistics now correct some high-technology goods, like computers, but not many services, like medical services, educational services, information and communication technologies, research activities and financial services.

Their second recommendation was to improve the measurement of welfare. This requires moving away from only measuring production, looking instead from the household perspective at income and consumption, factoring in wealth and its distribution, not just the average income, and broadening the income measures to non-market activities, including the value of leisure.

Their third recommendation was to create another independent instrument to measure the sustainability of resources. The element of sustainability is important because it determines whether the current level of welfare can be maintained for future generations. Coming back to your car's dashboard, this instrument is the indicator for the fuel tank that tells you how long you can drive for. This fuel gauge should reflect physical indicators of the proximity to dangerous levels of environmental damage, associated with climate change or the depletion of natural resources, such as fishing stocks or the rainforest.

We don't have to throw away GDP; it is a useful measure. When the economy thrives, GDP increases and people are better off. But only paying attention to GDP means we forget the essential. We should develop a speedometer and a fuel gauge, without discarding GDP. Maybe it is the arrogance of economists to think that we can summarise the whole economy in only one number – one statistic to rule them all. We are not doomed to have only one instrument when analysing the effects of economic policies. If we had a more reliable measure of welfare, an economic speedometer, built upon the blueprints of Nordhaus and Tobin, it would show us the true effect of the four-day week: a shift of gear for the economy. Like in your car, there might be an initial jolt, but the economy would be better off, even if GDP might initially say otherwise. The four-day working week would show up in a speedometer, either directly because people would enjoy more leisure, or indirectly because more economic activity would move towards leisure industries.

How will the four-day working week affect our fuel tank? Could it help the environment and improve sustainability, the third pillar of the Stiglitz–Sen–Fitoussi report? This is often argued by proponents of the four-day working week, many of whom view it as a measure of de-growth, to reduce consumption and save the environment. One of the proponents is Juliet Schor, a sociologist from Boston College leading the team evaluating the recent four-day-week trials, and author of the book *The Overworked American*. She has done extensive research documenting the positive association between carbon emissions and working hours, across countries, across US states, over time, and even across households. Schor argues that it will be impossible to decarbonise the western economies under the current technological approach – shifting to renewable energies and improving energy efficiency – if the demand for energy keeps growing. Even with all our efforts on the technological side of energy production and conservation, the decoupling of GDP and carbon emissions, commonly known as green growth, is simply not happening. She argues that to decarbonise our economies we must control energy demand, meaning stopping economic growth altogether. We should aim at keeping GDP constant, and use the natural increases in productivity to lower working hours instead, the opposite of how we have reaped the benefits of productivity increases over the past eighty years. Her 'Aristotelian' plan is to reconfigure the economy, with an automatic mechanism to reduce working hours as productivity increases. Another more radical proponent of the four-day working week as a measure of de-growth necessary to save our planet is Jason Hickel, an anthropologist and author of *Less is More*. He is the poster boy of Extinction Rebellion, a grassroots movement that represents not only a global worry about climate change, but also an alarming backlash against capitalism. What makes the proposal of de-growth controversial is the requirement to keep purchasing power out of people's pockets to stabilise or even reduce society's material consumption.

A shorter working week might improve the environment, but not as much as supporters of de-growth hope. One analysis from the University of Massachusetts Amherst claimed that a four-day working week would reduce our carbon footprint by 30 per cent. People with more time engage in fewer time-saving, energy-intensive activities. They walk instead of driving. They sleep longer. They don't defrost their meal in the microwave. Reducing commuting will take CO_2 out of the atmosphere, as in Utah's four-day week. This is too optimistic. The four-day working week is not a policy of de-growth – it is a policy for smarter, more efficient growth. It is not a measure to reduce consumption – it is a measure to increase the consumption of what people care about. It is true that pollution in big cities will go down with longer weekends, but elsewhere pollution might increase. People might take more flights for city breaks, go to the countryside or the seaside and leave plastic in the forests and on the beaches. Barbecues burn coal. The size of the 'green dividend' of the four-day working week will depend on its implementation. The research showing the negative association between hours worked in the economy and pollution strengthens the case that the green dividend will be positive, but it alone cannot save our planet. We should do it for the economy, not for the environment. The four-day working week won't deplete our fuel tank, but it won't fill it to the top either. For that, we need much more decisive action and economists must rise to the occasion, repent their 'sin of omission' and work to find the solutions that only their science can imagine to save our planet. Maybe the four-day working week will bring economic security and give time for everyone to realise how vital it is.

17

Elinor

'In days of old, when men really did work from dawn to dark, fathers never had a chance to know their children. Perhaps the future will reveal that one of the most profound effects of shorter workweeks will be a change in the structure of the family itself, as the division of labour between husband and wife in the home is changed to redress the ancient curse of female drudgery.'

Paul Samuelson

There is one Economics Nobel Prize Laureate whose name isn't on any birth certificate. Elinor Awan was born in 1933 in Los Angeles. Her youth was shaped by her parents' divorce, the Great Depression and the Second World War. She learned to work hard, be independent and not expect the world to bring any gifts. She was a 'poor kid', lucky enough to attend, by an 'accident of geography', the prestigious Beverly Hills High School, where most students wanted to go to college. She suffered from a mild stutter and joined the poetry and debating societies to improve her speech. The debating society promoted both an interest in politics and mental flexibility from arguing for and against a particular issue. Because she didn't excel in algebra and calculus, and she was a woman, she was discouraged from pursuing more difficult subjects. Her school adviser asked her what use trigonometry would be when Elinor was 'barefoot and pregnant in the kitchen'.

She completed high school in 1951 and, without encouragement from her mother, she joined UCLA to study political science. She worked thirty hours per week at the library, dime store and bookstore and gave swimming classes in order to pay her fees. She graduated in 1954 and struggled to find exciting jobs because employers would only offer her 'women's jobs' like teacher or secretary. Battling her way up, she became an assistant personnel manager in a business firm, and started dreaming of doing a PhD. She wanted to pursue an academic career in economics, but when she contacted the economics department at UCLA, she was turned away because she had not studied enough mathematics at high school. She was deemed not good enough to be an economist. She then applied to the political science department, but even there it was a struggle. After forty years without a woman as faculty or as a PhD student, in 1961 the department awarded four assistantships to women, a decision that had been strongly criticised at a faculty meeting, seen by many as a waste of departmental resources. Elinor got one of the assistantships and entered the programme. There, she met Vincent Ostrom, a young associate professor whose seminars she attended. In 1965, the same year she finished the PhD, they got married and her name changed to Elinor Ostrom. Vincent got an offer of a professorship from Indiana University, and Elinor was offered 'work' – many teaching hours for low pay. But she was used to starting from the bottom, and so began one of the most outstanding careers in social sciences.

Elinor's career revolved around 'governing the commons', which was also the title of her most famous book, published in 1990. Her research sprouted from a stirring article by Garret

Hardin, an American biologist and philosopher, entitled 'Tragedy of the Commons' and published in *Science*. According to his theory, any natural resource that was shared by many people was destined to be over-used, because everyone would selfishly try to get the most out of it. The economic theory is flawless – rational actors render the collapse of the commons inevitable unless conservation is mandated by a strong government, or it is assigned as private property. But there is a long way between theory and reality. Through sheer stubbornness, Elinor documented example after example of the failure of the 'tragedy of the commons' in practice. She studied communities across the world that had developed their own rules to conserve the environment and their natural resources – who can use, when they can use, and how much they can use – and contradicting the flawless theory, 'in most cases but not all', they succeeded. Based on field studies of local *institutions*, created by the community for the community, in countries as diverse as Japan, India, Guatemala, Switzerland, Turkey, Spain and the Philippines, and from diverse resource systems including grazing lands, fisheries, forests and irrigation systems, she assessed what made them successful. She found that people resist rules imposed by a higher authority, but follow them if they had a say in their formulation. Sanctioning of offenders is crucial for successful rules, but the mechanisms need to be low-cost.

Being an independent thinker comes with many risks. Elinor saw a world full of colour, but people like to think in black and white. Some liberals saw her work as socialist, as she argued that communities can be successful in solving problems of environment and resource sustainability, rather than promoting market-based solutions. Plus, she was 'too' ecologist. On the other hand, Marxist economists accused her of ignoring issues of class struggle and applying economic logic to non-market areas of human society. Elinor was, at some point, the president of the Public Choice Society, a society of academic economists considered to be right-leaning. For Elinor, the blind ideological search for simplistic solutions – market-based solutions or government-based solutions – was misguided. Societies are complex and solutions can have multiple forms and operate at different levels, in what she called *polycentricity*. We do not always have to think about markets or the government; solutions can come from people.

People care about their communities and they are willing to spend their own time to improve the lives of those around them. Shambhu Manandhar is an osteopath in West London. He works three and half days per week. Originally from Nepal, he studied at the British School of Osteopathy. He has always worked part-time. For him, happiness does not come from material objects, so he just works enough to live comfortably and support his family in Nepal. His grandfather taught him that a meaningful life comes from helping others, planting the seed of kindness, without expecting anything in return. Shambhu does it in his job, but also in his leisure. Every two weeks, he volunteers for the charity Repaying The Kindness. The charity helps carers in a London borough, taking them to museums, galleries, gardens, organising music events and gatherings – more meaningful than clapping on a Thursday evening. Once every two months, Shambhu volunteers as an osteopath in the organisation Peace In The City. Through the Liberation Prison Project, he supports long-term prisoners, exchanging letters and teaching them mindfulness and meditation, bringing hope to dark places. He also teaches mindfulness to children in schools. He believes that small gestures can change lives, and he sees it every day.

Shambhu is not alone. In the UK, the non-profit sector employs 3.5 per cent of all paid workers, but it relies on the unpaid work of millions of volunteers. The report 'Time Well Spent' prepared by the National Council for Voluntary Organisations reports the results of a 2019 survey on volunteering experience. About 20 million people, two in five adults, volunteer every year. Forty per cent of them do it at least once a week. They do it in local organisations, whether in community centres, places of worship, schools, political headquarters, recreational or sports clubs. Volunteers raise money for cancer research or food for the homeless, mentor young children or visit older people, give water to the runners in the London marathon or Covid jabs in Nightingale hospitals, provide transport for disabled people, take care of the donkeys in the Donkey Sanctuary, clean the beaches, put out fires, organise political events or engage in human rights activism. They solve concrete problems and improve our societies immensely, outside of the marketplace or the structures imposed by bureaucrats. People volunteer to improve the world around them, to help others, or because they value a cause. The second main reason for volunteering is the availability of spare time. Part-time workers, students and retirees are more likely to volunteer than full-time workers. People spend twice the time volunteering at weekends. Lack of time is the main reason for people quitting volunteering or for not starting it in the first place. The book *4 Days, 40 Hours* reported that out of the people who moved to the compressed working week, 8 per cent joined a social club, 4 per cent engaged in political action and 10 per cent took part in church activities. The four-day working week will give people time to volunteer for the community and solve its problems in a different way.

Elinor Ostrom's work on institutions – the rules created by communities, markets or governments to organise the economy, particularly the ones on 'governing the commons' – was recognised by the Nobel committee in 2009. Elinor shared the view of *institutionalists*, a political economy doctrine that emphasises the role of history and socio-political factors in shaping economic practices. She may have won the Nobel Prize in economics, but she was clear that her discipline was not economics. According to her, social sciences were becoming silos, scientists were not working together, and worse, they couldn't understand each other. She was determined to change it. Her work was interdisciplinary. In her PhD committee there were academics from sociology, economics, engineering and political science. She did conquer all the methods of economists, from standard microeconomics, game theory, behavioural economics and laboratory experiments to statistics and econometrics, but she also did case studies, field studies and in-depth interviews, all methods that are not welcomed in economics, as they are considered 'too soft'. No economist responded to Schumpeter's call for methodological diversity with more conviction.

Perhaps because of her broad research methods, Elinor never felt she was an economist, but also economists never considered her as one of their own. One economist wrote on an anonymous website, when she died in 2012:

> The day I decide to read anyone outside modern economics, Ostrom might be one of the first, but as of now, other than broad understanding, her work does not inform my thinking or my work. I think I speak for mainstream economists when I say this. A nice lady and certainly a scholar. Just not to us.

The Nobel committee showed courage for a decision that raised many criticisms, but the statistics do not lie: Elinor Ostrom has more citations than Joseph Stiglitz, Robert Lucas and Christopher Pissarides combined, and the playing field was far from levelled. Elinor faced a double penalty in her career. First, being a woman is a penalty. In academia, women economists have a harder time publishing or being promoted. In the publishing process women are held to a higher standard and a paper co-authored between a man and a woman counts less for the woman's promotion committee. Papers submitted by women to *Econometrica* take six months longer to be reviewed than those by men. In the top forty US departments, women make up only 13 per cent of full professors, up from 2 per cent in 1972. In Harvard, the university of Schumpeter and Leontief, out of the forty-three senior members, only three are women. The Econometric Society feels like an exclusive gentlemen's club. Finding a woman in the list of members elected before 1980 is harder than finding a needle in a haystack. The share of females has increased but it is still embarrassingly small. Between 1990 and 2000, forty-four women were nominated to become fellows, competing with more than 1,000 men. The probability of being elected was 35 per cent for men and 27 per cent for women. In maths-intensive fields of research, only in economics is there evidence of gender inequality. Women economists earn less and are less likely to be chosen for keynote speeches compared to men. They face more hostile, aggressive and patronising questions in research seminars. In an anonymous survey of members of the American Economic Association, half of the women said they avoided speaking at a conference or seminar to guard against possible harassment, and many admitted having been sexually assaulted or victims of an attempted assault. As if this was not enough, women also face a penalty for thinking and doing things differently from men, and having different interests. Elinor's interdisciplinary work and her methodological diversity were seen by economists as too different, which explains why she was never a member of the Econometric Society. When she was the head of the department in Indiana – the first ever woman – she waived the extra salary because the department was struggling to hire junior faculty. She never had the arrogance and the alpha-male behaviour that is common among economists. At the time of her death in 2012, Nobel Laureate Kenneth Arrow wrote about Elinor:

Ostrom was a great human being and one of the most egalitarian academics that we have ever known. She never had to display her brilliance – she was not interested in display or prestige and only in understanding important problems more deeply. She was especially welcoming and nurturing of young people, and she was a frequent and gracious hostess to those people who wanted to visit and learn from her. Indeed, she always made them, and all with whom she interacted, feel that she was grateful for the opportunity to learn from them. She was persuasive in communicating this view, because she truly believed it herself.

Elinor Ostrom represents much of what economics is lacking: diversity, an interdisciplinary view, and openness to different methodologies. Of the ninety-one Nobel Laureates since its inception until 2023, only six were not white men: three women, Elinor Ostrom, Esther Duflo and Claudia Goldin; one black economist, Sir William Arthur Lewis; and two economists of Indian origin, Abhijit Banerjee and Amartya Sen. This is probably not a bias of the Nobel committee; it reflects a wider problem within the profession. Besides being dominated by men, economics is too centred in the US. Out of the sixty-seven Laureates since 1990, only twenty-one were not born in the US and only five spent most of their careers in a university outside the US. There was more variety in the early days. The first ten Nobel Prize Laureates were based in Norway, Sweden, the United Kingdom, the US, Austria and the Soviet Union.

You can argue that economics is not much different from other male-dominated sciences like physics or mathematics, but the consequences are dramatically different. Economics is not just losing 'brains' by excluding women; the science is forming a biased view of society, the central problems it faces and how to solve them. A falling rock is a falling rock for a Marxist or a liberal. But shortening the working week is not the same for Keynes or Schumpeter, men or women, a black or a white person, French or American. The lack of diversity impoverishes economics and contributes to the accumulation of the 'sins of omission'. To publish in the best journals and progress in their careers, the best academics from around the world choose topics that are fashionable in the US or look at US data, instead of answering questions that are relevant for their own countries or using other data. Twenty per cent of researchers are based in the US, but half of the research is on the US. The white-male view means that many economic and social issues are ignored. Juanjo Dolado, an eminent Spanish labour economist, has compiled data on the top fifty economics departments. Out of 1,900 faculty, only 15 per cent were women, but this share varied by field of research. Women represented 20 to 25 per cent of economists studying wages and income, economics of education, health care, demographics, social security, labour markets, unemployment and public goods. In contrast, they represented fewer than 10 per cent of economists studying financial markets and institutions, asset pricing, portfolio choice, monetary economics, public finance, corporate finance, general equilibrium, fluctuations and business cycles, and non-cooperative games. Which of the two previous lists is more down-to-earth? Another study found that American male and female economists have different views on many labour market issues, with women having more favourable views of regulation, minimum wage, labour standards, health insurance and redistribution.

The difficulties that female economists face are similar to those that all women face in their professional lives. They earn lower wages for similar jobs because employers think they won't work as hard as men, or that they will quit or to move to part-time after having children, or because of pure discrimination. They work a double shift, caring for their children and their parents after work. If they switch to part-time, they lose salary and promotion opportunities. They are more likely to be sexually assaulted or bullied. Even in statistics, women suffer a penalty. In 2016, the value of the

UK's unpaid household service work, ignored in GDP, was esti-mated at £1.24 trillion, 63 per cent of GDP. According to a 2015 UK time-use survey, women work twenty-seven hours at home, while men only do sixteen hours. Among households with children, mothers work forty hours at home, double that of fathers.

The gender imbalance in the economy and in economics is important in my case for the four-day working week. First, it explains why economists haven't shown interest in the idea. Women are more likely to support it. A 2020 survey asking Canadians whether they should implement a four-day working week found that 47 per cent of men and 59 per cent of women thought it was a good idea. It is no coincidence that in 60 per cent of the companies that were interested in the pilot project in Portugal, the person who contacted us was a woman (when women represent only 27 per cent of leadership positions in Portuguese companies). The minister who decided to study the four-day week is a woman. The team I worked with had seven women. All the reporters covering the topic in the main media channels are women. If women are marginalised in economics and the economy, so is the support for the four-day week. Adding the US domination, economics becomes even more suspicious of government regulation and less appreciative of leisure.

The second aspect is that the four-day working week can con-tribute to the gender balance in the economy. This is the claim of feminists like Vicki Schultz, a professor of law and social sci-ences at Yale Law School, who have called for a reduced working week in the US. She argues that a society divided between those who are overworked and those who are underutilised is penal-ising women. Overworked men push women to cut back their own hours, to devote more to home. On the other hand, if women don't have a choice and are pushed to work less, their partners are forced to work longer. Schultz is one of the many academ-ics who view the four-day working week as a way to empower women, increasing their bargaining power, at work and at home, and endowing men with the time to devote to their families, all crucial to achieve a better gender balance. Women will suffer less discrimination and encounter more equal opportunities in their full-time work. Women who aren't working will come across more part-time employment opportunities. These were also the theoretical arguments expressed by Samuelson in 1970, and which find support in the experience of Andrew Barnes. He found that the four-day working week was a level playing field for men and women, as women returning from maternity leave would usually negotiate switching to part-time work. For example, Barnes talks of a male worker who picked up his son from school for the first time. The Reykjavík shorter working time experiment drove men to participate more in home duties. One woman commented that working less 'increases the potential for women to be able to properly participate in the job market, instead of always being on the run, trying to cram everything into their schedules. This enhances gender quality, mental health, family life and relationships with the children.' One man testified, 'I often use the extra hours to clean at home, and without hesitation if I'm alone there [...] So I participate much more in cleaning and tasks around the house.' The four-day working week won't change mentalities overnight. Some men will have more free time but won't take on more duties at home. But, at least in their professional lives, women will be placed on a more equal footing.

Claudia Goldin, an American economist and historian from Harvard, was awarded the 2023 Nobel Prize for her research on women's labour market outcomes, a rare instance when the committee recognised the subject matter studied rather than a methodological contribution. Goldin's research documented the underrepresentation of women in high-earning careers and the large financial penalty they face due to motherhood. While childbirth often leads to large and lasting drops in mothers' earnings, men's careers are unaffected by parenthood. Goldin uncovered the main factor contributing to the motherhood penalty: the compensation of family-unfriendly working conditions. High-earnings occupations disproportionately reward long hours and continuous labour market engagement, and penalise career breaks. Examining pay schedules across occupations, she finds that sectors that embraced greater flexibility reduced the gender pay gap, compared to those promoting a long-hours culture, particularly in corporate, financial, and legal sectors. Changes in work organisation driven by policy interventions regulating part-time and flexible work, but also to initiatives by firms recognising the benefits of attracting and retaining female talent, can reduce gender imbalance in the labour market.

Gender imbalance is more than a social or a feminist issue; it is also a serious economic problem. According to the International Monetary Fund, eliminating gender inequalities would boost the world GDP by 35 per cent. Part of the costs are due to the problem of misallocation of resources. Economists study misallocation, in the context of entrepreneurship. A company in the hands of the grandson of the founder is an example of misallocation, because the grandson is not necessarily the best person to run it just because he inherited it. The reverse of the problem is the entrepreneur with a good concept who is unable to set up a company because she doesn't have enough funds. To address the problem of misallocation, economists, inspired by Schumpeter, pushed for financial reforms that promote better functioning credit and financial markets, to allow funds to reach the hands of the best entrepreneurs. The uneven fight of women also generates misallocation. In the UK only one in three entrepreneurs are women, meaning more than one million missing businesses. A report commissioned by HM Treasury estimates that up to £250 billion, more than 10 per cent of GDP, could be added to the UK economy if women started and scaled new businesses at the same rate as men. Research shows that companies with more gender-balanced boards of directors are more successful, and that a pound invested in developing women's enterprise provides a greater return than a pound invested in developing male-owned enterprises. Whatever the source of the entrepreneurship gap, whether it is due to the fact that women work the double shift and have less leisure time to devote to their passion, or because women are more afraid of failure, the four-day working week, by giving women more time to develop a business while keeping their job, will foster their entrepreneurship.

One period when women have their two shifts reduced to one is during maternity leave, and some women take advantage of this to develop or launch their businesses. 'Thinking of starting your own business? Maternity leave's the time to go for it,' is the title of an article on the internet forum *Made for Mums*. It continues: 'Always dreamed of starting your own company, but never had the time (or money) to do it? Well, your new pregnancy may be just the nudge you needed to kick-start those yet-to-be-fulfilled ambitions ...' Commonly they bet on e-commerce using platforms like Amazon or eBay, arts and crafts using Etsy, or on network marketing. Babies' clothes and related accessories brands like SweetDreamers, Blade & Rose, Gumigem, Funky Giraffe Bibs, Little Ducklings Boutique, Skip Hop, Cheeky Chompers and Bag All Done were started by mums during maternity leave.

Elinor Ostrom believed that a 'core goal of public policy should be to facilitate the development of institutions that bring out the best in humans'. She also taught us that we should look beyond right and left, markets and government, for solutions to our problems and start shaping our institutions to work for everyone, men and women. I cannot find a better description of the four-day working week.

Conclusion

A Bridge

'The ideas of economists and political philosophers, both when they are right and when they are wrong, are more powerful than is commonly understood. Indeed, the world is ruled by little else. Practical men, who believe themselves to be quite exempt from any intellectual influences, are usually slaves of some defunct economist.'

John Maynard Keynes

How do you feel when you have a three-day weekend? You rest more. You invite your friends for a barbecue. Maybe you go swimming, cycling or running. You travel or you go to the cinema. You watch a masterclass. Do you volunteer or do a bit of work like I do? You spend more time with your family. You spend less time with your family. Whatever you do, chances are that you are happier. What if every weekend had three days? Throughout the book I have avoided philosophical arguments about the good life or happiness, a concept that most economists distrust because it is vague and subjective. Economists prefer to focus on the economy. Whatever you choose to do, you will be contributing, directly or indirectly, to the economy.

The four-day working week, I have argued, will fuel the economy by raising consumer spending in leisure industries. It will reduce the pressures on mental health and improve the efficiency of workers during their work time, and push managers to change processes in a way that will accelerate technological adoption and increase productivity. It will foster innovation unlike any other measure because it will give people time to devote to their passion. It will mitigate technological unemployment and reduce inequality. It will improve the coordination of economic activity, give people more freedom to decide how much to work and, by sharing the gains of economic growth among everyone rather than a minority, it will reconcile a polarised society and protect the economy from the risks brought about by populist movements. The four-day working week is more than an economic policy or a win for workers – it is a powerful social innovation.

Shortening the working week will benefit everyone in the economy, but some more than others. Women who now face the high costs of going part-time will be placed on a more equal footing with men. Young workers, scourged by higher unemployment and low prospects, will find more opportunities to gain labour market experience at the weekends. Older workers will more easily prolong their working life, keeping social security systems sustainable. Workers will have the carrot; capitalists will face the stick. But capitalists will not lose with a better capitalism. Leisure industries will offer profit opportunities and new businesses will appear to satisfy the increasing demand. Other firms will emerge from the passion and free time of anonymous people, who will become our future business leaders and drive creative destruction, the essence of capitalism. Alternative scenarios, with populists harming the economy, or with expensive measures to reduce technological unemployment, fight inequality or stimulate aggregate demand, are much worse for entrepreneurs and capital owners. The biggest winner will be the economy. It will become leaner, freer, less wasteful and more innovative, and will work for everyone.

The economic problems societies are facing today are akin to a Rubik's cube. The boilerplate policies that the same old schools of thought propose, like trickle-down economics, deregulating markets, Keynesian stimulus, central bank intervention and giving people money, can improve one side of the cube, but will make the other sides worse. We must look elsewhere for solutions, and fast. The four-day working week won't solve all our economic problems, but surely it is one step to align all the surfaces of our cube. It is urgent, because the danger of breakdown of the system is all too real. We are at a stage where only radical thought can prevent unpredictable extremist change.

The pandemic, amid all the economic devastation, brought a unique opportunity. Our lives as they were before the pandemic are gone. And so is the status quo, offering an unprecedented opportunity because the world – workers, firms and politicians – are open to new institutions and new forms of organisation. The cost of implementing the four-day week, because of the disruption of the status quo, is now at its lowest, and its gains are at their highest. Now is not the time for incremental change, minor reforms or antiquated policies. Now is the time for a paradigm shift.

The criticisms levelled against the four-day working week come in three packages. First is the timeless ethical argument that leisure is a sin and people are better off working, which has no grounds in economic theory. The idolisation of working and the stigmatisation of consumption are pure economic schizophrenia, because they are two sides of the same coin.

Second are the criticisms that assume only one form of adjustment towards the four-day working week: wage cuts, additional hours in the remaining days, profit reduction, price increases or government subsidies. The four-day working week can be operationalised with a combination of eight adjustments, notably productivity and time, which can be shaped by different players and guarantee a smooth transition.

The final set of criticisms, instead of debating the pros and cons of the proposal, turn it into a debate between ideologies. Ignoring its multidimensionality as a social innovation, the critics first narrow the case for the four-day working week to only one reason, and then enter a sterile argument between schools of economic thought on the workings of the economy. One typical example is centring the case on whether it will reduce unemployment. In the 1964 US Congress hearings, Herbert R. Northrup, a professor of industry at the University of Pennsylvania, started his testimony by defining: 'The nature of the problem [...] is to what extent will a reduction of weekly hours [...] reduce unemployment.' As I have explained, different schools of thought hold different opinions about whether unemployment will go down after shortening the working week, which is why Marx made the point and not Schumpeter. Economics is not an exact science and economists disagree on the workings of the economy – that is our nature. But not being Marxist shouldn't automatically force you to reject the four-day working week. Supply-side economists, conservative and liberal critics probably do not agree that the four-day working week will lower unemployment (some don't even believe unemployment exists), but they should discuss instead the arguments that the four-day week will raise productivity, foster technological adoption, unleash innovation and entrepreneurship, promote freedom and counteract populist movements.

Throughout the book, you might have gotten the impression that some of my arguments clash with each other, beyond the economic doctrines. If people moonlight with a second job, they won't rest much, and their efficiency will not increase. If they enrol on the Graduate Diploma in Economics at Birkbeck, they won't start their own company. If they volunteer on Fridays, they won't go for city breaks and splash out some money. I don't expect everyone to do everything. People will be given time and freedom to choose what to do with it. People will choose what is best for them and that is usually what is best for the economy. If you are on the verge of burnout, you will rest more over the weekend. If you have higher income, you will spend more. If you don't, you will drive an Uber. If you feel your job is in danger, you will retrain. If you have an idea lingering in your head, you will try to make it real. This is the beauty of our system and why freedom and capitalism are the most powerful combination for human prosperity.

I supported my arguments on the authority of the greatest economists and Nobel Prize winners, by my count about thirty of them, using them as scaffolding to build my narrative. I did so to persuade you. Otherwise, these would just be the arguments of an unknown young economist – what does he know about the economy? But how much authority should we place on these economists? In his speech at the 1974 Nobel Prize banquet, Friedrich Hayek said:

> Yet I must confess that if I had been consulted whether to establish a Nobel Prize in economics, I should have decidedly advised against it. [...] It is that the Nobel Prize confers on an individual an authority which in economics no man ought to possess. This does not matter in the natural sciences. Here the influence exercised by an individual is chiefly an influence on his fellow experts; and they will soon cut him down to size if he exceeds his competence. But the influence of the economist that mainly matters is an influence over laymen: politicians, journalists, civil servants and the public generally. There is no reason why a man who has made a distinctive contribution to economic science should be omnicompetent on all problems of society – as the press tends to treat him till in the end he may himself be persuaded to believe. One is even made to feel it a public duty to pronounce on problems to which one may not have devoted special attention. I am not sure that it is desirable to strengthen the influence of a few individual economists by such a ceremonial and eye-catching recognition of achievements, perhaps of the distant past.

Gunnar Myrdal, who disagreed with Hayek on so many things, was as fierce a critic of the Nobel Prize. I know of several Nobel

Laureates who are clueless about the economy. I have attended one talk where a Nobel Prize winner claimed the Great Recession was caused by a self-fulfilling expectation of an increase in regulation imposed by Barack Obama, in response to the crisis, years before Obama was elected. Flabbergasting! I have a great admiration for the macroeconomist's methodological contribution, but such a view of the economy is nothing short of ridiculous. As Hayek warned, the influence of Nobel Laureates over the public can be dangerous.

Plus, although we tend to sanctify all these brilliant minds, they have many skeletons in their closets. Hayek, so worried about the rise of authoritarianism, later in his career endorsed the Pinochet regime in Chile, saying he preferred 'a liberal dictator to a democratic government lacking in liberalism'. He also sent his book *The Constitution of Liberty* to the Portuguese fascist-inspired dictator Salazar, to help him 'design a constitution which is proof against the abuses of democracy'. Marx called Mexicans lazy. Keynes once wrote to his former lover that he wanted to 'rape an undergraduate in the Combination Room' to shake the Cambridge establishment. Both would qualify for Trump's locker-room. Henry Ford received the Grand Cross of the German Eagle from Nazi officials in 1938, and the newspaper he owned was full of anti-Semitic articles. Adolf Hitler described Ford as the leader of US Fascism, and had a picture of his automobile on his office wall. James Meade was a strong believer in eugenics and was the treasurer of the Eugenic Society. Many of these economists were racist, anti-Semitic, egotistical and dismissive of women's intellect.

Why should we trust their views on the shortening of the working week? We should not believe them because they are Nobel Laureates or great economists. We should believe the power of their ideas, the only thing that matters. We should implement the four-day week not because Samuelson, Leontief and Meade supported the reduction of the working week, but because it is a social innovation that will free people, raise efficiency, reduce technological unemployment and inequality, and liberate women. We should implement it through government legislation not because it was accepted by Hayek or defended by Hicks, but because of their insight that firms and workers don't fully grasp the benefits that working less will bring to society and that a shortening of the working week will enhance competition. We should not do it because Keynes and Schumpeter saw it as the natural evolution of a growing economy, but because people do want to share the gains of economic growth by consuming more and enjoying more leisure. We should do it not because Henry Ford shortened the working week for his workers, but because he showed it can raise productivity and he exemplified the innovation that could arise from more time devoted to one's passion. Their ideas about the economic gains of shortening the work week stand tall, long after they are dead. We don't need any scaffolding. The power of the four-day week comes from the different mechanisms that show how this social innovation can bring about a renewal of the economy and make for a better capitalism.

Above all, they show that the four-day week can bridge opposite views of the economy and build a consensus – the coming together of the Yin and the Yang. That is the final, truly amazing lesson that we can learn from the fascinating characters in this book. Samuelson, the dull centrist who preferred to unite rather than polarise, wrote about Bertil Ohlin:

> I was told forty years ago that when Gunnar Myrdal and Bertil Ohlin chose different political parties, they resolved not to let this lead to personal bitterness of scientific dispute in the manner of their elders, Cassel, Bagge, Heckscher, and Wicksell. As far as the testimony of my own experience is concerned, such a pact was never broken. In any case, the force of this example has been important in my own life. Over what will soon be five decades, Milton Friedman and I have had some occasions to disagree on policy choices and doctrines, without that affecting our friendly relations. Not only is this better for manners and for the liver, it also makes for better science.

Keynes and Hayek had much respect, mutual admiration and friendship. Schumpeter and Frisch, even further apart ideologically and academically, had an even closer friendship. Elinor Ostrom ignored the markets and the government to forge her own path. Senator Eugene McCarthy, a strong Democrat who met with Che Guevara in New York, years later voted for Ronald Reagan. Jon Huntsman Jr always believed in working with the other side, and served President Obama as well as four Republican presidents. They all teach a lesson about coming together. Our ideology should be an anchor, not a chain that prevents us from seeing the world from a different angle. The problems we are facing are too difficult to think that only one side has the monopoly of the best solutions. The world has been polarising for too long. The four-day week can forge the bridge that we desperately need.

A Leap of Faith

'The success of everything depends on intuition, the capacity of seeing things in a way which afterwards proved to be true, even though it cannot be established at the moment, and of grasping the essential fact, discarding the unessential even though one can give no account of the principles by which this is done.'

Joseph Schumpeter

At 10 a.m. on 31 August 2012, I was standing in swimming shorts on a pier on the European side of the Strait of the Dardanelles in Turkey, ready to face my biggest challenge: swim from Europe to Asia. Inspired by Lord Byron, the first person in the modern age to swim across the strait in 1810, a race is celebrated annually. The 1km that separates the two continents is impossible to swim directly because of the strong current, so the race starts 3km upstream. That day wasn't the best to swim across the Dardanelles, we were told during the induction twenty-four hours earlier. Adding to the treacherous currents, heavy winds would make the sea very choppy. As I stood on the pier, waiting to jump, the only question in my mind was: can I do it?

I started learning to swim at the age of 6, and I hated it. I had developed asthma two years before, with frequent overnight visits to the hospital to get oxygen. My parents forced me to take on swimming. I struggled to cross the 25m swimming pool, gasping for air with every stroke. My only comfort was backstroke, which came seldom after several lengths of terrifying front crawl. I grew out of the asthma, but the swimming became part of me.

The jump from the pier into the water was a leap of faith, not in God, but in me. I wasn't sure I would make it, but I trusted myself and I wasn't scared. I had trained for months, ten weekly hours of swimming. A few weeks before the race, I spent days hopping Greek islands with a friend, swimming in open waters continuously for one or two hours. As the race started, I had to adapt to the rough conditions, starting with breaststroke to cut the tireless waves and only switching to front crawl later in the race. It was lonely. Within minutes, the 400 participants disappeared from sight, swimming at different paces or more against or in favour of the current depending on their fear of ending up in the Aegean Sea. I just kept going, stroke after stroke, convinced that I had it within me to finish – and I did. It took me two hours to swim across the Dardanelles. Lord Byron wrote about his crossing: 'I plume myself on this achievement more than I could possibly do on any kind of glory, political, poetical or rhetorical.' I feel the words of Byron as my own. Reaching the Asian shore in Canakkale was my life's biggest achievement, one that a 6-year-old asthmatic boy could never have dreamt possible, and even in those moments standing on the European shore before jumping it was anything but certain.

Societies also progress through leaps of faith. These leaps of faith are associated with doing something for the first time, something that has its risks, but which has been studied in detail and is backed by science. It was a leap of faith when Vasco da Gama embarked, on 8 July 1497, on a journey, sailing to India for the first time with a small fleet of four boats. It was a leap of faith for himself and his men, but also in the cartography, astronomy and navigation skills of the Portuguese, which at the time were second to none. It was a leap of faith when Charles A. Lindbergh piloted, on 21 May 1927, the first solo, nonstop transatlantic flight in history, in the *Spirit of St Louis*. It was a leap of faith when the Americans launched *Apollo 11* to send men to the moon – one based on the US capacity in engineering, mathematics and astrophysics.

Ultimately, implementing the four-day working week across the entire economy is also a leap of faith – faith in the science of economics. Can I tell you with precision that wages are going to grow by 6 per cent, inequality shrink by 2 per cent, technological unemployment fall by 4 per cent, the share of votes in nationalistic parties collapse to 1 per cent, private consumption accelerate by 3 per cent? No. None of the effects are seriously quantifiable because we cannot predict exactly what people will do with their extra time, or how the economy is going to adjust. Economics can help us understand what trends to expect, but any quantification is nothing more than a guess. I have explained the reasons for shortening the working week, but in the end, we need the courage to jump into the unknown. As Keynes explained with his usual brilliance, we shouldn't be afraid:

> There is no reason why we should not feel ourselves free to be bold, to be open, to experiment, to take action, to try the possibilities of things. And over against us, standing in the path, there is nothing but a few old gentlemen tightly buttoned-up in their frock coats, who only need to be treated with a little friendly disrespect and bowled over like ninepins. Quite likely they will enjoy it themselves, when once they have got over the shock.

A long bowling alley lies ahead. We first need people like you, interested, thoughtful and with enough grit to finish reading this book, to be ambassadors for the four-day week, whether you are left- or right-leaning. We need pressure from below, with more people taking on part-time roles and more firms adopting the management practice. Join the 4 Day Week Campaign. Send an email to your MP supporting the idea, explaining the reasons why (those more in line with your MP's ideology) and telling your story about what you and your family would do with the extra day and how that would contribute to the economy. Feel free to recommend my book. Second, we need someone to fill Henry Ford's shoes – a great entrepreneur at the helm of a large firm who can see what Henry Ford saw and have the audacity he had, to show the world that the four-day week is more than a gimmick used by a few small firms for publicity. Third, we need more economists, like Samuelson or Leontief, to push for the four-day working week. I am sorry to disappoint you, but I am no Samuelson. Maybe this book will persuade some to embrace the idea. Fourth, unions must return to their glory days and rally behind this idea, but be open to make concessions on how it is implemented. Finally, we need politicians with the vision of Jon Huntsman, the values and the courage of Eugene McCarthy, and the power of Richard Nixon, to make the same leap of faith President Franklin Roosevelt made when implementing the five-day week. Jeremy Corbyn, a British politician and former leader of the opposition, was not the one. It must come from the centre. Jacinda Ardern and Sanna Marin, former prime ministers of New Zealand and Finland, talked about the four-day working week, but more politicians need to be persuaded to get the ball rolling. The bowling alley ahead might be long and narrow, but as I realised when writing this book, the more you study and think about the four-day week, the more persuaded you are by the idea. So, I am sure that sooner or later, we will do it. We will bowl down those pins. Friday will become the new Saturday.

The six-day week was the epitome of the nineteenth century. The five-day week was the epitome of the twentieth century. The four-day week will be the epitome of the twenty-first century. Once we achieve it this book will seem useless, but don't rush to sell it on eBay. Please leave it quietly on your bookshelf. When you get older, pass it on to your grandchildren. It might become useful again at the turn of the next century, when the first firms start operating on a three-day week and critics respond: 'it is a utopia, we have always worked four days!'

Classroom

Friday is the New Saturday is not meant to be an academic book. Unshackled, I avoided breaking the flow of the reading with endless footnotes explaining minor exceptions, and parentheses with proper citations behind every statement or quote. Most quotes, you can find easily by googling them together with the author's name. I used Wikipedia a lot. In this classroom, you can find the main references used in each chapter, related to working hours and the shortening of the working week. On my webpage (sites.google.com/view/pedromaiagomes), I include the following list of references with the links to be found on the internet.

Chapter 1

4 Days, 40 Hours, edited by Riva Poor, Pan Books, 1970.
The Four-Day Workweek, Robert Grosse, Routledge, 2018.
The 4 Day Week, Andrew Barnes with Stephanie Jones, Piatkus, 2020.

A Shorter Workweek in 1980s, William McGaughey, Thistlerose Publications, 1981.

Nonfinancial Economics: The Case for Shorter Hours of Work, William McGaughey and Eugene McCarthy, Praeger, 1989.

'The Superiority of Economists', Y. Algan, M. Fourcade, and E. Ollion, *Journal of Economic Perspectives*, 29(1), pp.89–114, 2015.

Samuelson's page in the Nobel Prize Archive.

Chapter 2

'The Five Day Week', William Green, *The North American Review*, 223(883), pp.566–74, 1927.

The Five-Day Week in Manufacturing Industries, National Industrial Conference Board, 1929.

'The 5-Day Week in the Ford Plants', Henry Ford, *Monthly Labor Review*, 23(6), pp.10–14, 1926.

'In Defense of the Longer Work Week', Harold Moulton, *The Annals of the American Academy of Political and Social Science*, 184, pp.68–71, 1936.

Hours of Work, edited by C. Dankert, F. Mann and H. Northrup, Harper & Row, 1965.

How to Achieve Shorter Working Hours, Lord Skidelsky, Progressive Economic Forum, 2019.

In Praise of Idleness and Other Essays, Bertrand Russell, George Allen & Unwin Ltd, 1935.

'The 40-Hour Week', *The Economist*, 20 June 1936, p.666, *The Economist Historical Archive, 1843–2015*.

Chapter 3

'Teamworking and Organizational Performance: A Review of Survey-Based Research', A. Delarue, G. Van-Hootegem, S. Procter, and M. Burridge, *International Journal of Management Reviews*, 10(2), pp.127–48, 2008.

'Where Has the Time Gone? Addressing Collaboration Overload in a Networked Economy', Rob Cross and Peter Gray, *California Management Review*, 56(1), pp.50–66, 2013.

'Coordination of Hours within the Firm', Claudio Labanca and Dario Pozzoli, *IZA Discussion Paper* 12062, 2018.

'Time as a Network Good: Evidence from Unemployment and the Standard Workweek', Cristobal Young and Chaeyoon Lim, *Sociological Science*, 1, pp.10–27, 2014.

'Time Inseparable Labor Productivity and the Workweek', Maya Eden, *The Scandinavian Journal of Economics*, 2021.

'Work and Leisure in the U.S. and Europe: Why So Different', A. Alesina, E. Glaeser and B. Sacerdote (Section 5.2), *NBER Macroeconomics Annual*, 20, pp.1–100, 2006.

'Following the Crowd: Leisure Complementarities Beyond the Household', S. George-Kot, D. Goux, and E. Maurin, *Journal of Labour Economics*, 35(4), pp.1061–88, 2017.

'Nobody to Play With? The Implications of Leisure Coordination', Stephen Jenkins and Lars Osberg, in *The Economics of Time Use*, edited by D. Hamermesh and G. Pfan, 2005.

'Does Wife's Labor Supply Influence Labor Force Participation of her Elderly Husband? Lessons from France', Idriss Fontaine, *Applied Economics*, 2021.

'The Astonishing Human Potential Wasted on Commutes', Christopher Ingraham, *The Washington Post*, 25 February 2016.

'Trends in Commuting Time of European Workers: A Cross-Country Analysis', J. Giménez-Nadal, J. Alberto Molina and J. Velilla, *IZA Discussion Paper* 12916, 2020.

'Stress that Doesn't Pay: The Commuting Paradox', Alois Stutzer and Bruno Frey, *The Scandinavian Journal of Economics*, 110(2), pp.339–66, 2008.

'Does Commuting Affect Health?' Annemarie Künn-Nelen, *Health Economics*, 25(8), pp.984–1004, 2016.

Chapter 4

'Labor Supply of New York City Cabdrivers: One Day at a Time', C. Camerer, L. Babcock, G. Loewenstein, and Richard Thaler, *Quarterly Journal of Economics* 112(2), pp.407–41, 1997.

'Do Workers Work More if Wages are High? Evidence from a Randomized Field Experiment', Ernst Fehr and Lorenz Goette, *American Economic Review*, 97(1), pp.298–317, 2007.

'Does Labor Legislation Benefit Workers? Well-Being After an Hours Reduction', D. Hamermesh, D. Kawaguchi and J. Lee, *Journal of the Japanese and International Economies*, 44, pp.1–12, 2017.

'The Effect of Adult Children's Working Hours on Visits to Elderly Parents: Evidence from the Reduction in Korea's Legal Workweek', E. Kim, C. Lee and Y. Do, *Population Research and Policy Review*, 38, pp.53–72, 2019.

'Sins of Omission and the Practice of Economics', George Akerlof,
    Journal of Economic Literature, 58(2), pp.405–18, 2020.
Frisch's page in the Nobel Prize Archive.

Chapter 5

'Economic Possibilities for our Grandchildren', John Maynard Keynes,
    Essays in Persuasion, Macmillan & Co., 1930.
John Maynard Keynes 1883–1946: Economist, Philosopher, Statesman,
    Robert Skidelsky, Paperback, London, Penguin (Non-Classics), 2005.
'The Times they are Not Changin': Days and Hours of Work in Old and
    New Worlds, 1870–2000', Michael Huberman and Chris Minns,
    Explorations in Economic History, 44, pp.538–67, 2007.
Hours of Work, Hearings Before the Select Subcommittee of Labor of
    the Committee on Education and Labor, House of Representatives,
    Eighty-Eighth congress. Statement by Mr Ira Nunn, pp.411–15, US
    Government Printing Office, 1963.

Chapter 6

The General Theory of Employment, Interest and Money, John Maynard
    Keynes, Macmillan, 1936.
John Maynard Keynes 1883–1946: Economist, Philosopher, Statesman,
    Robert Skidelsky, Paperback, London, Penguin (Non-Classics), 2005.
'The 5-Day Week in the Ford Plants', Henry Ford, *Monthly Labor Review*,
    23(6), pp.10–14, 1926.
'Recent Growth of Paid Leisure for U.S. Workers', Peter Henle, *Monthly
    Labor Review* 85(3), pp.249–57, 1962.
'The Causes of Japan's "Lost Decade": The Role of Household
    Consumption', Charles Y. Horioka, *Japan and the World Economy*,
    18(4), pp.378–400, 2006.
'The Paradox of Toil', Gauti Eggertsson, Federal Reserve Bank of New
    York Staff Reports, 2010.
'Secular Stagnation: Theory and Remedies', Jean-Baptiste Michau,
    Journal of Economic Theory, 176, pp.552–618, 2018.

Chapter 7

Prophet of Innovation: Joseph Schumpeter and Creative Destruction,
    Thomas K. McCraw, The Belknap Press, 2007.

History of Economic Analysis, Joseph A. Schumpeter, edited from manuscript by Elizabeth Boody Schumpeter, Oxford University Press, 1954.

The Macroeconomist as Scientist and Engineer, Gregory Mankiw, 2006.

'The 5-Day Week in the Ford Plants', Henry Ford, *Monthly Labor Review*, 23(6), pp.10–14, 1926.

Diminishing Returns at Work: The Consequences of Long Working Hours, John Pencavel, Oxford University Press, 2018.

'Recovery from Work and the Productivity of Working Hours', John Pencavel, *Economica*, 83(332), pp.545–63, 2016.

'Working Hours and Productivity', Marion Collewet, Jan Sauermann, *Labour Economics*, 47, pp.96–106, 2017.

'Time Inseparable Labor Productivity and the Workweek', Maya Eden, *Scandinavian Journal of Economics*, 2021.

'The Effect of Work Hours on Adverse Events and Errors in Health Care', Danielle Olds and Sean Clarke, *Journal of Safety Research*, 41(2), pp.153–62, 2010.

'Extended Work Shifts and the Risk of Motor Vehicle Crashes Among Interns', L.K. Barger, B.E. Cade, N.T. Ayas, J.W. Cronin, B. Rosner, F.E. Speizer, C.A. Czeisler and Harvard Work Hours, Health, and Safety Group, *New England Journal of Medicine*, 352(2), pp.125–34, 2005.

'The Impact of Overtime and Long Work Hours on Occupational Injuries and Illnesses: New Evidence from the United States', A. Dembe, J. Erickson, R. Delbos and S. Banks, *Occupational and Environmental Medicine*, 62(9), pp.588–97, 2005.

'The Working Hours of Hospital Staff Nurses and Patient Safety', A. Rogers, W. Hwang, L. Scott, L. Aiken and D. Dinges, *Health Affairs*, 23(4), pp.202–12, 2004.

'Extended Work Hours and Risk of Acute Occupational Injury: A Case-Crossover Study of Workers in Manufacturing', S. Vegso, L. Cantley, M. Slade, O. Taiwo, K. Sircar, P. Rabinowitz, M. Fiellin, M.B. Russi and M. Cullen, *American Journal of Industrial Medicine*, 50(8), pp.597–603, 2007.

Work-Related Stress, Anxiety or Depression Statistics in Great Britain, Health and Safety Executive, 2019.

'Nearly 80% of Employees Say this One Thing is more Stressful than Having Too Much Work', *Forbes*, 14 August 2019.

www.mentalhealth.org.uk/statistics/mental-health-statistics-global-and-nationwide-costs.

'National Health Costs Could Decrease if Managers Reduce Work Stress', Michael Blanding, Harvard Business School.

*Why Sleep Matters: The Economic Costs of Insufficient Sleep. A
    Cross-Country Comparative Analysis*, M. Hafner, M. Stepanek,
    J. Taylor, W.M. Troxel and C. van Stol, Rand Corporation, 2016.
'Japan Wakes Up to Sleep Shortage Problems', Leo Lewis, *Financial
    Times*, 20 November 2018.
'Stressed, Tired, Rushed: A Portrait of the Modern Family', *New York
    Times*, 4 November 2015.
The Four-Day Workweek, Robert Grosse, Routledge, 2018.
The 4 Day Week, Andrew Barnes with Stephanie Jones, Piatkus, 2020.
*Shorter: How Working Less Will Revolutionize the Way your Company Gets
    Things Done*, Alex Soojung-Kim Pang, Penguin Random House, 2020.
4 Days, 40 Hours, edited by Riva Poor, Pan Books, 1970.
'The Four-Day Week: An AMA Research Report', K.E. Wheeler,
    D. Tarnowieski and R. Gurman, American Management Association,
    1972.
'The Effects of Working Time on Productivity and Firm Performance:
    A Research Synthesis Paper', Lonnie Golden, *Conditions of Work and
    Employment Series* No. 33, International Labour Organization, 2012.
'Technology and Labour Regulations', Alberto Alesina and Joseph Zeira,
    NBER Working Paper 12581, 2006.
'Automating Labor: Evidence from Firm-level Patent Data',
    A. Dechezlepretre, D. Hemous, M. Olsen and C. Zanella, *CEP
    Discussion Paper* 1679, 2020.
'Demand Shocks that Look Like Productivity Shocks', Y. Bai,
    K. Storesletten and J. Rios-Rull, 2011.
'Success Of A Five-Day Week Experiment', *The Times*, 6 November 1934,
    p.16. *The Times Digital Archive*.
'Second 5-Day Week Coal Output', *The Times*, 21 May 1947, p.4. *The
    Times Digital Archive*.

Chapter 8

'Aristotle on Leisure', Joseph Owens, *Canadian Journal of Philosophy*,
    11(4), pp.713–23, 1981.
'Should I Quit my Day Job? A Hybrid Path to Entrepreneurship', Joseph
    Raffiee and Jie Feng, *Academy of Management Journal*, 57(4), 2013.
'Entrepreneurs, Don't Give Up Your Day Jobs (Yet)', *Wired*,
    19 February 2016.
'Henry Ford (1863–1947)', *Forbes*, 29 July 2005.
My Life and Work, Henry Ford, Digireads.com Publishing, 1922.

Mass Flourishing: How Grassroots Innovation Created Jobs, Challenge, and Change, Edmund S. Phelps, Princeton University Press, 2013.

We-Think: Mass innovation, Not Mass Production, Charles Leadbeater, Profile Books, 2009.

'Are Ideas Getting Harder to Find?', N. Bloom, C.I. Jones, J. Van Reenen and M. Webb, *American Economic Review*, 110(4), pp.1104–44, 2020.

In Praise of Idleness and Other Essays, Bertrand Russell, George Allen & Unwin Ltd, 1935.

Chapter 9

'The 35-Hour Workweek in France: Straightjacket or Welfare Improvement?', Marcello Estevão and Filipa Sá, *Economic Policy*, 23(55), pp.417–63, 2008.

'Public Sector as Pioneer: Shorter Working Weeks as the New Gold Standard', P. Jones, R.C. Jump and L. Kikuchi, *Autonomy*, 2020.

Work Sharing During the Great Recession: New Developments and Beyond, edited by Jon C. Messenger and Naj Ghosheh, International Labour Organization, Edward Elgar Publishing, 2013.

'An Economic and Business History of Worksharing: the Bell Canada and Volkswagen Experiences', Michael Huberman, *Business and Economic History*, 26(2), pp.404–15, 1997.

'In Medio Stat Victus: Labor Demand Effects of an Increase in the Retirement Age', P. Garibaldi, T. Boeri and E. Moen, *Journal of Population Economics*, 2021.

Chapter 10

'Why Are There Still So Many Jobs? The History and Future of Workplace Automation', David Autor, *Journal of Economic Perspectives*, 29(3), pp.3–30, 2015.

'The Consumption Smoothing Benefits of Unemployment Insurance', Jonathan Gruber, *American Economic Review*, 87(1), pp.192–205, 1997.

'Recessions and the Cost of Job Loss', Steven Davis and Till von Wachter, *Brookings Papers on Economic Activity*, 43(2), pp.1–72, 2011.

'Job Displacement and Mortality: An Analysis Using Administrative Data', Daniel Sullivan and Till von Wachter, *Quarterly Journal of Economics*, 124(3), pp.1265–306, 2009.

'The Distribution of Work and Income', Wassily W. Leontief, *Scientific American*, 247(3), pp.188–205, 1982.
Leontief's page in the Nobel Prize Archive.

Chapter 11

Efficiency, Equality and the Ownership of Property, James Meade, G. Allen & Unwin, 1964.
'Work in the Age of Robots', Christopher Pissarides, Presentation at 6th Lindau Meeting on Economic Sciences.
'The Declining Worker Power Hypothesis: An Explanation for the Recent Evolution of the American Economy', Anna Stansbury and Lawrence Summers, *Brookings Papers on Economic Activity*, 2020.
'Understanding the Price Effects of the MillerCoors Joint Venture', Nathan H. Miller and Matthew C. Weinberg, *Econometrica*, 85(6), pp.1763–91, 2017.
'Evidence for the Effects of Mergers on Market Power and Efficiency', Bruce A. Blonigen and Justin R. Pierce, *NBER Working Paper* 22750, 2016.
'Anti-Competitive Effects of Common Ownership', José Azar and Martin Schmalz, *Journal of Finance*, 73(4), pp.1513–65, 2018.
Capital in the 21st Century, Thomas Piketty, Harvard University Press, 2014.
The Price of Inequality: How Today's Divided Society Endangers Our Future, Joseph E. Stiglitz, W.W. Norton & Company, 2012.
'The End of Cheap Chinese Labor', H. Li, L. Li, B. Wu and Y. Xiong, *Journal of Economic Perspectives*, 26(4), pp. 57–74, 2012.
Meade's page in the Nobel Prize Archive.
Pissarides's page in the Nobel Prize Archive.

Chapter 12

The Road to Serfdom, F.A. Hayek, Chicago University Press, 1944 (Chapter 3).
Hayek on Hayek: An Autobiographical Dialogue, F.A. Hayek, Liberty Fund Paperback Ed., 2008.
'Labor Supply in the Past, Present, and Future: A Balanced-Growth Perspective', Timo Boppart and Per Krusell, *Journal of Political Economy*, 128(1), pp.118–57, 2020.
'Part-Time Jobs Help Women Stay in Paid Work', *The Economist*, 5 September 2019.

'Only a Fraction of Uk Job Ads Offer Flexibility, Study Finds', *The Guardian*, 24 May 2016.

'British Workers Want Flexible Working – But Only 6% of Job Ads Offer It', Katie Allen, *The Guardian*, 9 June 2015.

Theory of Wages, John Hicks, Palgrave, 1932.

'Working Hours and Top Management Appointments: Evidence from Linked Employer–Employee Data', A. Frederiksen, T. Kato and N. Smith, *IZA Discussion Paper* 11675, 2018.

'Working Hours, Promotion and the Gender Gap in the Workplace', T. Kato, H. Owan and H. Ogawa, *IZA Discussion Paper* 10454, 2016.

Spending Time: The Most Valuable Resource, Daniel S. Hamermesh, Oxford University Press, 2019.

Hayek's page in the Nobel Prize Archive.

Chapter 13

The Populist Temptation: Economic Grievance and Political Reaction in the Modern Era, Barry Eichengreen, Oxford University Press, 2018.

John Maynard Keynes 1883–1946: Economist, Philosopher, Statesman, Robert Skidelsky, Paperback, London, Penguin (Non-Classics), 2005.

'A Few Remembrances of Friedrich von Hayek (1899–1992)', Paul Samuelson, *Journal of Economic Behavior & Organization*, 69, pp.1–4, 2009.

'Time Inconsistency', Gregory Mankiw, Gregory Mankiw's Blog, 2006.

'Did Austerity Cause Brexit?', Thiemo Fetzer, *American Economic Review*, 109(11), pp.3849–86, 2019.

'Global Competition and Brexit', Italo Colantone and Piero Stanig, *American Political Science Review* 112(2), pp.1–18, 2018.

'The Trade Origins of Economic Nationalism: Import Competition and Voting Behavior in Western Europe', Italo Colantone and Piero Stanig, *American Political Science Review* 62(4), pp.936–53, 2018.

'The European Trust Crisis and the Rise of Populism', Y. Algan, S. Guriev, E. Papaioannou and E. Passari, *Brookings Papers on Economic Activity*, (2), pp.309–400, 2017.

'Importing Political Polarization? The Electoral Consequences of Rising Trade Exposure', D. Autor, D. Dorn, G. Hanson and K. Majlesi, *American Economic Review*, 110(10), pp.3139–83, 2020.

'Populist Leaders and the Economy', M. Funke, M. Schularick and C. Trebesch, *American Economic Review*, 2023.

'Why it Has to Be Biden', *The Economist*, 29 October 2020.

Bertil Ohlin's page in the Nobel Prize Archive.

Chapter 14

'How the Rational Expectations Revolution Has Changed
Macroeconomic Policy Research', John B. Taylor, in J. Drèze (ed.),
Advances in Macroeconomic Theory, International Economic
Association, Palgrave Macmillan, London, 2001
The 4 Day Week, Andrew Barnes with Stephanie Jones, Piatkus, 2020.
Robert Lucas's page in the Nobel Prize Archive.

Chapter 15

'Optimal Public Sector Wages', Pedro Gomes, *Economic Journal*,
125(587), pp.1425–51, 2015.
'The Macroeconomics of Public Employment: New and Old Lessons',
Pietro Garibaldi and Pedro Gomes, 2021.
'The Impact of Austerity Measures on the Public–Private Sector Wage
Gap in Europe', Maria Michael and Louis Christofides, *Labour
Economics*, 2020.
'Four-Day Work Weeks: Current Research and Practice', Red Facer and
Lori Wadsworth in *Symposium Redefining Work: Implications of the
Four-Day Work Week*, special issue of the *Connecticut Law Review*,
42(4), pp.1031–46, 2010.
'The Four-Day Work Week: Old Lessons, New Questions', Robert Bird, in
Symposium Redefining Work: Implications of the Four-Day Work Week,
special issue of the *Connecticut Law Review*, 42(4), pp.1059–80, 2010.
'A Performance Audit of the Working 4 Utah Initiative', Report to the
Utah Legislature, 2010.
'Four-Day Workweek in the Philippines: Policy, Practice, Prospects',
Policy Briefs, 1(2), Labor and Social Relations Research Division,
Institute for Labour Studies of Philippines, 2011.
*Conference on Shortening Working Hours: Background and Summary of
Talks*, edited by Guðmundur D. Haraldsson, ALDA Association for
Sustainable Democracy, 2019.
The Case for a Four Day Week, A. Coote, A. Harper and A. Stirling,
Polity, 2020.
'A Review of the Evidence on the Four-Day School Week', Christine
Donis-Keller and David Silvernail, Research Brief, Center for
Education Policy, Applied Research and Evaluation, 2009.
'The Four-Day Week – What Are the Advantages for Schools?',
Robert Richburg and Douglas Sjogren, *NASSP Bulletin*, 67(459),
pp.60–3, 1983.

'The Economics of a Four-Day School Week: Community and Business Leaders' Perspectives', J. Turner, K. Finch and X. Uribe-Zarain, *Applied Economics and Finance*, 5(2), 2018.

'Does Shortening the School Week Impact Student Performance? Evidence from the Four-Day School Week', Mark Anderson and Mary Walker, *Education Finance and Policy*, 10(3), pp.314–49, 2015.

'Work Hours Constraints and Health', D. Bell, S. Otterbach and A. Sousa-Poza, *Annals of Economics and Statistics*, 105/106, pp.35–54, 2012.

'The Effect of Working Hours on Health', Maria Ines Berniell and Jan Bietenbeck, *Economics and Human Biology*, 39, 2020.

'The Association Between Physical Activity and Hospital Payments for Acute Admissions in the Australian Population Aged 45 and Over', A. Marashi, S.G. Pour, V. Li, C. Rissel and F. Girosi, *Plos One*, 2019.

Chapter 16

GDP: A Brief but Affectionate History, Diane Coyle, Princeton University Press, 2014.

The Case for a Four Day Week, A. Coote, A. Harper and A. Stirling, Polity, 2020.

'Is Growth Obsolete?', William D. Nordhaus and James Tobin, in *The Measurement of Economic and Social Performance*, edited by Milton Moss, pp.509–64, 1973.

'The Measurement of Economic Performance and Social Progress Revisited', Joseph E. Stiglitz, Amartya Sen and Jean Paul Fitoussi, Commission on the Measurement of Economic Performance and Social Progress, Paris, 2009.

'Reducing Growth to Achieve Environmental Sustainability: The Role of Work Hours', K. Knight, E.A. Rosa and J.B. Schor, University of Massachusetts Amherst Working Papers, 2012.

The Ecological Limits of Work: On Carbon Emissions, Carbon Budgets and Working Time, Philipp Frey, Autonomy, 2019.

'Could Working Less Reduce Pressures on the Environment? A Cross-National Panel Analysis of OECD Countries, 1970–2007', K.W. Knight, E.A. Rosa and J.B. Schor, *Global Environmental Change*, 23(4), pp.691–700, 2013.

'Does Decreasing Working Time Reduce Environmental Pressures? New Evidence Based on Dynamic Panel Approach', Qing-long Shao and Beatriz Rodríguez-Labajos, *Journal of Cleaner Production*, 125, pp.227–35, 2016.

Kuznets's page in the Nobel Prize Archive.

Chapter 17

Governing the Commons: The Evolution of Institutions for Collective Action,
Elinor Ostrom, Cambridge University Press, 1990.

Time Well Spent, A. McGarvey, V. Jochum, J. Davies, J. Dobbs and
L. Hornung, National Council for Voluntary Organisations, 2020.

The Case for a Four Day Week, A. Coote, A. Harper and A. Stirling,
Polity, 2020.

'Gender and the Dynamics of Economics Seminars,' P. Dupas,
A.S. Modestino, M. Niederle, J. Wolfers and the Seminar Dynamics
Collective, 2021.

'Academic Sexism: A Dispiriting Survey of Women's Lot in University
Economics', *The Economist*, 23 March 2019.

'Women and Economics: Economics is Uncovering its Gender Problem',
The Economist, 21 March 2019.

'The Determinants of Econometric Society Fellows Elections', Daniel
Hamermesh and Peter Schmidt, *Econometrica* 71(1), pp.399–407, 2003.

'Gender Differences in Peer Recognition by Economists', D. Card,
S. DellaVigna, P. Funk and N. Iriberri, Econometrics Library, UC
Berkeley, 2020.

'Are Men and Women-Economists Evenly Distributed Across Research
Fields? Some New Empirical Evidence', J.J. Dolado, F. Felgueroso and
M. Almunia, *SERIEs*, 3, pp.367–93, 2012.

'Half of Canadians Support Concept of a Shorter Standard Work Week;
One-in-Five Say it's a Bad Idea', Angus Reid Institute, 2020.

'Feminism and Workplace Flexibility', Vicki Schultz, in *Symposium
Redefining Work: Implications of the Four-Day Work Week*, special issue
of the *Connecticut Law Review*, 42(4), pp.1203–22, 2010.

The 4 Day Week, Andrew Barnes with Stephanie Jones, Piatkus, 2020.

The Alison Rose Review of Female Entrepreneurship, review commissioned
by HM Treasury, 2019.

Ostrom's page in the Nobel Prize Archive.

'Economic Gains From Gender Inclusion: New Mechanisms, New
Evidence', D. Ostry , J. Alvarez, R. Espinoza and C. Papageorgiou, IMF
Staff Discussion Note, 2018.

Index

Note: *italicised* page references indicate illustrations.

About the Author

A leading researcher on public sector employment, Professor Pedro Gomes' work has influenced policy makers across the world. He studied for his BSc in Economics in his hometown of Lisbon and received his PhD from LSE in 2010. Previously an Assistant Professor at the University Carlos III de Madrid and a Visiting Professor at the University of Essex, he is now a Professor of Economics at Birkbeck, University of London. In 2022, he was invited by the Portuguese Government to coordinate their four-day-week trial. He lives with his wife and daughter in London.